THE RECURRING DREAM OF EQUALITY

Communal Sharing and Communism Throughout History

James R. Ozinga

University Press of America, Inc.
Lanham • New York • London

Copyright © 1996 by
University Press of America,® Inc.
4720 Boston Way
Lanham, Maryland 20706

3 Henrietta Street
London, WC2E 8LU England

Library of Congress Cataloging-in-Publication Data

Ozinga, James R.
The recurring dream of equality : communal sharing and communism
throughout history / James R. Ozinga.
p.   cm.
Includes bibliographical references and index.
1. Collective settlements--History. 2. Communism--History. I. Title.
HX626.095   1995   335'.9--dc20   95-42407 CIP

ISBN 0-7618-0188-X (pbk: alk: ppr.)

⊖™The paper used in this publication meets the minimum
requirements of American National Standard for information
Sciences—Permanence of Paper for Printed Library Materials,
ANSI Z39.48—1984

FOR

MY

GRANDSONS

KURT STEPHEN OZINGA

AND

JAMES MATTHEW OZINGA

Preface

The dream of equality has recurred throughout the long story of human development. Only recently, in the last century and a half, has the dream been captured by the word "communism." So effectively was this done that the alleged death of communism 1989-1991 was taken by many as the death of the dream. But the dream of equality is by no means dead. Marxist communism may be either dead or dying (actually it died decades earlier than 1989-1991), but the recurring dream continues to haunt the human spirit as a goal that powerfully focuses human aspirations as it has for so long in the past.

Because of the confusion between the failed ideology and the dream, I thought it might be fun to uncover historical examples of that dream of communal equality in order to see if anything might be learned from such a survey, not only for supporters but also for detractors. If people who push for greater equality could be made to see that the abolition of private property or the *removal* of income gaps does not help people nearly as much as a moderation of those gaps does, something positive would be accomplished. If opponents of any more equality could be made to see how long the struggle has gone on and how long it probably will continue, they may reluctantly conclude that moderating income gaps might also be in *their* interest.

It is for these goals that this book is written, so that people could see the many, many variations of communism throughout history. It was stimulated by a long standing curiosity, but the immediate trigger, as you might imagine, was the collapse of Marxist communism in Russia and Europe. I have taught communism on a university level for thirty years and, except for the last few years, felt it necessary to spend most of the time discussing Marxism and the Soviet Union. Also, until quite recently, the textbooks I used (and the ones I wrote) mainly concerned themselves with these things; the Marxian variant of communism, its ill-fated implementation in Russia, and its awkward clones in China, Cuba, and elsewhere. When European communism collapsed in 1989, there was an immediate need to either move my Communism course from the Political Science department across campus to the History department or substantially to revise the content of the course. I chose the latter path and this book is the result. But the other motives were there all along: sharing the breadth of communism so readers could appreciate how much wider it is than its Russian variant and the desirability of circumventing the need for it.

As my research progressed, it was interesting to discover how much of the material was written by women and concerned women and gender equality. It was not my intention at all to write something that might find a place on a "women's study" shelf in a library. Yet because nearly half of the material is from female sources, this might actually occur. Additionally, as my research progressed, I was impressed with how much the dreaming of equality was mixed up with religious or spiritual feeling. Even though a man like Karl Marx was purportedly an atheist, he and others before and after him articulated ideas that were basically religious in content. Marx's communist future bears a very strong resemblance to the heavens depicted in various scriptures. Also, when I began I had no idea what my conclusions would be in the final chapter. If I had been forced to answer that question at the beginning of my research I would have argued that what I hoped to accomplish was to convince people that communal sharing ideas were very old and varied well before Marx was even born. That's all. What I did discover is a large number of interesting experiments, some conceptual and some real, that together tell a fascinating story. Then when I tried to sum up what could be learned from the real life examples, the lesson from all this began to crystalize. If one considered the size of successful communal experiments as well as their duration, some interesting conclusions could be drawn that others might find as interesting as I did.

I am grateful to my students who put up with rough drafts of this book that I used as lecture notes and then revised the material so often that I sometimes forgot where I was going and where I had been, or wrote questions for exams on material that had not been covered. My most ardent thanks must, however, again go to my *sine qua non*, my wife, Suzanne, who very faithfully read every version I wrote even though she often had other things she would rather do. Her kind observations did more to keep me honest than harsh criticism would have done. My colleague of nearly thirty years, Professor Thomas W. Casstevens, earned my gratitude and proved his friendship once again by doing the final proofing of the entire text despite a busy schedule and tired eyes. Errors remaining after all that effort have their nerve.

My biases are quite obvious in the text. I believe that more equality would be a good thing in most societies, and so I am sympathetic to the experiments this book covers. However, my sympathy does not arise from an affinity for communism but from a strong distaste for the hypocritical anti-communism that dresses greed in the cloak of liberty and pretends that individual rights are possessed by all. I have tried, therefore, to be kind to the people whose work I include here, but I am quite willing as well to point out when they displease me. I would not want to live in More's Utopia--it's too regimented; nor do I share the anti-civilization goals of the Shining Path in Peru, even though I understand their nostalgia for a simpler peasant life. I must also confess to a remarkable fondness for liberation theology and its desire to *practice* Christianity (what a strange idea!) and spread a divine love to all God's children even though I probably would be the last person selected to live in a theocracy. I would like to see the human condition substantially improved, and I think what drives my liberal philosophy is a strong desire to see equality and liberty in a better balance so that equal liberty or a **real** equality of opportunity for both genders and all races comes to pass. Then, if we are really lucky, in time the power of love might overcome the love of power, and the world of people, plants, animals, and things could finally know a harmonious peace.

After all, a life without hope is dead in the water.

TABLE OF CONTENTS

Introduction

Communal Sharing: the Basis of the Dream

Prior to 1785 the dream of equality would not have become involved with ideas of communism or Marxian notions of history. In its beginnings the dream did not refer to an economic theory about the inevitable movement from capitalism to the social ownership of the means of production, or to a bureaucratic society governed by little people interested in power for themselves while maintaining the facade of social sharing. Previous to the late eighteenth century, the word "communist" did not even exist.

The word was first placed in print by a French journalist named Restif de la Bretonne in 1785 in a review of a book describing a communal experiment in Marseilles. In the review Restif cited a 1782 letter from the book's author who described himself as an *auteur communiste* (communist author). The author, Joseph Alexandre-Victor Hupay de Fuvea was a utopian intellectual who had written *The Project for a Philosophical Community* in 1779, which James Billington called "...the first full blueprint for a secular, communist society in the modern world."[1] With the emergence of the word communist, thus, also came the beginnings of communism.

By 1840 the word referred to an ideal social revolution. A March 1840 German newspaper wrote disparagingly that the communists had in view nothing less than a leveling of society; substituting for the presently existing order of things an absurd, immoral, and impossible utopia of a community of goods.[2]

The word could take on that meaning as soon as it was coined because there was a long standing concept of social leveling to which it fit; what I call the dream of equality--a concept calling for a community of goods, a society of sharing, of innocence, a society whose *raison d'etre* was the equality of its members, a sister/brotherhood, a caring kind of loving in which alienation can find no root.

In this sharing community private property was normally transcended. It was a type of cooperative organization, but was also something more. Melnyk used the word "cooperative" to describe an organization deliberately created to permit people to help themselves, ranging from loose associations like Italian fishermen's co-ops for administering member's insurance to rigidly organized and very cohesive Israeli kibbutzim with community ownership, work, and life.

In between the two extremes exist a large range of cooperative types.[3]

Obviously, many organizations both formal and informal can fit this cooperative definition. For example, a suburban housing development with drainage ditches alongside the roads can become an occasional, temporary cooperative to clean out the ditches in the springtime. So volunteers might gather on a Saturday morning and march through all the ditches, cleaning as they go. This is an informal cooperative group. A formal organization would be like a grocery store that occupies a building and has regular and permanent contracts with suppliers so as to serve the members of the consumer co-op on a regular basis.

In these cooperatives private property is usually left alone. The sharing is partial, i.e., geared to that specific thing like cleaning the ditches, members insurance, or the grocery store. Where the cooperative movement slips over into more full time communal sharing, or becomes extreme in Davidovic's words, is when private property is surpassed, prevented, and/or abolished and the cooperative approach is not partial but covers nearly everything within the society. Articles of personal consumption, for example, remain or become private property because their use destroys their utility for others. Husbands, wives, and children remain private in most sharing systems, but not in all of them, as the following chapters will show. So, although the social ownership can become quite extensive, it is not necessarily all inclusive. Nonetheless, the social ownership of most property or the lack of private property makes communal societies distinct from other forms of social cooperatives.

In such a communal society individual liberty is constrained by equality, but in earlier historical periods the loss to liberty was slight. The freedoms then enjoyed by common people were few and far between. The freedom to be better off than someone else was impossible for the majority who had no education, the wrong clothes, no connections, or the wrong accents in their speech. When social superiors no longer appeared god-like but as social parasites who took what belonged to all and used it for themselves alone, this upper crust had to be scraped off and discarded in order to allow the vast majority to flower and grow. Communal sharing or equality then meant a new freedom to enjoy life for the vast majority even as it constrained the freedom of the very few to steal life's essentials from the many. Liberty's constraint was not originally seen as a problem.

By the twentieth century, however, at least for the industrialized West, the spread of wealth and education that had taken place created phenomenal differences from the stratifications of earlier centuries.

Meaningful liberty was enjoyed by vast numbers of people and so the implementation of communal sharing and a loving kind of equality in the modern day would mean constraining freedom far more than in previous centuries. Because this was so, the issue of the proper balance between liberty and equality became a much more important question than it was in the past. The question has never been satisfactorily handled, and because it has not, the fear of losing liberty is often used to restrain the growth of equality.

The resulting danger is that equality will continue to be the victim of too much zeal for liberty. However important liberty is, it should never be used to bludgeon equality into subservience. Instead of attempting to **balance** equality and liberty, liberty is frequently highlighted as the only important part of the equation, and equality plays the role of a barely tolerated poor relation come to dinner.

The result for most people is a frustration arising from the apparent impossibility of balancing two precious concepts. There seems to be a strong impulse for equality in the human psyche that is in contradiction to selfish and acquisitive freedoms. Such a conflict is often characterized as a battle between idealism and realism because the urge to equality is often expressed as an ideal; or as a battle between naivete and pragmatism because equality is so frequently nested in a cloud of innocence. For example, people say that equality will not work because human nature will not permit it. Arguing against this notion makes one seem idealistic and innocent, out of touch with the realities of the so-called real world. The point is often missed that the dream does refer to a real world, the world of equality and loving sharing, not the artificial and distorted world of grasping egos who overcame alienation with illusions of power supported by possessions, alcohol, and drugs.

Robert Fulghum is a man who felt that his education could have stopped at the kindergarten level. Beyond that point, he said, his learning about the distorted world and how to live in it had not helped. Fulghum pointed out that the top two components of a list of significant things learned in kindergarten were to **share everything** and to **play fair**.[4] There are other significant elements in a kindergarten that come to mind when considering the five year olds we urge to share and play fair; they're so innocent, and so free of the hatreds that characterize the so-called real world of the adults. This innocence is a powerful part of what life could be like. Look at children playing with each other as though size, gender, religion, or skin color made no difference. No one cares about this stuff in the world of children. It's not perfect, but its characteristics would certainly make the adult world a great deal better; perhaps even creating a life where no one hated because the other party was a little different, a life where women were cherished as the source of life rather than treated as second class citizens, a life where war was an unthinkable abomination, and where cruelty to others and to the world of nature was the only sin worth discussing. The dream of equality in this instance would be rather like returning to kindergarten, but older and wiser than one was the first time around.

So prior to Karl Marx in the 1870s and Russia in 1917, and prior to Restif's use of the word "communist," the dream of equality represented a way of life that emphasized the social bonds that connect people rather than the property or racial differences that distinguish them. Social *sharing* was underscored rather than attempts to justify a private extraction of wealth from that which had earlier belonged to everyone. The dream articulated an ideal difficult to implement, but it also represented a happy abundance, sharing, cooperation with others, and a balance with the surrounding world.

Because the dream of sharing often represented an ideal alternative to existing society, it became fashionable to consider the dream utopian. This practice underscored the impossibility of implementing any real equality because the word "utopia" meant "nowhere" as though communal sharing were automatically impossible. This practice suited the enemies of equality very well because it made the dream appear to be an oxymoron. Heaven on earth is impossible, isn't it?.

What is seldom understood is that the contradiction between ideal and reality is only as "real" as the observer makes it; either a small hurdle or an insurmountable barrier. Those who feel drawn to sharing or even to communism argue the former while those opposed the latter; but neither seems to understand that the barrier rises or falls according to their perception rather than any reality possessed by the barrier.

For example, people sometimes argue that humans are too selfish ever to live in a society of equality and sharing. "Too selfish" is never operationalized. How distinct, for example, is the selfish human in contemporary, capitalist society from the sharing human in a proposed communist society? No one knows. Everyone accepts that people have both altruistic and selfish tendencies, but there is never any attempt to say how much of one or the other is possessed on average. There is seldom any attempt to define the two words.

If altruism is defined as acting in another's interest at some expense to yourself, and selfishness as acting for your own interests at some expense to the interests of others, then perhaps the question can be answered. For example, suppose a study were made of how often and under what circumstances people would stop to help someone stranded on the expressway or, contrariwise, simply drive by without stopping. When confronted with such a situation there is an instant calculation of risk that either causes the brakes or the accelerator to be pushed. Is it possible that an altruism/selfishness ratio could be developed that would describe humans on average? Perhaps 70 percent of the time a person would drive by the stranded people, while 30 percent of the time people would stop.

The point is not whether this is true or not, but simply that if our altruism/selfishness ratio were, say, 20/80 or 30/70, what would it have to become in a sharing society so that the greater equality became less impossible to imagine? Perhaps the change in the ratio would not be a large one for most people; perhaps only a move from 30/70 to 50/50. Perhaps a small change in the ratio would make a significant alteration in behavior. Thinking such as this may make communal sharing seem more possible and less "utopian," but very few are willing, at least on the theoretical level, to consider *greater* equality as possible, so deeply has the "utopianism" been ingrained.

Despite this difficulty, however, on the practical level people have very slowly implemented some equality. Lewis Mumford reminded his readers in 1922 that it was our utopias or dreams of ideal societies that make the mundane life worthwhile; it was our partially implemented dreams of equality that made any sort of progress possible.[5] Partial implementations, however, don't stop the dream; they may even **encourage** continuations of the full dream as hopes for a future in which war and hatreds will disappear, when children are no longer taught to hate. The dreams do not disappear; they continue even if they have been partially implemented, and even though recent implementations have been heavily tarnished.

This persistence may be because these dreams of equality, peace, and prosperity often presume a time set far in the past when the dream was a reality. The implementation, then, would actually be a return to the time when people behaved as brothers and sisters and survival was simply a matter of putting out one's hand to receive the food provided by the group or by the earth.

This common presumption suggests that these dreams have definite sources in the early life of the human race, and that this is a major reason why they continue to recur. A study of the "communisms" in history, therefore, should first consider the speculative beginnings of the dream and then go on to consider its many examples.

Endnotes
Introduction

1. James Billington, *Fire in the Minds of Men: Origins of the Revolutionary Faith* (New York: Basic Books, 1980), pp. 79-80.

2. Ibid., p. 242.

3. G. Davidovic,. *Towards a Co-operative World* (Antigonish, Nova Scotia:; Coady International Institute, 1967), p. 12; cited in George Melnyk, *The Search for Community: From Utopia to a Cooperative Society* (Montreal: Black Rose Books, 1985), pp. 3, 4.

4. Robert Fulghum, *All I Really Needed to Know I Learned in Kindergarten* (New York: Ballantine Books, 1986), p. 4

5. Lewis Mumford, *The Story of Utopias* (Gloucester, MA: Peter Smith, 1959), p. 1.

Chapter One

Communal Sharing
Source and Goal of Human Existence

Prehistoric Modes of Social Organization
Stories of Creations and Future Heavens

There is a feeling about equity and sharing that exists in all of us, a sense that seeks more--more sharing, more equity, more balance than is present in contemporary society. Perhaps the origin of that sense is a small voice left over from our kindergarten experience, a sort of super ego or conscience that pushes us in the direction of sharing and loving rather than grasping and hating. Going to the other extreme, maybe it is a philosophically heavy, categorical imperative to seek virtue. Nonetheless, we have this capacity within us to act quite differently from the way most people act most of the time. And perhaps we would act in these more loving ways more often if others would as well.

From where does this strong impulse come? A dream of equality and sharing was not part of the Ten Commandments or the Code of Hammurabi, nor does there appear to be a gene for sharing and connectedness that does battle with one for selfishness and alienation, however logical that sort of conflict may appear. The ideas about equality and sharing seem to owe their existence to a memory buried deep in the primitive brain, a memory of things past when sharing and loving was much more in vogue than in contemporary life; a memory of something that used to be.

Prehistoric Modes of Social Organization

Long, long ago people that were barely human learned that group protection meant individual protection, and that individual survival could best be achieved by group action. This group orientation seems to have been more than a cold hearted survival technique; it was also a compassionate, basic instinct of the new humans. The sharing and the caring were what made them humans with great potential rather than a line of development that would quickly die out. Moreover, the compassion was not just an invention of the weak to control the strong, nor was it developed by unrealistic women who stayed safely in camp while men went off to hunt or fight. Rosalind Miles wrote that just because group defense was a critical part of a man's work did not mean necessarily that females were the only ones with tender, caring feelings with males living only to fight or fornicate.

The first men, as well as women, she argued, only became human when they learned to care for others. John Stewart, the anthropologist, described an interesting skeleton he found in the Shanidar caves in Iraq. The male had been crippled and blind, and had been for some time. The bones also suggested that he was an old man for that Neanderthal time. He obviously had needed care, and this suggested that his primitive society had a highly developed social sense.[1]

Archeological data suggest, therefore, that long before recorded history there existed a practical communal sense that survived to modern times in isolated areas. Not only did this early communal sharing exist, but **the fact of its existence defined a group as human**. It is no wonder that something so important is remembered by us all. That even today sharing and caring are sometimes associated more with women than with men may be a throwback to those very ancient days on Crete or in northern Africa when society was organized by women much more than by men.[2] If this is true, it explains the sense one develops that the dream of equality seeks to make society more feminine, and it suggests strongly that women cease trying to be like men and insist instead that men become like women.

This primitive communism was a practical social order in the sense that individual survival clearly depended on group organization. It was also a **natural** phenomenon in the sense that the sharing, equality, and caring which characterized it flowed out of the extended family network on which the tribe was based. It wasn't hammered in from the outside.

This meant that the social bond uniting individuals was stronger than the individuals making up the society. In such a system, found as well in Greek city states, individuals found a substantial part of their own meaning in belonging to the whole. One's life was lived as a **member** rather than as an atom. The separateness of one's existence was partly overcome by the sharing within the larger group.

Indeed, because individual survival was linked to **membership**, the group may have been thought of as more important than the individual. This dichotomy was not real back then, however, because in these early societies the issue would not have arisen. The individual identified with the group to the extent that individually selfish activity must have seemed suicidal, or at least as mentally deranged.

This early communalism was also driven by the need to cooperate in order to survive. This notion among humans may have derived from the surrounding animal world. Donald R. Griffin, a cognitive ethologist, cited several examples of animal groups which consciously coordinated their activities so as to gain food, to escape danger, or just to communicate.[3]

This cooperation was also such an impressive part of animal activity in the wilds of Siberia that Prince Piotr Kropotkin used it as an example in *Mutual Aid* to support his ideas of social anarchism.[4]

If it is correct that people got the idea from animals, these early humans took animal cooperativeness further, creating a communal society. These people needed food, warmth, and security, and in these small communities with high birth and death rates, the **social** context of work, play, and reward made more survival sense than any articulation of raw individualism. The image of a totally self-sufficient primitive individual standing alone against the hostile world owes more to ideas coming from alienated philosophies like Stoicism and Cynicism, and to the glorification of Spartan manhood by less disciplined Athenians, than it does to real life in these tribal communities.

Having named them social, however, does not imply that these individuals were like social insects such as ants or termites who live only for the community, whose altruism/selfishness ratio might be described as an impossible 98/2, for example. Such a view of humans in a communist society is based on caricature, like the one provided by Ayn Rand, for example, in *Anthym*. When a discussion appears to reduce individualism a bit in order to make some room for socialism, those opposed often go too far and make automatons out of former individuals. In a discussion of selfishness vs altruism in human nature it is rare to hear someone acknowledge the **degrees** of difference between the two positions rather than to leap instantly from one absolute to the other.

This is an important issue to consider at the beginning of a discussion of communism as it will be again at the end. Early communalism among primitive people was not total. They didn't share everything. The social life of early people contained several examples of individual work and individual consumption. Gathering fruits, nuts, and edible roots, for example, was a female group activity that provided daily sustenance, and these foods appear to have been eaten individually in the woman's family unit. These foods were eaten individually, not dumped into a common pot from which everyone drew family supplies. On the other hand, the meat provided by the males' hunting such as the cooperative buffalo hunting by the Piegan Indians in Alberta around 3700bc described by Reeves[5] resulted in food that was shared on a tribal level.

Stories of Creations and Future Heavens

So the memory of communal sharing may come from those ancient times. Other sources include ancient myths such as the ones about golden people or a golden age in the very distant past. Hesiod, from the vantage point of the 8th century before Christ, wrote in his poem *Works and Days* of the really ancient times when, he thought, it was obvious that men and gods had a common descent. In the beginning, he wrote, the immortals whose homes were on Olympus created the golden generation of mortal people. They lived in Kronus' time, when he was the king in heaven, living as if they were gods; hearts were free of all sorrow and there was no hard work or pain. No miserable old age came their way because their hands and feet did not alter. They took their pleasure in festivals, lived without troubles and, when they died, it was as if they had fallen asleep. All goods were theirs. The fruitful grainland yielded them a great and abundant harvest of its own accord while they at their pleasure quietly looked after their works in the midst of all the good things.[6]

A later example of the same golden age myth was provided by Ovid (43BC to 17AD), a Roman poet. In Book I of his *Metamorphoses* he poetically described the golden past in a lengthy creation myth that comes just after Ovid has the Maker imbue formless, rude clay with human form. Contrary to the probably incorrect notion of a very short time-span in the Garden of Eden followed by a lot of hard work, Ovid suggested that early humans lived well over a lengthy period. When the world was very young and humans were rather new, Ovid felt that things were very nice. The golden age, he wrote, was lived without law or force. People did the right things without coercion. There wasn't any punishment nor even the fear of it. A person didn't have to pray for mercy, there was no need. Everyone was secure and safe without walls or moats or horns or trumpets, and certainly there was safety without swords or shields. Nations could doze through the ages because they were safe without armies. The earth freely gave all that people needed without being worked by either spade or plowshare. Spring lasted throughout the year. Warm winds blew softly over the flowers that bloomed without seeds. Like the flowers the untilled earth brought forth profuse crops of grain from uncultivated fields. Life was easy and very pleasant in the golden age.[7]

According to Ovid, this is what we had, but we lost it; and the rhythm of the pattern is that things go from gold to silver to brass and by the age of brass people know what cold and ice are and are learning the relation between work and survival. Then came the Age of Iron when, Ovid stated, modesty, truth, and faith withdrew, replaced by tricks, deceit, brute force, treachery, and a lust for gain. And so we lost what we had, and in recalling it we remember how good it once was and we try to get there again.

Taoism, a Chinese religion and philosophy following the teachings of Lao-tse who lived in the 6th century BC, speaks of a time that used to be when people lived with birds and beasts and all creation was one. There was no good versus bad, for everyone was equally without knowledge and without evil desires; virtue could not err and everyone was in a state of natural integrity.[8]

Shakespeare, in the early 17th century, contrasting the Romantic tradition of his day with the Machiavellian politics he had been describing in *The Tempest* put golden age ideas into the speech of Gonzalo, the trusted Counsellor (Act II, Scene 1). Had I the planting of this isle, he said, and were I the king on it, I would not admit any sort of traffic, nor magistrate. Letters would be unknown. In this evidently ignorant island community there would not be any riches, nor poverty, nor service or contract or succession. No one would be bound to the land. There would be no use of metal, corn, wine, or oil. There would be no occupations because everyone would be idle, even the women, who would be innocent and pure. Of course there would be no sovereignty. Nature would produce all things in common without sweat or endeavor. There would thus be no need for crime of any sort, no need for weapons. Nature would bring forth a plentiful abundance that would feed my innocent people. Then would I, he said, govern with such perfection as to surpass the golden age.[9]

Is it too speculative to argue that the memory of such idyllic pasts of sharing, equality, and equity may be lodged in the oldest, reptilian part of the human brain?. Or is it in the air we breathe? The brain seems more logical even though placing the memory there is speculative. But, since all potential sources of the dream emerge from ancient periods when written records were not kept, speculation is all one has. Such memory, like a person's unconscious recollection of the womb, might reflect the two and a half billion years when life was a part of the nourishing and sustaining ocean.[10] Or it could reflect the very long centuries of life before warfare, violence and greed became common.[11]

Such a memory would be reinforced by later stories in all the religions, such as the Judeo-Christian version of the beginnings in the Garden of Eden, written and preserved in the book of Genesis which begins the Bible. This story, widely accepted as an alternative to human evolutionary beginnings, placed a man and a woman (Adam and Eve) in a garden that was probably located in a part of the Middle East near Iran. There in the garden these two people lived in innocent happiness.

There was no mention of private property because there probably wasn't any. Not because it had been destroyed or transcended, but because no one had yet thought of it. This was just the beginning of human relations and human interaction with the environment. In the innocence of Eden, private property would not have fit.

There are two conflicting accounts about how the two people got to the Garden. The first account occurs in the first chapter of Genesis. Male and female were evidently created simultaneously on the sixth day of the creation story, on the same day that animals had been made. Genesis 1:26-27 describes not only the simultaneity but also the strong likelihood that both genders were created in the image of God. In verse 27 particularly, the author slips from singular to plural as though the word "man" really meant both genders.

The two new people were then told to do what comes naturally: be fruitful and multiply and replenish the earth. Why the word replenish when they were the first people was an unexplained mystery. Nonetheless, there they were, living in harmonious peace with every beast of the earth, fowl of the air, and all the creepy things on and under the ground. Everything was theirs to use as needed, everything in common. Also, everything at this point was good. No mention was made of avoiding the fruit of any tree, nor was there any reference to any particular tree. It was a story that seemed to resemble other stories of golden beginnings. But this was not true of the other creation story in Genesis 2, where a good dose of theology was introduced. The second chapter may have had a different author because so many things were changed. The deity portrayed was a sterner concept of God and the relationship between God and people was correspondingly harsher. This second chapter stated that only the **male** was created by God in the image of God out of the dust and mist. Immediately the reader is confronted with not just the male that God had created but also the **trees** in the Garden like the tree of life and the tree of the knowledge of good and evil. This is no longer a creation story, but the story of how sin entered the world. That's why the trees are needed up front in the Chapter Two account. This new man, Adam, was placed in the Garden and was told not to eat of the tree of the knowlege of good and evil because if he did he would surely die in the same day.

Having set this stage, the Genesis two author realized that there was no female in the picture with whom Adam could be fruitful. So animals were created, after the human rather than before as in Genesis one, and the man was asked to name all the animals. The subtext of Adam's naming activity was that he was looking for a mate among the animals. (Genesis 2:20) Somehow, even though the impression was given that creation was complete when the man named Adam was created, it wasn't complete at all and the oversight was incredible: the single human had no reproductive capacity as did the animals Adam named. Presumably the animals were all male and female, and naturally Adam did not find a woman companion because at this point in Genesis two a human female wasn't yet there. She wasn't there when the Genesis two God told Adam not to eat of a certain tree, either. Since Adam did not find a companion among all the creatures brought before him, the Genesis two author remedied this situation by making a woman out of the rib of the man. (Genesis 2: 21-22) As James Frazer put it, the author of Genesis two hardly hides his contempt for women in the lateness of her creation and that from a part of the man.[12]

Even worse, all the troubles of the human race were ascribed to Eve's credulity in dealing with the serpent, despite the fact that it was Eve's innocence or naiveté (as well as Adam's) that made the Garden of Eden what it was. The unrealistic implication was that people who have never seen a street should be streetwise.

At any rate, the Genesis one or the Genesis two couple lived harmoniously with the animal and plant world surrounding them. They had no desire for clothing and no sense that being naked was anything unusual. In addition, there was no need to work for food, shelter, or happiness. Presumably it was a warm climate because there was no suggestion that clothing was needed for warmth, and the earth provided for human hungers and needs apparently without any effort expended by Adam or Eve. It was Adam's duty to dress and keep the garden (Genesis 2:15), so there was some activity that could be thought of as work, but it would be work that didn't seem like work to Adam. Nineteenth century socialists and communists often spoke like this too. People would work in the future society, but it would be like doing a hobby. In Adam's case one gets the impression that it was easy work because all the animals were as irenic as the two people. Did Eve help with this work? Probably.

The two people probably related sexually in the Garden although there is no specific mention of it. Nor is there a clear idea of how long the two people stayed in the Garden before being forced out. Some scholars have said that Eden lasted a few hours after creation was finished, others say a few weeks, while still others insist on several years.[13] Nor is there a mention of the birth of the woman who became Cain's wife. Whether children were born in the Garden or not is an open question. When Cain was banished or exiled from the area where Adam and Eve lived, the reader discovers that Cain was already married. Strange that it was not recorded. In support of Frazer's contention of the Genesis two author's misogyny, the woman Cain married had to have been an **unmentioned** sister. The verses 16-17 of Genesis chapter four told the story succinctly:

when Cain went to the land of Nod he made his wife pregnant with Enoch, and Cain built a city after the name of his son.

What comes across from both the myth of the golden age and from the story of the garden is the overwhelming innocence of the people involved. The lack of clothing, for example, in the garden story. They didn't even know they were naked. This is still true of children. Even after children learn what nudity is they will still bathe unconcernedly with siblings of the other gender. They are innocents like Adam and Eve were, or as kindergarteners appear to be. And not only were they supposed to be innocents in the beginning, Jesus later taught that this was something people should **become**; like little children--or else entering the Kingdom of Heaven was said to be unlikely. (Matt 18:3) The Kingdom was to be made up of people resembling little children. (Luke 18:16) It seems strange that Eve (or Adam) should be blamed for trusting the serpent when trusting others is what an innocent child mostly does.

Just as with the Golden Age, or many later examples of communal sharing, the Garden of Eden experience was not as long lasting as one might have hoped, although Agostino Inveges (1649) speculated that the Garden of Eden experience began at dawn on Friday March 25th and ended at 4:00pm on Friday April 1st.[14] In Ovid's poem the suggestion was made that the movement of the gods caused the golden age to slip into silver: Saturn was sent to gloomy hell and Jove ruled the world. Plato's *Republic* saw the overvaluing of honor as compared with wisdom as the culprit, and one moved from philosopher kings and queens to something he called a timocracy. The "perfect" society, in other words, develops a virus and begins to degenerate. Jean Jacques Rousseau's state of nature seemed very similar in that the perfections of the early beginning could not safeguard against emergent private property. Karl Marx, reflecting his Hegelian background, saw the virus or flaw as alienation which emerged in the ancient society when people developed religion as a function of their alienation and allowed the notion of private property to evolve without serious challenge. As a result both religion and private property were institutions that separated people from their own best characteristics. All of this was very similar to the development of alienation described in Genesis 3 as having happened in the Garden of Eden.

One of the trees in the garden bore fruit that the Genesis 2 creator specified as off limits. This tree was called the tree of the knowledge of good and evil. Pushing a fruited tree back into the creation story seems to be a fairly common thing. A fifth century BC vase, for example, shows the serpent-dragon of the Hesperides guarding the Tree of the Golden Apples.

The woman involved is Athena, the goddess of wisdom.[15] Actually the **fruit** in the Garden wasn't the problem, it was the act of eating it that was evil because it would be an act of disobedience. This story wisely defined goodness or virtue as seeking to do the will of God. Evil then is whatever pulls one away from God, separates, creates a gap, and creates alienation or an unnatural separation. Alienation is a philosophical word that means the same thing as the more religious word sin, although many philosophers seem unaware of this. So knowledge of good and evil was not the problem; the problem was the **experience** of alienation brought about by the act of disobedience.

The story was told in such a way as to discredit the serpent or snake that formerly symbolized the Goddess that early people worshipped before male gods took over.[16] The story was also told in such a way as to discredit the female. The serpent spoke to Eve who ate of the fruit, and she in turn talked Adam into taking a bite. This, if accepted as true, makes the woman, Eve, responsible for her own alienation from God, as Adam was responsible for **his** choice. To make Eve responsible for the abstract alienation implied in original sin, something like the sin of the world, is nonsense, because it depends on the heretical notion that sin or alienation is genetically transmitted down through the generations.

In the Garden of Eden alienation emerged and there was an immediate loss of innocence: the two humans now knew they were **naked**, and that they weren't supposed to be. They sought coverings of fig leaves. Curiously, their loss of innocence was described positively as an opening of their eyes (Genesis 3:7), but in the next breath both Adam and Eve were hiding from the Creator because, as Adam said, I was afraid because I was naked. (Genesis 3:10) Presumably he had not as yet put on his apron of fig leaves. God then asked, understandably: who told you that you were naked? (Genesis 3:11) But innocence, alas, could not be easily regained. The nakedness could be covered but the alienation could not.

More results were soon forthcoming. The Creator, unhappy that his/her command was disobeyed, cursed the serpent who now had to slither on its belly to get around, cursed the woman with dominance by her husband and with "sorrowful" childbirth, and cursed the man with hard work; he would live by the sweat of his brow. Nature was also cursed: thorns and thistles were now to interfere with human enjoyment and their subjugation of the earth. Death entered the world, presumably for the first time, suggesting that life in the garden was intended to be eternal. The tree of life which gave eternity was not a forbidden tree in the beginning, but after alienation occurred it was; both Adam and Eve were expelled from the garden to prevent their eating from that tree. Interestingly enough, that tree of life shows up again in the book of Revelations as a source of eternity and peace among nations.(Rev 22:2) A bit further in that same chapter, a tight connection was made back to the Garden of Eden, because only those who do God's commandments were entitled to eat of the tree of life.

The Genesis story, like other ancient stories, very clearly informs the reader that we had something once, a life without toil, without sorrow, in harmony with nature and with others, and a life of innocence that was not intended to end. We had it, and we lost it, and all of our life we remember and try to regain it.

Other religions tell the same story in a different way. Zoroastrianism, for example, replaces Adam and Eve with a similar pair named Moshya and Moshyana. For many cultures and religions it all began with a bird sitting on an egg.[17] In Mithraism, information drawn from drawings and monuments in chapel caves suggests that Mithras was born from a rock surrounded by snakes, bringing forth a lighted torch symbolizing the sun or the light of the world. He came forth naked, plucked fruit or leaves from a tree, and the next scene shows him clothed. No written records were left, but the beginnings seem similar to the Judeo Christian tradition. Mithras had the light, lost it, and must regain it by slaying a heavenly bull so that life could exist on earth.

But it is a flawed or tainted life, and religions try to solve the problem of alienation from God by exhorting a closer relationship between the human and the deity. Very few humans seem to listen. If everyone actually **practiced** Christianity, or presumably other religions, the alienation problem would be solved. Close relationships with God would ensue as people genuinely sought virtue and avoided vice. The visible result would be the Kingdom of God on earth: there would be harmony among people who would think of others as sisters and brothers. Sharing would be a way of life, love would be the dominant motivator, egalitarianism would characterize all human relationships, and peace, joy, and happiness would prevail throughout the world as hunger, disease, and poverty disappeared. This would be what things looked like if all actually practiced Christianity. It would in fact be heaven on earth, and many people believe that this will one day happen.

What would distinguish the heaven in the skies from such a heaven on earth would be eternal life and proximity to God in the sky heaven. In fairness one should also add that the sky heaven alone has a counterpoint: a hell into which all those who did not seek virtue were to be placed.

The limited access of the heaven suggests elitism; the very opposite of equality and sharing, as though the idea in the minds of the people describing it curtailed the loving and sharing to one's own group. This elitism makes heaven imperfect, because one can imagine a **better** place where forgiveness is the foundation of a more general loving.

The sky heaven, if the elitism is ignored, is a state of bliss enhanced by access to the tree of life and proximity to God, considered a good in itself. As in the beginning there is to be no sadness, hunger, difficulty, pain, or work. No tears, death, or sorrow. (Rev 21:3-4)

The new city, sometimes called the new Jerusalem, or heaven, was to be a city of pure gold, with walls made of jasper, and foundations constructed of twelve layers of semi-precious stones: jasper, sapphire, chalcedony, emeralds, sardonyx, the ruby-like sardius, chrysolyte, beryl, topaz, chrysoprasus, jacinth, and amethyst. The city had walls, it also had gates: twelve of them, and each of the twelve gates was a single pearl. The one street of the city was pure gold, as transparent as glass, a distinct contrast to More's *Utopia* where gold was an object of shame.

The new city was blessed with the glory of God, which lit things up so well that the city did not need a sun or a moon. There was never any night. At some focal point the throne of God could be seen, and flowing out of that throne came a pure, clear river. John called this the water of life and the trees of life were also nearby on both sides of the river. The leaves of the trees of life allegedly healed the nations.

Certain things were not allowed into the heavenly city: anything that defiled, or abominated, or lied. Here there would no longer be any kind of curse, or night, or death.(Rev 21 and 22) Interestingly enough the bad things were right outside the city, presumably outside the walls. Rev 22:15 stated that right outside the city were dogs, sorcerers, fornicators, murderers, idolaters, and liars.

This is the Christian view of the life after death or heaven. The Jewish heaven is not that different, except that there seem to be many interpretations of it. Milton Steinberg wrote that there might be more varied descriptions of life after death among Jews than any other tenet of Judaism.[18] The form of the hereafter is called Paradise, Heaven, or Eden, and the opposite is called Hell or Sheol or Gehinnom. At any rate there is a deathlessness, a resurrection, a judgment day, and a reward or punishment in the Jewish faith even if these terms vary considerably in the assumed meaning from one Jew to another.

Even so, there is general agreement that a Kingdom of God is coming, a time when God's law prevails and God's nature (goodness) asserts itself in all of the world's affairs. Although coming in the future, intimations of the Kingdom exist even now. Steinberg wrote that such earnests (downpayments) in the midst of the sinful, wicked world are all those activities and behaviors that are warm, sweet, right, and compassionate. Such a heavy emphasis on the Kingdom in Judaism becomes understandable, Steinberg wrote, when one considers that the Kingdom of Heaven embodies the most precious hope of the human spirit.[19]

This Kingdom of Heaven awaited the inaugural efforts of the Messiah. The prophet Isaiah wrote about this with typical Hebrew parallelism and pointed unerringly, once again, at the childlike innocence expected. In Isaiah 11:6 he wrote of wolves dwelling with lambs, and leopards lying down with young goats. Calves and young lions will be together, and a little child shall lead them. Besides all this, the author later said that there would be no hurting and no destroying "...in all my holy mountain." (Isaiah 65:25)

Instead of arguing that wolves do not dwell peacefully with lambs, or that only a fool would believe that they could feed together without incident; instead of biting the prophet's finger, the prophet asked his listeners to see where the finger was pointing: toward an age of innocence, of sharing, of love.

The Islamic heaven is expectedly similar in many respects because Islam is based on the Judeo-Christian tradition. However, one interpretation of the Muslim heaven appears to be more for men than women. In this view the heaven is a giant banquet with the men being served by young boys or pretty women.

In Buddhism life is seen as a dissatisfied existence searching for an otherworldly goal, rather like a moth being attracted by the impossible, such as the moon or a star. The cause of the dissatisfaction, or alienation, was attachment to things of sense, to things of the material world. Peace was not to be found in the acquisition of things, but in release through the limitation of desire. This release allows an ethical conduct and a serenity that wears down the karma that insists on rebirth, resulting in the breaking of the chain of material life.

Buddhism does not have much use for individualism or materialism. It is an idealist system in the philosophic sense. Wearing down the karma is the wearing down of that which binds together the interconnected elements or ideas comprising an individual. Obviously, erosion of the force that connects these things allows the dissolution of the individual as the parts fly free of the constraint.

The goal is often called nirvana, a word that means the going out of fire, especially the fire of greed. Synonyms for nirvana are blessedness, bliss, release, or the other shore. The stress in Buddhism is on ethical conduct and while within the ranks of monks there is equality, there is toleration for the inequality among people in the outside world. The goal of Buddhism is individual salvation not the establishment of the Kingdom of Heaven on earth. Nonetheless the force of the religion/philosophy is on the pursuit of virtue, equality as the ideal, and a condemnation of greed. The love expressed by the early Buddhist was (is) a calm, quiet, unemotional goodwill toward all the world. Later evolutionary developments in the religion changed some of the religious precepts. For example, the calm love was replaced by a more active loving, which necessitated good works rather than a calm good will toward another. Later changes made Buddhism more of a religion than it was in the beginning.

Hinduism emerged about 1500BC and was at the outset a collection of religions, and it never lost its ability to assimilate new ideas. Many Gods play many functions, like Varuna who keeps the rivers running, for example. Brahman, for another example, represents unity, a unity that lies behind all temporal manifestations and their accidental difference. Visnu, the God of the sun, was a major deity. Conduct of one's life was (is) very important to the Hindu, and the distaste for this-worldiness suggests a Buddhist-like ideal, although this is difficult to square with caste separations in Hindu lands such as India.

Nirvana to the Hindu as to the Buddhist means the extinction of rebirths. The individual soul is blended into Brahmin, the World Soul. This resembles a Christian union with God and can take place while a person is still alive. Nirvana represents the end or loss of alienation or separateness and the bliss of connection with the deity.

Both Hinduism and Buddhism tend more toward abstract notions of heaven, but then they don't have much of a beginning story to match the Garden story of Christianity, Judaism, or Islam. Except for the possible gender distinctions in the Islamic heaven, there is in all religious belief a strong commitment to an egalitarianism that marks the end of distinctions between people. All are brothers and sisters, all that is that have made it to the promised future. Many do not, and for those unsuccessful ones there is an egalitarianism of despair in the place called hell or a continuation of life in another form.

One begins for most religions, therefore, with love, innocence, sharing, and equality as in the Garden of Eden. Those characteristics, however, were lost when alienation from God occurred. Overcoming that alienation permitted those seeking virtue to find earnests of that future Kingdom in this world and a full Kingdom of Heaven later. The religious views and secular descriptions of golden ages when life began are astonishingly similar. Dreams of future equality are similar as well.

An example of this occurs in Dolores Ibarruri's autobiography, the story of her leading rôle in the evolution of Spanish communism. She had become a parliamentary deputy for the Popular Front in the 1936 elections and took her new job very seriously. When a man approached her office and said his pregnant wife, about to give birth, had been refused treatment in the maternity home because she could not pay, Dolores went back with him and demanded to see the manager. A nun went to get him and returned with him. The manager refused to readmit the woman even though her labor had begun. Dolores turned to the nun and said: "You're despicable!" "Where's your charity, your love of your neighbor?"[20] Communism and Christianity had, for Dolores Ibarruri, the same kind of virtue. It is most understandable.

Endnotes
Chapter One

1. Rosalind Miles, *The Women's History of the World* (New York: Harper & Row, 1988), pp. 15-16.

2. Ibid., pp. 3-17. See also Riane Eisler, *The Chalice and the Blade* (San Francisco: Harper & Row, 1988).

3. Donald R. Griffin, *Animal Thinking* (Cambridge: Harvard University Press, 1984), pp. 84-87.

4. Piotr Kropotkin, *Mutual Aid, A Factor of Evolution* (London: William Heinemann, Popular Edition, 1915), pp. 11-62.

5. B. Reeves, "Six Millennia of Buffalo Kills," *Scientific American* vol 249, no 4, (October 1983).

6. Doyne Dawson, *Cities of the Gods: Communist Utopias in Greek Thought* (New York: Oxford University Press, 1992), p. 13. For a slightly more difficult translation see Hesiod, *Works and Days*, lines 110-121, translated in Apostolos Athanassakis, *Hesiod: Theogony, Works and Days, Shield* (Baltimore: John Hopkins Press, 1983), p. 70.

7. Ovid, *Metamorphoses*, Book I, can be found in George Sandys, *Ovid's Metamorphosis; Englished, Mythologized and Represented in Figures*, edited by Karl K. Hulley and Stanley T Vandersall (Lincoln: University of Nebraska Press, 1970). An easier to read, partial translation is by Robert M. Adams, ed., and trans., in the critical volume on Sir Thomas More's *Utopia* (New York: W. W. Norton & Co., 1975), pp. 96-97.

8. Chuang Tzu 9, cited in Andrew Wilson ed., *World Scripture: A Comparative Anthology of Sacred Texts* (New York: Paragon House, 1995), p. 224.

9. William Shakespeare, *The Tempest*, in William Aldis Wright, *The Complete Works of William Shakespeare* (Garden City: Doubleday & Co., 1936), p. 1308.

10. Monica Sjoo & Barbara Mor, *The Great Cosmic Mother: Rediscovering the Religion of the Earth* (San Francisco: Harper & Row, 1988), p. 2.

11. Riane Eisler, *op. cit.*, Chapters 1-3.

12. James G. Frazer, *Folklore in the Old Testament: Studies in Comparative Religion, Legend and Law*, vol. 1 (London: Macmillan, 1919), p. 5.

13. Jean Delumeau, *History of Paradise: The Garden of Eden in Myth and Tradition*, Matthew O'Connell, trans. (New York: Continuum, 1995), p. 181.

14. James G. Frazer, *op.cit.*, pp. 183-184.

15. Buffie Johnson, *"Lady of the Beasts" Ancient Images of the Goddess and Her Sacred Animals* (San Francisco: Harper & Row, 1988), pp. 154-156.

16. Sjoo & Mor, *op. cit.*, p. 125.

17. Buffie Johnson, *op. cit.*, pp. 30-33.

18. Milton Steinberg, *Basic Judaism* (New York: Harcourt Brace Jovanovich, 1975), p. 161.

19. Ibid., p. 165.

20. Dolores Ibarruri, *They Shall Not Pass: The Autobiography of La Pasionaria* (New York: International Publishers, 1966), p. 175.

Chapter Two

Communal Sharing as a Method
of
Maintaining Purity or Virtue

Pythagoras
Plato
Diogenes
Settlement Houses

Among the philosophers living before Socrates there was little evidence that communism was an attractive dream that would fit with their political ideas. This may be due to the fragmentary evidence from which knowledge of their opinions is drawn. The lack of communal sharing in their philosophy may also be due to the Greek tendency to keep myth and fact apart, meaning, for example, that they wouldn't blend metaphors drawn from the myth of Kronus into their political philosophy. It may also be that they never got beyond quite simple thinking. For example, a sixth century BC figure named Thales is well known for believing that water was the basis of all things. He was honored because he successfully predicted an eclipse as well as a successful harvest, but he is generally considered the first real philosopher because his belief about water as the source moved him away from theology and toward empirical science.

Even so the religious notion of purity by abstinence from external contamination was well known. The Orphics of ancient Greece, or followers of the mythical Orpheus, believed in the transmigration of souls, and that the human soul could achieve immortal happiness or eternal pain as a result of how one lived one's life. The Orphics thought that they could become pure partly through ceremonies and partly through abstaining from contaminating things like animal food or meat. Through abstaining from such contamination and through ceremonies of intoxication, alienation was ended and union with the deity was achieved. To escape the wheel of life that turned through endless cycles of birth and death in a world of pain and weariness, one sought the ecstasy of union with God--possible only through purification and abstinence.[1]

Anaximander was another sixth century figure who believed that all

things came from a single primal substance that was then transformed
into other primary substances such as fire, earth, and water which
coexisted in a self-limiting kind of balance loosely understood as
justice.   Justice in this sense limited or restrained the primary
substances from overpowering each other. It was the balance between
them that made life possible, and the balance was the result of the
restraining justice.

This was the context in which Pythagoras, also a sixth century figure,
lived and made his contribution. The communal sharing articulated by
Pythagoras was a major characteristic of the religious-mathematical
societies he established in the Greek cities of southern Italy, especially
at Croton. Communal sharing and other rules of the society secured a
purity for the entire Pythagorean group withdrawn from the
contamination of the larger cities.   At first glance this makes
Pythagoras's communism appear different from Plato's because in *The
Republic* the sharing was a device to prevent corruption only among
rulers and perhaps the guards, but not the producers--the majority of
society. By introducing communal sharing, Plato hoped to keep his
Republic from degenerating into less desirable forms of government.
Communism whether for the whole society or just for the rulers (and
perhaps the guards) was used here rather like an innocence pill that
anxious parents might want to prescribe for their teenage children--
something to retard evil, to keep temptations at a resistable distance.
Pythagoras meant his sharing and the other taboos for his religio-
scientific community as devices to keep it apart from a corrupting world
which he wanted to influence, while Plato was an elitist who meant the
sharing to be applicable to the upper class of philosopher kings and
queens (and perhaps to the protectors) who could act as a similar
virtuous group, but definitely not to the majority of the population who
were the producers and merchants. Diogenes, on the other hand, meant
his communal sharing to characterize the entire society.

Pythagoras

Plato may have drawn some of his ideas about "communism" from
Pythagoras, a person about whom there is more myth than fact.
Nonetheless, Pythagoras' influence seems to have gone beyond Plato to
help shape the later "communism for the wise" developed by an
evolving Stoicism, even though when taken as a whole the Pythagorean
communities were "a peculiarly disciplined organization, resembling no

other pagan Greek school or sect then or later. "[2]

Pythagoras was a native of Samos, an island off the coast of what is now Turkey. He lived around 532BC, the son of a rich family of Greek colonists that was part of the Greek imperialism with reference to this part of the ancient Asia Minor. From Samos he moved to Croton, in south Italy, where there were also prosperous Greek cities more distant from threatening Persia than was Samos.

At Croton and other Greek cities in southern Italy, Pythagoras founded societies or collectives of disciples that became influential in the political life of the cities. The influence was probably briefer than Pythagoras intended because legend has it that the Croton citizens, at least, rose up against the school and Pythagoras had to move. After his death he was quickly turned into a mythical figure, credited with miracles and magic powers, and all this myth and magic surrounded his genuine contributions in mathematics.

The rules of his societies were rather strange and seem rather primitive. They also seem more related to bad magic than to communism or mathematics. The first rule was to abstain from beans, while the second one prohibited the picking up of something that had fallen. Other rules prohibited eating from a whole loaf or leaving the imprint of the pot in the fire or one's body in the bed.[3] These were only a few of the fantastic regulations for the group. They were not to stir a fire with a knife, kill white roosters, or urinate on their own nail parings. It was a strange form of communal organization.[4]

Although one might feel superior to any organization that operated according to those or similar rules, Pythagoras was light-years ahead of his contemporaries in that his commune admitted women equally with men. This elevated attitude toward women was not designed to create a basis for communal sex, because this was a practice the Greeks normally thought of as barbarian. Dawson states that the Pythagorean communities practiced an austere form of sexual morality in that adultery for either men or women was severely punished.[5] The property of the commune or that of individuals was shared in common although the details of that sharing or redistribution are missing from the record.[6] His society had a strong emphasis on education focused on geometry, arithmetic, astronomy, and music. His school taught the importance of **order** in the society and this probably placed the Pythagorean school on the side of the aristocrats and against the mob government of poor democrats in the Greek version of democracy.

Pythagoras argued that everything was number, and that number patterns were the basis of the universe. He thought of numbers like shapes, speaking of squares and cubes but also oblongs and triangular numbers that resembled the molds into which he poured pebbles. The number of pebbles required to fill a mold was the number represented by that shape.[7] This may not sound too intelligent, but remember that only fragments of his philosophy have survived. His greatest discovery was the constant relationship of elements in a right triangle. The square of the hypotenuse was equal to the sum of the squares of the sides coming off of the right angle. This was the famous Pythagorean Theorem: $A^2 + B^2 = C^2$ and underlying this as well as other mathematical statements was the belief that numbers follow rational patterns. So his philosophy was a kind of rationalized mathematics tied up with ratios, and anticipating pure number forms in the heavens. Qualitative things like musical harmony were based on numerical ratios like 1:2, 2:3, 3:4, for example, as a student of musical composition would know. His emphasis on arithmetic proved troublesome, so even in Pythagoras' time there was a movement from arithmetic to geometry, a trend perfected by Euclid, a follower of Plato.

Pythagoras' society shared everything in common, was unbiased as to gender, and was religious. His community was a means by which individual souls could escape the wheel of life (transmigration). Even scientific and mathematical discoveries were deemed collective.[8] Private property, in this understanding, was evil, leading a person to evil because it pulled one away from contemplation, the noblest activity of a human being. After contemplation, came competitive sports as the next most valued activity, and then at the bottom of the heap was buying and selling, or what Adam Smith called "trucking." So the communal sharing as used by Pythagoras prevented the falling away of at least the higher members of the society who were engaging in contemplation or looking on, and stood the best chance of understanding the numerical basis of the universe and escaping the wheel of life. We are strangers in this world, he said, and the body is the tomb of the soul, but we shouldn't try to escape by self-murder because we are the chattels of God, our herdsman. Without his command we have no right to make our escape. In this life, he said, as would Plato, that there are three kinds of people, just as there are three sorts of people who come to the Olympic Games. The lowest kind was made up of those who come to buy and sell; above them were those who came to compete; but best of all were those who came to look on, because it was these who contemplated. The greatest purification of all was science and those who have devoted themselves to science were the contemplators, the true philosophers who had effectually released themselves from the "wheel of birth."[9]

Plato was an admirer of Pythagoras, and he pulled many Pythagorean ideas into his own thinking. Plato's notions of an ideal society and the need for communal sharing to arrest degeneration among the upper classes could have come from Pythagoras as well. But Plato was more complicated than Pythagoras, or at least more of Plato's work was left to posterity, so an understanding of Plato's scheme for an ideal society is essential to understanding his use of "communism."

Plato

Plato lived about four centuries before Christ. He was a friend and student of Socrates whom he met in 407BC. For the next eight years, or until 399, Plato devoted himself to the study of Socrates' ideas. He was deeply affected by Socrates' arrest and conviction on charges of impiety and corrupting the youth. Socrates' execution in 399BC was a blow to the young Plato. His dislike of democracy may date from this event because Socrates' condemnation came from a democratic court. In the Athens of the day, democracy was less of a compromise system and more a class government favoring the poor; democracy allowed the greater numbers of the poor to dominate the fewer rich. Conversely when the rich were in power they tended to rule through oligarchies that benefitted the wealthy at the expense of the poor. Normal government, then, even to a biased Plato, was far from balanced; it was a seesaw reverting from one class oppression to the next. Politically he might prefer an oligarchy of conservative individuals like himself, but practically it was not a wise choice because of the near constant seesaw between oligarchy and democracy as the rich and poor fought their continuing battle.

This is why when he thought of an ideal government he did not choose either democracy or oligarchy, but a form of society new from the ground up. For them, of course, it wasn't new at all; it represented an ideal government present in Athens before Atlantis was lost. In Plato's *Timaeus* Critias said to Socrates that the city and its citizens you described to us yesterday as if from a fable (the ideal society described in *The Republic*), we will now transport hither into the realm of fact; for we will assume that the city you described was that ancient city of ours, and declare that the citizens you conceived are in truth our actual ancestors of whom the priest told.[10] Critias here articulated the belief that this ideal society existed in ancient Athens before Atlantis was submerged.[11] It was not so much new, then, as it was a re-creation of that which had been lost.

The Republic is a long dialogue that begins with a discussion of the meaning of justice. The reader soon realizes that justice would characterize the new society, and the nature of that justice would be the proper balance of the various forces in the society. Everyone in their right place performing what they did best, according to their natures.

The three basic natures of society corresponded, Plato wrote, to the three components of the human soul: **desire** with its seat in the loins, **emotion** with its seat in the heart, and **intellect** with its seat in the head. An individual functioned best when emotions and desire were harnessed to the direction of intellect. The goal of that balanced soul, directed by reason and pushed or pulled by emotion and desire, was to return to the divine world of ideas from which it had originally come. Human souls existed prior to the individual's birth, living in that heavenly world of ideas. When the soul lost its wings and could no longer stay aloft it sank to the earth and took up residence in a human body. The goal of the soul from this point on was to regain its lost position. The same was true for society as a whole because society, in Plato's view, was simply an individual writ large. It was rather like projecting the human soul onto a large screen; the parts of society were the same but they looked and *were* so much larger that they could be analyzed much easier. So society, like the individual, was made up of three forces, **producers** corresponding to desire, **protectors** corresponding to emotions, and **philosopher kings and queens** corresponding to intellect. Just as with the individual the social order must reflect a proper balance of its parts. The producers would create the food and goods but neither protect nor rule, the protectors would make the society secure, both within and without, but would neither produce nor rule. The philosopher kings and queens would rule, and would neither protect nor produce.

This was a proper balance. Plato argued that disaster occurred when either desire or emotion ruled over the intellect in the individual, and that this was the same for society. If life were a chariot racing to heaven, then the two horses pulling the chariot should be desire and emotion, and the charioteer had to be reason. Similarly, in society, the philosopher rulers must guide the protectors and producers to avoid social disaster and disintegration.

This was the desired balance in the society, and he decided he had to be ruthless in order to achieve it. He would send out of the society everyone over the age of ten, leaving children ten and under to begin a schooling that determined, through testing, their place in the three class structure. By starting with the young children Plato felt the new society had a chance because the old would have been rubbed off with no chance of contaminating the next generation. Full equality of educational opportunity would be given to each child from the outset because there was no way of telling where the light of talent or genius would break out. The equality of educational opportunity was for every race, rank, and gender without partiality, an astonishing thing for someone to suggest near the beginnings of four centuries before Christ. The implication here is that the vocational or skill differences between males and females were due to differences in education, something not otherwise recognized until the **twentieth century**. As late as the nineteenth century in Britain, women of the upper classes were prohibited by custom from reading the entire newspaper because their delicate natures supposedly could not handle it. Some of these same women wallowed through mud and blood and incredible incompetence as they followed the lead of Florence Nightingale during the Crimean War to establish nursing as a respected profession.

Plato's equal education was separated into three parts with each part lasting ten years. The first ten years' education was primarily physical. The entire curriculum was gymnasium, playground play, and sports. The goal was to develop healthy bodies with regular diets and exercise so that medical care was unnecessary.

The second ten year period began education proper with what Plato called music, harmony, and rhythm. By music he meant all the arts presided over by the Muses: music itself, of course, and art, letters, culture, and philosophy. In addition the musical milieu provided an attractive ambience for the teaching of mathematics, history, and science. This was to be done freely, with no compulsion. A moral basis was to be provided through religious training, somewhat cynically, because Plato believed that a belief in God reduced evil doing, and a sense of personal immortality guaranteed courage in battle.

Tests at the age of twenty would create the first separation; those failing it would become the producers. These people would staff industries, farms, fisheries, and stores. They could own property, marry, have their own families, and live normal lives. This would probably be the majority of the population.

Those passing the test would continue in school for another ten years.

The emphasis would be on mathematics during this period so that gradually the student might develop the basis for an insight into the harmonious order of the whole world that mathematics provides. The second test occurred when the remaining students were thirty years of age. Those failing this test became the protectors of the society, staffing the military and police forces throughout the land.

Those **passing** the test at age thirty continued with more intensive education for the next five years during which time insights into the harmonious order of the world provided a vision of the divine: the world of the forms, the reality that underlay all material existence. These forms (*eidos*) or ideas were the patterns after which the world was made, and harmony on earth was a reflection of the harmony of these heavenly forms. Sensing this dialectical truth was so important that only those who remained in school from age thirty to thirty-five could be the philosopher kings and queens. At age thirty five these rulers-to-be were removed from school and for fifteen years given practical training in a variety of professions. At age fifty, after all this training and practical experience, they became philosopher rulers.

This was Plato's ideal state, but he wanted to do more than simply suggest its beginning, he also wanted to show how it could maintain itself over time. In the Republic everyone was imagined to be in their proper or right place, doing whatever vocation was appropriate for that individual. It was to be a virtuous society because it was based on and led by knowledge. Knowledge was virtue, and the highest form of knowledge was the dialectic, knowledge of the world of ideas, the divine forms or models of reality--more real in Plato's mind than the material world which reflected the ideal ideas or patterns.

Plato knew that societies were not static, they evolved and changed over time. He was describing a Republic that had supposedly existed in the ancient Athenian past. In addition, one of the constants of social existence was the tendency of the ruling class to perpetuate itself as a ruling class through its children. But the children of philosopher kings and queens might or might not be appropriate rulers; they might in fact not even be meritorious enough to be protectors. To control all of this Plato invented what Mumford called a "medicinal lie."[12] This lie was necessary, Plato felt, because it argued that even though all were equal, the social divisions in the society had a divine origin.

Plato has the main character in *The Republic* say that he would try to convince first the rulers, then the soldiers, and finally the whole community that the education and nurturing they had received was an illusion; that in fact they had been spawned by the earth itself. This would accomplish two things: it would make the earth and the land that they inhabit seem to them to be both mother and nurse whom they must protect at all costs; and all people would appear to each other as brothers and sisters, born of the same soil.[13]

Although all in the land were siblings, for some God mixed gold in their composition, while in others was mixed silver, and for yet others iron and brass. The golden children were the rulers, the silver the protectors, while the iron and brass were the producers. The first and most important divine commandment to the rulers was that, for the good of the state, the mixture of metals in their children must be watched very carefully. If a child of their own were born with a mix of iron or brass, they must, without the smallest pity, assign that child to the lower level in the society. If, on the contrary, the producer group produced a child with either gold or silver in its composition, that child should be promoted either to the ranks of the protectors or of the philosopher kings and queens. The people must be told, Plato insisted, that even though they were all brothers and sisters, ruin would come to the state if its rule passed into the keeping of a woman or man of iron or brass.[14]

Plato thus tried to explain that class divisions had a divine origin. He was by no means the last to attempt this specious argument. His motives are understandable, however, for what he is trying to accomplish is some longevity to his ideal state. He knows that to allow heredity to govern the selection of the next generation of leaders, protectors, or producers would bring a quick end to the Republic. People would seek the benefit of their children rather than the good of the state.

The class for whom this divine commandment was the most difficult was the top class. In the lower two classes a child of gold would be something to be pleased about, but a child of iron and brass to a ruler/parent would be seen as a disaster and probably covered up. In this sense the rulers had a more difficult task than the other two classes.

Here is where communal sharing entered the picture; certainly not to affect the entire society, not to create equality where it had not existed before, not to open doors for everyone to experience brother/sisterhood and a new age of innocence but to preserve the virtue of the ruling class. To put it negatively, the sharing was intended to retard spoilage. The communal characteristics he introduced were specifically for the philosopher kings and queens, though they may have also been for the protectors as well. It certainly did not apply, despite what Aristotle thought, to the majority of the society who were producers.

The communal sharing made sure that philosopher queens and kings did not push their own children into the golden occupations without regard for their merit. Nor would they hope to gain in some monetary manner by making their children rulers. The communal character of their society guaranteed the innocence of the rulers and kept them from becoming corrupt.

They would not have any property other than that which was vitally necessary. They would not have, for example, a private house, but instead they would be provisioned like disciplined Spartan warriors. Plato had a barracks existence in mind for these rulers. They would eat meals in common and live together in a harmony of activity like soldiers in a camp. Although they would be supported by the producers in such a way as to underwrite all of their expenses, they themselves would **never** handle money. Money, in Plato's judgment, was a base thing. All of their goods except those of personal consumption were owned in common with others.

This equality would be in existence right from the beginning of the ideal society, so that one did not have to imagine taking property away from some people so as to equalize it for everyone. This was the case when agriculture was collectivized in the Soviet Union under Stalin in 1928-33. Those with property in land lost it to the new collective farms, and those with livestock lost their animals as well. The ones gaining from collectivization were those who had little or nothing to begin with. So for some in Russia, the introduction of communism meant a loss, or a lowering of their standard of living; for others, of course, a raise. In the case of the philosopher rulers, they all started out with no personal possessions and all needs were supplied by the lower two classes.

Without a doubt Plato intended this communalism to extend well beyond economics and property. Relations between the sexes would not only be regulated by the philosopher rulers, but these relationships must **not** result in private affairs. No person, for example, would have private rights over any other person. That meant no monogamous marriages among the philosopher rulers and probably among the protectors as well. Plato had no affection for free love either. Although the sexes would work closely together and exercise in the nude, not only would indiscriminate mating be strictly forbidden, the whole sense of *eros* was absent. The rulers, like the protectors, had to rise above physical desires. Note that Plato was also transcending the Greek notion of beauty = youth by insisting that both sexes exercise together in the nude whether young or old, wrinkled or smooth.[15]

The reason Plato was so strict about this was that he intended eugenics to apply to human mating as it did to the mating of animals and presumably plants. He argued that eugenics was absolutely necessary in order to develop the finest human stock. And if the ideal state were to succeed, it would need fine rather than sickly stock. Just as people would stand guard over a female animal to safeguard future stock, so the human sexes would come together to mate only with prior permission. Spontaneous mating, thus, was ruled out, and permission would be given only if the mating made eugenic sense. Sanctions were severe: only if the mating were approved would the resulting child be allowed to live.

There would be a drawing of lots to see which female got which male, but the drawing would be rigged by one of the rulers so as to avoid incest and to make the most eugenic sense. The child resulting from such approved coupling would be removed at birth from its parents and be brought up communally. One could not even know who were one's own children, not even the mother, because knowing your own children would naturally cause the parent ruler or parent protector to favor that child over another, and the whole merit system in the schools would collapse. On the contrary, each child would be raised communally. They would not know who their parents were, nor would parents know their own children. Children would become possible sons or daughters of all the adults, and all adults would be possible mothers and fathers to the children, close kin-relationships anticipating the extended family notion at the core of African socialism as well as the child-rearing characteristics of Israeli kibbutzim.

Eugenics involved more than just the selection of the pair allowed to mate. It involved optimal times for mating as well. Specific ages were given for approved procreative mating: men between the ages of 30 and 45 and women between the ages of 20 and 40. Prior to these age periods, procreative mating might receive permission, but a resulting child had to be deported to another area, or, if defective, exposed. Nurture was limited to those children born to pairs within the prescribed age limits. The goals were an improvement of the human stock and control of the population size to reduce the risk of war and dependence on foreign trade.

It can be argued that this was not a pro-female argument at all, that in the process of making everyone the same the female was expected to become a weaker male. One can point to Plato's <u>Laws</u> to show a far less favorable attitude toward women. One could argue that Plato used females as a symbol useful in his critique of Athenian society.[16] However, the point here is not Plato's feminism, which can be doubted, but the fact that female equality was an integral part of Plato's overall communism in *The Republic*.

It is also difficult to believe that Plato saw much difference between the protectors and the rulers because his age limits for females focused on the female at the age of twenty when the educational system had not yet determined whether she would guard or rule. The males presumably **could** be rulers, but no specific mention of that ranking suggests that it was not important to Plato; reinforcing the notion that the protectors and the rulers were, in many respects, to be thought of as one group.

Rather strict communal sharing in this instance was to occur within an ideal state as a method of maintaining virtue for the upper classes, a form of social control and protective isolation of the rulers and perhaps the guards from the corruption of money and individual property. The majority of the population, the producers, had private property, private families, and whatever else their acquisitive natures could acquire. This communalism was for the upper class(es) alone.

These uncorrupted rulers would be both male and female; the philosopher king could well be a queen. This notion of gender equality was a revolutionary idea perhaps taken from Pythagoras and articulated at a time when Athenian women were cloistered and took no part in public affairs, a state that would last for centuries. Plato raised the question in *The Republic* whether there were some occupations that women could not hold because they were females. The answer was at least two millennia ahead of his time. He wrote that if one found that either the male or female gender was specially qualified for any particular occupation, then, of course, that is what ought to be assigned to them. But if the only difference seems to be that the male begets and the female brings forth, then we should conclude that no relevant difference between man and woman has yet been produced. Guardians and their wives, he wrote, should share in the same pursuits because there is no occupation concerned with the management of social affairs that belongs to either sex. Natural gifts are to be found here and there in both genders, and every occupation should be open to both, so far as their natures are concerned, though woman is for all purposes the weaker.[17]

Even with the communalism in place to preserve the virtues of the philosopher kings and queens, Plato expected that his republic would degenerate at some time in the future. The degeneration would follow, he felt, a cyclical pattern through **timocracy, oligarchy,** and **democracy,** to **despotism.** The degeneration would begin when the rulers' virtues were forsaken for something less enduring, like honor. Communism, in other words, could keep the wolf of degeneration away from society's door for a considerable period of time, but eventually the battle would be lost. Of course, the degeneration could be reversed by a blending in of virtue, and communism for the rulers could again be implemented. But the purpose again would be to retard social degeneration for as long as possible.

Plato's ideas were lodged in his famous dialogue, but they were never tested anywhere as he intended. Of course, his notion of a society divided into rulers, protectors, and producers did characterize the medieval period, as well as many other later periods. But these later frameworks would hardly have been called ideal by Plato because they would fit military dictatorships or practically any form of despotic government. To fit Plato's model the rulers would need to be very well educated, free of gender bias, and living in communist simplicity as brothers and sisters.

Diogenes

Thinkers after Plato tried to accomplish this but in a way that did not include the extensive educational system Plato had erected nor did they initially involve the whole society. A strong tendency among the Cynics and Stoics for the next two centuries was to expand and extend the Socratic image, a wise man trying to teach a city, into a **community** of wise, ascetic, and virtuous people who would benefit the larger city-state in which they lived. An early example of this trend was Diogenes, the Cynic, whose somewhat uncertain dates are 412-323BC, making him roughly the contemporary of Aristotle, Plato's most famous pupil.

Diogenes was a pupil of Antisthenes who was a disciple of Socrates, but a bit older than Plato. Antisthenes lived an aristocratic life until after the death of Socrates, when he began an active philosophizing on his own; dressing like a commoner and speaking as one, believing that people should return to a natural simplicity and do without government, property, marriage, religion, or any artificial pleasure. He despised both slavery and luxury at a time when slavery was an assumed part of the environment and luxury was the goal of almost everyone.

Diogenes was a pupil of Antisthenes whom the teacher allegedly did not want to have around. Diogenes was the son of a disreputable money-changer who had been imprisoned for defacing the coins in his care. Legend suggests that Antisthenes tried to discourage Diogenes by beating him away with a stick. This may have helped Diogenes to grow up with a strong antipathy toward authority as well as to its representation on coins. He determined to live naturally, like a dog does, and for this reason Diogenes became the first of a group called "cynics" or canines.

Like a dog Diogenes rejected all conventions of manners, dress, housing, food, and even decency, and proposed a sister/brotherhood with all people everywhere as well as all animals. Like Francis of Assisi, Diogenes lived by begging. He sought virtue by liberating himself from desire, or from any attachment to the material goods some people value so highly. One needs independence from the external world, so free yourself from external goods, and value only virtue.[18]

In *The Republic* allegedly written by Diogenes there was an expectation that the entire world would become a Cynic success story, but the main thrust of his teaching was that the communal sharing of the wise community would gradually leaven the entire society and make it better. The communalism Diogenes had in mind was much more than a community of property. Sexual sharing or free love, possibly drawn from legends about barbarians so as to shock puritanical Greeks, was a very strong part of his *Republic*. He proposed a community of women, for example, with a free choice of partners, sounding like Rosa Graul's "Hilda's Home", a story serialized in a 19th century magazine,[19] and quite unlike the regimented eugenic system of Plato. Like Plato, Diogenes insisted on raising the children in common. Choice of sexual partner was left quite free. Indeed, Dawson wrote, the ideal city of Diogenes permitted every kind of incest, bold promiscuity on the part of both genders, a homosexuality so unrestricted that the system might be called a "community of boys," and even rape if necessary. Women in his city dressed and behaved exactly like men, even exercising with them in the nude.[20]

This may have been a parody of Plato's *Republic* or it may have been a forgery attributed to Diogenes and written by a later Stoic who wanted to show a Cynic dependency on Stoicism. These questions, happily, can be left to others; what is important here is that these ancient Greek ideas expressed admiration for widespread social sharing in communities that were subsets of a larger whole which the communities hoped to influence. Pythagoras, Plato, and Diogenes were all quite similar in that regard. Plato stands out from the other two, however, in that the communist community was the ruling group (and perhaps the guarding group as well) of the entire society.

These ideas remained untested in large part, but were remembered attempts at implementing ideas from the golden age or from the idyllic Garden. These attempts were reminders of what could be and how it might be brought about even though one might disagree as to method and possibly even parts of the goal. For centuries after Christ, the ideas of Pythagoras and Plato remained influential, and even the more ascetic ideas of Diogenes found fertile soil in Zeno and the Stoics, creating ideas that lasted through the Roman times into and beyond the middle ages. Christian notions about ideal societies were adapted to fit ideas of heaven and the end of the world when appropriate rewards and punishments would follow universal judgment. Life on earth in such formulations was left unchanged. Basic contentment with the idea that communal sharing and brother/sisterhood were ideals attainable only in heaven after death lasted until the 12th century when communal sharing ideas began to emerge in a different form in the thinking of Francis and Joachim. Later, both Thomas More's *Utopia* in 1516 and Thommaso Campanella's *The City of the Sun* in 1637, literary communist utopias that stressed knowledge, owed a great deal to Pythagoras, Plato, and Diogenes. So do the Settlement Houses in the early twentieth century.

Settlement Houses

The settlement house movements created by Jane Addams (1860-1935) at Hull-House in Chicago, Lillian Wald (1867-1940) at the Henry Street Settlement in Manhattan, and Mary Simkhovitch (1867-1951) in Greenwich Village were attempts by women to create a social environment in which a virtue could flourish that would spread beyond the settlements to impact on a much broader civic life.

A dictionary definition of settlement houses describes them as welfare centers providing community services in an underprivileged area.[21] Lillian Wald used a different dictionary and provided a definition that carried with it an aura of participatory action: "...an establishment in the poorer quarter of a large city, where educated men and women live in daily contact with the working class for coöperation in social reform."[22]

Jane Addams was born in Cedarville, Illinois. College educated in an era when female graduates of colleges were rare, she visited Europe in 1887 and was deeply influenced by Toynbee Hall, the first social settlement located in East London that had been founded in memory of Arnold Toynbee who had become interested in the neighborhood poor while a student at Oxford. Jane Addams returned to Chicago determined to replicate Toynbee Hall in the United States. Jane wrote that it was difficult to tell exactly when her ideas matured, but she gradually became convinced that it would be a very good thing to rent a house in the poorer part of town where both primitive and actual needs were to be found. In the house young women who had spent much time in study might learn of life from life itself, try out some of the things they'd thought about and put truth to the test.[23]

After some searching for a good site and lots of advice from intellectuals, city officials, and newspaper reporters, the house was found, a run-down old structure that took its name from its early owner, a Mr. Charles Hull. They quickly gathered volunteers and began kindergartens, girls and boys' clubs, a coal cooperative for the neighborhood, and a boarding club for girls who worked in nearby factories but felt they couldn't stay on strike because they would not be able to pay for their board and room. They would be the first of the workers to capitulate and go back to work because they were the most vulnerable. So the cooperative was formed to provide for this need, and two comfortable furnished apartments were rented near Hull-House.[24] The ladies tried to fill gaps wherever they were perceived. One such was an old lady of 90 years who was left alone all day while her daughter cooked in a restaurant. In frustration the old lady would pick at the plaster on the walls, ruining the walls and forcing the family to keep moving. The Hull-House group diverted her to making paper chains, and when it was learned that she spoke Gaelic, scholars from the university came to visit her. The neighbors became very proud of her and began to cherish her.[25] Hull-House gradually became an important part of Chicago life, as did the house on Henry Street in Manhattan.

Lillian Wald's house in New York City was built in the slums on the lower East side. It was a crowded part of the city; in one neighborhood there were 1,000 people per acre. In the midst of this poverty and dirt, the women of Henry Street lived together, travelled together, and worked together. In the process they created a network of love and support that sustained them and the area around them.

They voluntarily chose to live together in a society that offered very little economic freedom for women. Their private sexual lives were criticized by outsiders, and often, especially during the suffrage movement, they were harassed and jailed. During World War I their anti-military activities branded them as social enemies and brought them large quantities of hate mail. They dared to stand up and be counted and many other people tried to push them down again. They were described as communists during the Red Scare of the 1920s and 1930s; and by communists the critics meant Marxists or Bolshevists. Lillian Wald and Jane Addams and most of their co-workers were described as part of a red web of traitors who threatened America. In 1935 when Jane Addams died, she was described as the most dangerous woman in the United States.[26]

In part these silly charges come from a total misunderstanding of the politics of settlement house leaders. Jane Addams remarked this even before she had begun Hull-House. While looking for a house to rent, the group (which included a newspaper reporter) looked at a house which contained an anarchist sunday school where a young German was teaching children to sing the poetry of Koerner. The newspaperman was suspicious of the singing and when Jane translated the simple poetry for him he still was not satisfied. When she told him that the poetry was to be found in any decent library, that it was not some secret anarchist material, the reporter looked at her askance. She said that then and there she got the idea that to treat a Chicago man who is called an anarchist as you would treat any other citizen was to lay yourself open to deep suspicion.[27] To a person who only sees black and white her behavior was suspicious. A Marxist, however, she was not.

Jane Addams herself clearly pointed out that the most significant change brought about by the success of Bolshevism in Russia was the fear engendered throughout the rest of the world, a fear for the safety of private property and established governments, a fear that frequently hamstrung progressive change and enshrined the tendency to play things safe. The same characteristics affected European society after the French Revolution and Napoleon. In words that could equally well apply to the disastrous period known as the Cold War, she found it a great detriment to American national development that foreign policy was directed so largely by the panic-stricken and by those skeptical of the essential integrity of human nature.[28] Jane Addams was far more concerned with abolishing toothaches for children than private property for adults.[29]

When Lillian Wald and the Henry Street group are considered as possible Bolshevik sympathizers, the same sort of disbelief arises. Lillian Wald made very clear in the mid-thirties that she and her sisters identified with the progressive elements of Bolshevism but not with the whole. She was as critical of Bolshevism as she had been about the tsarist autocracy that had preceded it.[30]

Through all this carping criticism the ladies of Henry Street pursued their vision of social justice and social change not from an ivory tower miles from danger, but from the heart of the slums of New York City. Lillian Wald described the lower East side in terms reminiscent of descriptions of contemporary slums. Bad as the streets were, she wrote, the conditions of most houses were worse. Filth and grime accumulated on the stairs, sanitation was primitive and bathtubs were scarce. Rear tenements in which there was no running water overlooked yards filled with debris; children played on heaps of offal, while families of six or more crowded together in one or two rooms.[31]

Miss Wald and her female cohorts in the Settlement House determined to correct these problems. They did not do so in charity because they felt that charity merely prolonged the problem by reinforcing poverty and its humiliating character. They sought institutional change that would be both permanent and public. They began such things as playgrounds, public health programs, maternity programs, parks, school lunch and other child welfare programs, but they believed that final responsibility must be taken over by the government as a permanent service to the community. So they and other settlement houses were lobbying groups to gain support for greater governmental responsibility for the poor in their areas.

Henry Street financial support came from a variety of sources. The most public was probably Jacob Schiff, a particular friend of Lillian Wald. But this support was simply to get started; the group insisted that social welfare was the state's responsibility, not that of private citizens.[32]

There were many victories. Cleaning up garbage collection in Chicago. Helping young women who by the age of 14 were already professional prostitutes. Forming the Hull-House Social Science Club, which heard radical speakers from all over the world. Thousands of little things that helped real people get through real life better than they would have otherwise. At Henry Street it was no different. By 1897 they had persuaded the New York City Health Department to send 150 physicians to spend one hour per day in New York's public schools. A regular school nurse program was established, eventually resulting in a visiting nurse for each school in the system. School lunches came out of this Settlement House program.

They created the Social Halls Association and built auditoria for public lectures, concerts, and political meetings; dining halls; ballrooms; pool rooms; and social centers as well as study halls for children that had nowhere to study or practice musical instruments. A national playground association was formed in 1898 along with the Outdoor Recreation League. The Visiting Home Nurse Service, founded by the ladies at the Henry Street Settlement, made over 600,000 calls by 1932. The nurses that set out from Henry Street each day gave advice on nutrition and disease prevention. They practiced holistic medicine before the term was popular among the avant garde. Lavinia Dock stated in a 1907 speech that the contemporary age rejected the theory that misery and sickness were unpreventable. People had learned to place prevention before amelioration and to respond to the thrill of the discovery that the human race was capable of construction and of indefinite development and improvement. Human society, she argued, could be voluntarily and consciously built into nobler and fairer forms than those of the past.[33]

Jane Addams argued that the settlement houses provided a proper outlet for educated young people who valued the sentiment of human brotherhood, who felt a fatal lack of harmony between their theory and their lives, the lack of coordination between thought and action. These young men and women, she argued, are longing to socialize their democracy so as to universalize a life of refinement and cultivation. Places like Hull-House provided an outlet for active mental faculties and an aware social conscience.[34]

These were steps in the direction of a broader movement that would bring the fruits of settlement house activity to everyone. The best speculative philosophy, Jane Addams stated, was that which set forth the solidarity of the human race, for the highest moralists have taught that without the advancement and improvement of the whole, no one can hope for any lasting improvement.[35]

Lillian Wald likewise insisted that the activities of the Henry Street Settlement House were only the beginning. Her goals were by no means limited by the Henry Street neighborhood. She wanted to end war, poverty, unemployment, and to establish freedom, security, and a global harmony based on the notion that we are all one family. These accomplishments, she felt, would depend on the activity of future generations with commitments similar to those of the courageous Henry Street settlers.[36]

A third example of the settlement house idea occurred at about the same time in Greenwich Village. Mary Melinda Kingsbury Simkhovitch was born in Chestnut Hill, Massachusetts and graduated from Boston University. She did graduate work at Radcliffe College and at the Universities of Berlin and Columbia. In 1899 she married Vladimir G. Simkhovitch who became a professor of economics at Columbia in 1904. From 1898 until 1902 Mary was associated with a settlement house called the Friendly Aid House on New York's lower east side, and in 1902 she helped to establish Greenwich House. She was its director for the next 40 years, and tells the story of those years in her autobiography of Greenwich House called *Neighborhood*.[37]

The Cooperative Social Settlement Society was founded in May of 1901 and this organization lay behind the Greenwich House in Greenwich Village. They found a house in a neighborhood populated by people from twenty-six different countries. They shared space on the street with five saloons and nine boarding houses. Greenwich House had also been a boarding house and a tenement house and had an Anarchist Society's headquarters in the dining room. This was where the women lived, while the men rented space for themselves nearby, coming to Greenwich House for their meals. The whole idea, Mary wrote, was that the group of friends, together with the neighbors would through common experience build up enthusiasm for common projects. This would be better than the charitable approach because the participation of everyone would make for sound improvements.[38]

She did not confuse the community movement that she saw herself a part of with the class struggle and the labor movement. This wife of an academic economist and the founder of a prestigious economic club was well aware of the "class struggle" but she saw the community movement in which she and other settlement house people were involved as the larger whole in which the labor movement could occur.[39] But, like Jane Addams and Lillian Wald, Mary Simkhovitch was quite able (unlike her critics) of understanding where her position was with reference to either German/Italian fascism or Russian communism. She saw no difficulty in supporting the Progressive Party in 1912, and saw herself as defending old-fashioned liberalism. This liberalism she understood to be an attempt to understand the complexity of the times, to effect change in a step by step manner, and to rebuild on the basis of factual knowledge and new desires. Such liberalism, she wrote, "...is the only road possible for adult men and women who see the destruction that necessarily takes place in the train of revolution...."[40]

Mary K. Simkhovitch, like Jane Addams and Lillian Wald, was no radical, if by radical one means the adoption of some far out political and economic philosophy. The ladies of the settlement houses were activists but not revolutionaries. They were active in being living examples of the social virtue that Mary Ansell hoped for and Sarah Scott depicted (See Chapter 7). The light of virtue and purity which Pythagoras saw the need of so long ago, could have been kept alive by religious groups but it wasn't. Settlement Houses and other experiments like them did so instead. If there had been more of them perhaps the dream of communal sharing might have been achieved.

Endnotes
Chapter Two

1. Bertrand Russell, *A History of Western Philosophy* (New York: Simon & Schuster Touchstone Book, 1945), pp. 19-21.

2. Doyne Dawson, *Cities of the Gods: Communist Utopias in Greek Thought (New York: Oxford University Press, 1992), p. 15.*

3. Russell, *op, cit.*, p. 31.

4. Dawson, *op, cit.*, p. 14.

5. Ibid., p. 18.

6. Russell, *op. cit.*, p. 32.

7. Ibid., p. 35.

8. Ibid., p. 32.

9. John Burnet, *Early Greek Philosophy*, 4th Edition (London: Adam & Charles Black, 1930), p. 98.

10.   Plato, *Timaeus*, trans. R.G. Bury, Loeb Classical Library (Cambridge: Harvard University Press, 1961), pp. 45, 47.

11. Frank E. and Fritzie P. Manuel, *Utopian Thought in the Western World* (Cambridge: Harvard University Press, 1979), p. 120.

12. Lewis Mumford, *The Story of Utopias* (Gloucester, MA: Peter Smith, 1959), p. 46. Original copyright 1922.

13. Francis MacDonald Cornford, *The Republic of Plato* (New York: Oxford University Press, 1979), pp. 106-107.

14. Ibid.

15. Arlene W. Saxonhouse, *Women in the History of Political Thought* (New York: Praeger Publishers, 1985), pp. 40-41.

16. Ibid., pp. 48, 57-58, 62.

17. Cornford, *op, cit.*, pp. 152, 153.

18. Russell, *op, cit.*, pp. 230-232.

19. Rosa Graul, "Hilda's Home," serialized in *Lucifer, the Light Bearer* (1883-1907), cited in Carol Farley Kessler, ed., *Daring to Dream: Utopian Stories by United States Women, 1836-1919* (Boston: Andora Press, 1984), pp. 192-204.

20. Dawson, *op, cit.*, pp. 146-147.

21. William Morris, ed., *The New College Edition of the American Heritage Dictionary of the English Language* (Boston: Houghton Mifflin Co., 1976), p. 1186.

22. Lillian Wald, *Windows on Henry Street* (Boston: Little Brown & Co., 1936), p. 5.

23. Jane Addams, *Twenty Years at Hull-House* (New York: Penguin Books, 1938), p. 72.

24. Ibid., p. 105.

25. Jane Addams, *Twenty Years, op, cit.*, pp. 86-87.

26. Blanche Wiesen Cook, "A Utopian Female Support Network: The Case of the Henry Street Settlement," in Ruby Rohrlich and Elaine Hoffman Baruch, eds., *Women in Search of Utopia: Mavericks and Mythmakers* (New York: Schocken Books, 1984), p. 114.

27. Jane Addams, *Twenty Years, op, cit.*, p. 77.

28. Jane Addams, *The Second Twenty Years at Hull-House: September 1909 to September 1929* (New York: The Macmillan Co., 1930), p. 154.

29. Ibid., p. 156.

30. See Lillian D. Wald, *Windows on Henry Street, op. cit.*, pp. 251-284. This chapter in her book descibes a lengthy period of Henry Street involvement with Russia before, during, and after the 1917 upheavals. Lillian Wald was by no means one of Paul Hollander's political pilgrims swayed by the latest leftist propaganda. To sense the contrast with Lillian Wald, see Paul Hollander, *Political Pilgrims: Travels of Western Intellectuals to the Soviet Union, China, and Cuba 1928-1978* (New York: Oxford University Press, 1981).

31. Ibid., p. 111.

32. Ibid.

33. Ibid., p. 113. Speech taken from "Lavinia Lloyd Dock," *Nursing Outlook* (June 1969), pp. 72-75.

34. Jane Addams, *Twenty Years, op. cit.*, pp. 92-93.

35. Ibid., p. 100.

36. Ibid., p. 115.

37. Mary K. Simkhovitch, *Neighborhood: My Story of Greenwich House* (New York: W. W. Norton & Co., 1938).

38. Ibid., p. 93.

39. Ibid., p. 93.

40. Ibid., p. 176.

Chapter Three

Communal Sharing
as part of a
Spiritual Revolution

Early Christian Sharing
Francis of Assisi
Joachim of Fiora
Liberation Theology
Dorothy Bryant's The Kin of Ata

So long as spiritual goals are kept sufficiently abstract, the Kingdom of Heaven is difficult to imagine as something that could occur in this world in this life. In part this reflects the success of the apocalyptic version of the Jesus message over the sapiential one. In other words the notion that the Kingdom was yet to come won out over the idea that the Kingdom was already here--a divine kingdom with no respect for proper protocols, a kingdom, as he had said, not just for the poor but for the destitute, the beggars.[1] This separation between the futuristic heavenly and the present earthly evaporates, however, when one discovers the interchangeability of communal sharing, loving, and acts of kindness with high levels of spirituality. The two go together. If either one is sought the other seems to follow. If one feels a decided increase in spirituality, it is most likely that the expression of that spirituality will look very much like communism is supposed to look. So it ought not be surprising that communal sharing and positive spiritual change go together.   It doesn't matter where one starts, one will cause the other to occur. The examples of communal sharing in this chapter demonstrate this phenomenon.

Early Christian Sharing

The early followers of Jesus located in Jerusalem after the alleged ascension of Jesus into the heavens had the intention of establishing a revolutionary kind of community because of the spiritual change that had taken place within them. The evidence for this is quite scanty, and what there is comes from a few verses in the book of Acts in the Bible's New Testament. But what does exist is very good evidence that both Jesus and the early believers intended to create a sharing community. The egalitarianism was not simply in Jesus' message, it stemmed as well from the peasant society (Nazareth) from which Jesus emerged.[2] It was not just a small part of, but a major component of the heritage Jesus left to his followers.

"Jesus' Kingdom of nobodies and undesirables in the here and now of this world was surely a radically egalitarian one, and, as such, it rendered sexual and social, political and religious distinctions completely irrelevant and anachronistic."[3] Jesus proclaimed that neither broker or mediator should exist between humans and the divine or between humans. The miracles and parables, his healing and even his eating were calculated to force people into unmediated physical and spiritual contact with God and each other, a religious and economic egalitarianism that negated all hierarchical and patronal aspects of either Jewish or Roman society.[4]

Apparently there were over 3,000 converts in the very early days of Christianity before the new religion even had a name. The group was large enough to make a strong impression on the author of Acts yet small enough to be cohesive and tightly organized. The converted Jews were baptized in the new style John the Baptizer had made popular, and it was reported in the book of Acts that they all continued steadfastly in the doctrines of the apostles, in their eating and prayers. All that believed remained together and had all things in common.[5]

To reach the plateau of all things in common, they all sold their goods and possessions and shared the resulting money with everyone. All the believers were of one heart and soul--they were really together. One dimension of that spiritual togetherness was that none of them had any thought for individual possessions. Instead they had all things in common.[6]

No one lacked for anything in this new spiritual society because as many of them as had been possessors of houses or lands sold them and brought the monies to the group, laying them down at the feet of the apostles.[7] Subsequent redistribution of this new wealth was to everyone according to his or her need.[8]

This new process of selling one's possessions and sharing with others was not at all understood to be an accidental or casual arrangement. The author of Acts made it very clear that the communal sharing these people were practicing was a very serious *spiritual* affair. A man named Ananias and his wife Sapphira sold their possessions but kept back some of the money. They laid only a part of the proceeds at the feet of the apostle, pretending that it was all. Peter said immediately that this was totally unacceptable. It was a major error and he apparently meant the lie rather than the holding back of possessions. The lie alienated the individual from God whereas the common sharing brought the individual closer to the deity. In Peter's judgment there was no gray area in between the two positions. Peter told Ananias that his actions revealed that Satan rather than God was inside them. Satan, he said, has filled your hearts. Ananias fell down dead, and three hours later when his wife Sapphira, who didn't know what had happened, repeated the lie, she too fell down dead. As one might imagine, these events caused fear to spread throughout the entire church.[9]

No more is mentioned of this early sharing by Christians. A strong reason for its continuation would be the expected early return of Jesus. As long as that was possible, one can imagine that the communal sharing would possibly continue, although there is no evidence either way. As long as that second coming was anticipated daily, there was no point in going on with life as it was before. But when it was obvious that the second coming of Jesus Christ was being postponed to the indefinite future, the reason for staying together would slowly disappear. If that disappearing reason happened to coincide with the destruction of the temple in 70AD and the wrath of the Roman armies, then the dispersion of the early Christians becomes quite understandable. As time passed the Kingdom of Heaven increasingly became something one expected after one's life or at the end of the world rather than some time in the near future. Spirituality diminished and expectations of communal sharing became part of the anticipations of heaven.

It also became more abstract and separated from daily life. During the middle ages the older strain of ideal sharing from the Pythagorian communities, Plato's *Republic*, and even Diogenes' *Republic* were pulled into the Christian theological version of the last days. The ideal was the heavenly, the spiritual, the mystical; the goal for which one strived, but which was not expected to be any part of one's daily life. The ideal was not an earthly goal at all. Passages in the Bible that apparently referred to a quick return of Christ or the imminence of the Kingdom of Heaven were interpreted to mean something compatible with the failure of Christ to return and the fact that the Kingdom had not begun.

Life on this earth was not believed to be a soul's punishment for losing its wings, as Plato had put it poetically, but thought to be a pilgrimage in a strange place; a long waiting room that for some reason was seen as necessary before one received the entry pass into heaven. For the successful, for those who became involved in the politics of society or the church and grew wealthy at the expense of the many, this separation between the earthly and the ideal life blurred the attractiveness of the ideal because the earthly life was so gratifying. The ideal counterpart to the mean pilgrimage dimmed to insignificance compared to the pleasure of gaining power and expanding it. If the successful thought about heaven at all it was to imagine an afterlife which rewarded people like themselves.

For the less successful, however, the separation between earthly life and ideal life provoked a fear that involvement in the affairs of the world would jeopardize their spiritual lives. Sometimes such people found refuge in monastaries or convents; or they just tried to live pure (defined as celibate) lives, sometimes seeking greater spiritual depth by denying bodily needs other than sex or even punishing their body. This could involve living in strange circumstances like down a well, for example, or atop a small tower, or rising from their sleep several times during the night for prayer and meditation. The theory was that the more miserable the body was during this life the happier the later life of the spirit would be.

Such a sense (or nonsense) of things depended on the idea that virtue and sin were represented by spirit and matter, an old Gnostic notion that Christianity never outgrew. In this view matter equalled sin and spirit equalled virtue, so that one's body was evil and had to be denied in order that one's soul could be freed from its bodily imprisonment. Within this general conception sexual intercourse was not viewed as a song of joyful love sung to one's creator, but was contrariwise imagined an evil barely tolerated to maintain the human race. This was why celibacy was so highly valued; because sex was viewed as so sinful.

In this context, of course, ideas of communal sharing, of brother/sisterhood, had to be relegated to the far-off future after one died. There was no room for it in this vale of tears, this dismal waiting room for strangers in a foreign land filled with people patiently enduring so as to win the prize.

Sometime in the twelfth century this attitude and approach to life underwent a significant change. The parochial isolation of the Middle Ages was broken by the Crusades that began early in the twelfth century, by the rising conflict between the new kings and the papacy, by the presence of more than one pope at the same time, and by the success of another major religion, Islam.

These may only appear to be the reasons, but the fact of the matter is that the dream of a future life became the catalyst for adventurous deeds designed to bring to earth some form of the Kingdom of Heaven. A few people stood out as leaders, implying that it was sinful to wait passively for the blessedness of the next world; demanding instead the early consummation of the times in the immediate, earthly founding of the glorious Kingdom of God. The main area of prophetic contagion was Central Europe and the Rhineland, but the movement quickly spread throughout the continent.[10]

Ideal beliefs and notions of social revolt were coming together, but this was by no means only a secular drive. Even secular revolutionaries were turning to the Bible for a model of a desirable society to replace the odious one they were rejecting. This was a strong enough movement that the Roman Catholic church caused the Council of Narbonne in 1229 to forbid lay reading of the Bible. What was there in the Bible that the establishment feared? Only visions of paradise and a Lord's Prayer that asked: "Thy kingdom come...**on earth** as it is in heaven."

The rational, ideal society such as that articulated by Plato would not become generally known in Europe until the fifteenth century when it would become part of the explosion of learning that was not even anticipated in the twelfth century. In the 1100s echoes from ancient utopias may have lingered in popular folklore, but they would be weak in comparison with images of paradise drawn from the pages of the Bible. What was different was that these images of an ideal society were taken to mean that this is how earth should be *now* rather than how it might look in the distant future after death. In the 1300s in England John Ball and the Lollards found sanctions for social and political protest in the Scriptures because it showed them how the world could be and how it began: equal and sharing rather than stratified and grasping. "When Adam delved and Eve span, who was then the gentleman?" was the resulting question. If there weren't lords and ladies in the beginning, why are there now? Do away with them! The Hussites of Bohemia and Moravia dreamed of a patriarchal order whose rulers would imitate the Fathers of the Old Testament. Flemish weavers went further back to the Garden of Eden and built an ethics on the nudity and simplicity of the first couple. They called for the naked truth, or no hiding at all.

A beginning of all of these protests was a critique of the church for its great wealth and enormous distance from the common person. These critiques, like those from the theology of liberation in the twentieth century, came from individuals **within** the church. But the critiques and personal examples were more than protests against Vatican wealth, they were in fact calls for the entire world to turn itself around from ways that Plato too would have found reprehensible. The two most prominent activists were Francis of Assisi (1182-1226) and Joachim of Fiora (1130-1202) who saw money, possessions, the pursuit of wealth, and the sense of "mine" as opposed to "yours" as the soil from which evil, dissension, and social degeneration grew.

Both Francis and Joachim were Italians who represented a more widespread spiritual movement early in the twelfth and thirteenth centuries. Both called for an end to the hypocrisy of automatically supposing that great spiritual force and great material wealth could coexist in the same institution or in the same person. They condemned the institution of private property, gaps between rich and poor, and called for the sharing of both material and spiritual wealth among all of God's children, but especially the poor.

Francis of Assisi

Francis was born in 1182 of a wealthy merchant family named Bernardone living in Assisi. His name at birth was John, and legend has it that because he spoke French the name Francis replaced the name John. He learned both Italian and French from his parents and Latin from the priest, but he had no other formal schooling. He entered his father's business, but soon began to spend more than he made. His generosity became well known and his friends multiplied, as one might imagine.

In 1204 he volunteered for military service in the army of Pope Innocent III. He fell ill, however, and in a fever heard a voice asking him a difficult question: "Why do you desert the Lord for the servant, the Prince for his vassal?" meaning, one gathers, why are you serving the Pope instead of me? Francis asked what he should do and was instructed to go home and wait for more information. So he returned to Assisi, but this was a different man than the one who had so recently left. He began to implement a personal communism with a very high spiritual content. He gave all of his possessions and some belonging to his father to the local chapel priest. He overcame his disgust with leprosy so that he could help lepers. He ate little, stayed near the chapel, and soon became a target of derision from passing children because his appearance disintegrated: he became thin, ragged, and often confused. The children thought him mad.

Although this new life upset his father very much, Francis never seems to have looked back. He continued to give away anything that others gave him, even the clothes on his back. He begged along the roadway and then gave what he received away to others whom he perceived as more needy. This intensity of loving could not have been kept up had Francis not had a small support network to assist him, but this fact should not detract from his great generosity.

In February 1209, while listening to a church service, he heard the priest read Jesus' words to his disciples who were evidently preparing to go on a missionary journey: As you go, preach, saying the Kingdom of Heaven is at hand. Heal the sick, cleanse the lepers, raise the dead, cast out devils: freely you have received, freely give.

Provide neither gold, nor silver, nor brass in your purses, nor script for your journey, neither two coats, neither shoes, nor yet staves, for the workman is worthy of his meat.[11]

What Jesus may have originally meant by these words is perhaps an open question, but Francis took them as a literal confirmation of what he was doing with his life. The words provided him with the ideological context into which his life could fit. He began to preach a gospel of material poverty and spiritual richness. He denounced money as evil and urged everyone to sell all that they owned so that they could give the proceeds to the poor. He called for an end to private property which would also end the need to defend it with arms. His communism was his understanding of the Kingdom of Heaven, both the method of reaching it and the goal itself.

This is not surprising when activities of the early Christian church are recalled. Francis probably read the Acts 4:32-35 description of the early church group in Jerusalem and wanted to recreate it in Italy. The passage suggested that because of the communism the believers were all of one heart and one soul; something that would really appeal to Francis. The believers had everything in common. This increased the fervor of their spirituality and increased the grace they were given. No one lacked for anything because each person's needs were satisfied from the social wealth created by everyone's having sold all their possessions and giving the money received to the apostolic leaders.

There was nothing halfway about Francis' communism. He pushed it to its logical limits within the spiritual context, and perhaps even beyond logical limits. Prefiguring Hegel and Marx's great concern with overcoming alienation, Francis preached against **anything** which divided the individual from the whole. And the whole included all things, not just other people. He could not stand for anyone to be poorer than he was, and his followers had difficulty keeping him clothed. He communicated with animals and plants, and even hated, it was said, to put out a candle flame because the fire might not wish to be extinguished. He preached a sermon to birds who allegedly listened avidly. He felt a oneness, a unity, with the whole universe that precluded alienating elements such as private property, wealth, individualism, or a sense of separation from nature. This unity was even extended to other religions. A hymn written by Francis in 1225 bridged the gap between Christianity and other religions more oriented to nature. The hymn was called *The Canticle of Brother Sun* and it named the sun as brother and as one of God's creatures. The moon was his sister as were the stars. The wind was his brother, water was his sister as was mother earth. He was one with people and nature, as well as other understandings of spirituality.

If Francis had not preached such a difficult lesson for others to follow, his teaching could have led to a rebellion against both church and state. Occasionally, after his death, his ideas **were** the basis of rebellion against authority. Some have argued that Francis had in mind a clear rebellion against the economic and political power held by the church and against the many corruptions he saw in the monasticism of the early 1200s.[12] His Friars Minor, as early Franciscans were called, were often mistaken for other rebels such as the Albigensians or the Cathari. The Franciscan demand for purity of life, the need to devote one's life to God and Gospel, the tendency to follow the idealism of the Sermon on the Mount, the repudiation of private property, and the call for a full equality of goods among people gave the Franciscans a revolutionary cast, even if Francis had never intended to begin anything other than a spiritual revolution.

However, the order founded by Francis quickly discovered that his spiritual life of generous simplicity was very difficult to emulate. His order gradually became like other monastic movements, except for a small group of dedicated followers who called themselves Spiritual Franciscans or Left Franciscans or Zealots who continued the attacks on property by calling for Christian poverty. In this view poverty is a virtue because it is the opposite of an evil: great wealth. This sort of thinking would lead others to the idea that the poor are the salt of the earth, virtuous and deserving **because** they are poor. The followers of

Francis had an enormous influence, even though a pope in 1323 declared that the need for Christian poverty was a false doctrine. The establishment that Francis hoped would repent gutted the heart of his movement.

Francis of Assisi or John Bernardone was a most unusual man, a rare individual standing as a model and ideal for others to try to emulate. He probably wasn't perfect, but he must have been so close that it didn't really matter. In a time when individualism was touted over communism as an expression of conservative Christianity, Francis stood out as a prominent exception. He did not stand for individualism; in fact he stood for the opposite so strongly that he might have prayed "Lord remove the bondage of self that I may serve you better." The prayer that has always been attributed to Francis is again a model very difficult to follow because it expressed such a high degree of altruism that very few, if any, are able to implement its words. This model unfortunately underscores the impossibility of following in his footsteps; preventing the very thing it purports to create.

Lord make me an instrument of your peace.
Where there is hatred, let me sow love;
Where there is injury, pardon;
Where there is doubt, faith; where there is despair, hope;
Where there is darkness, light; where there is sadness,joy.
Divine Master, grant that I may seek not so much
To be consoled as to console;
To be understood as to understand;
To be loved as to love;
For it is in giving that we receive;
It is in pardoning that we are pardoned,
And in dying that we are born to Eternal Life[13]

If such men are necessary **before** communal sharing and loving can arrive it is doubtful that they will ever come. Finding other people equally or even almost as unselfish as Francis would be very difficult. If such a person were to be the result of a communal society, it might almost be believed possible. But that the sharing depended on the prior existence of such humans makes the dream of equality even more difficult to imagine.

Joachim of Fiora

Giovanni dei Gioacchini di Fiori is a second example of spiritual communism. What distinguished Joachim of Fiora, as he came to be better known, was that his communist ideas were lodged, as were Marx's, in a theory of history. He was born at Celico in the region of Calabria, Italy around 1130AD and lived until 1202. His noble father was Mauro the Notary who held office at the court of Roger II of Sicily, and initially Joachim's career was patterned after his. He became a well educated young man in the era of European crusades to free the Holy Land from the Moslems and various attempts to unify Italy under first one king and then another.[14]

He was sent to Constantinople as part of an official party but he parted company with the others and journeyed to the Holy Land to find himself and his purpose in life. The poverty of the people he passed was evidently greater than what he had witnessed in southern Italy. It impressed him so much that he dismissed his servants and continued on to the Holy Land as a humble pilgrim. His sense of a need for dramatic atonement was so great that when he got to the Holy Land he punished his body by spending the entire Lenten period living in an old well on Mt. Tabor near the Sea of Galilee.

How he accomplished this hermit-like existence is not clear. Perhaps he had servants bringing him food and drink during that lengthy period, but it must have been difficult nonetheless, because sensory deprivation would be punishment all by itself. At any rate, at the end of his lengthy stay in the well, Joachim allegedly had a vision. He later said that this vision caused him to understand not only all the Scriptures, but also the past, present, and future of the world. It was, in other words, a major flash of insight that completely changed his life. He said that he had received the "fullness of knowledge."[15]

For a while Joachim became a hermit near Mt. Etna in Sicily. He then returned to Calabria as a wandering preacher where he was ordained as a priest and later became a monk. In a biography written by Joachim's secretary, Luke of Cosenza, Joachim was described as a humble and kindly man of great devotion, given to prayer and study. He often wore the oldest clothing he could find, slept little, and ate little, and yet was robustly healthy. His humility was a visible characteristic because he would often volunteer to do the lowest work of the monastery like the cooking or scrubbing the infirmary floor. He became popular and was elected Prior and then Abbot of his monastery in 1178. Five years later, however, he left all this administrative detail to begin dictating the ideas and concepts that whirled in his head. The Pope released him from his duties as Abbot and encouraged his writing. The next pope, Clement III, again encouraged Joachim in 1188 and requested that his writing be examined by the papal curia when it was finished.[16]

Joachim and a friend sought to live as hermits in cells, but seclusion proved impossible. People sought him out and wanted to be his followers. The result was the formation of St John of Fiore Abbey on Mt. Nero, with rules of poverty and prayer. He began to write, he felt, under divine inspiration, and in 1200 he sent his writings to Pope Innocent III for papal censorship. Two years later he died.

Joachim's vision on that Easter Sunday gave him the strong feeling that human history was a **divine** story that had a beginning, middle, and a culmination corresponding to the three parts of the Trinity. History, in short, was divided into three ages. The Age of the Father he characterized as a human society ruled by fear. It was a harsh period, loosely equivalent to what he imagined was "Old Testament" history, when repressive threats of vengeance were necessary to maintain order. This eye for an eye period was supplanted by the Age of the Son, the second historical age, which was less harsh but still very controlled. This second age was associated with the organized church whose discipline functioned as a social and political educator. The age would last many years but it had a shorter shelf life than many thought. Joachim felt that the church became too attached to material things and as a result its discipline and message became corrupt. When the gap between wealth and poverty became great enough, and he felt it was very visible then, the Age of the Spirit would arrive. Joachim predicted, unwisely perhaps, that the new age would begin in 1260 well after his own death, but at a point, he computed, when twelve centuries would have passed since the resurrection of Jesus which began the Age of the Son.

The important part of this is not the date, but the contents of the new age supposed to begin in 1260. The Age of the Spirit would have **neither** a religious **nor** a secular hierarchy, although West and Zimdars-Swartz argue that Joachim intended a new and different sort of monastic group to direct the affairs of church and state in the third Age.[17] It became widely believed at the time, however, that in the new age no person would ever be subordinate to any other again, a sort of spiritual anarchy. For this reason Joachim's ideas were extremely popular with mendicant orders. Material goods would be held in common, because there would be no private property. The rule of fear, replaced by the discipline of the church, would now become the rule of love. This new age would come sooner if its goals were taught more widely and if people lived lives of voluntary poverty and urged the church to do the same. When the new day dawned, the Holy Spirit would take over. Real freedom, love, and oneness would prevail, but in the last days of the second stage, just before the new Age of the Spirit, Joachim predicted more troubles, wars, and ecclesiastical corruption.

Followers of Joachim spread these ideas over a very large territory and thousands of people accepted his apocalyptical vision as literally true. The idea that a reign of love was coming soon, a reign of love on earth that would supersede property, wealth, and the law was enormously appealing, especially to the poor. Judgment Day was postponed to the end of this new period when the Holy Spirit would reign on earth. The imminent earthly Kingdom of Heaven, of course, softened and blurred the otherwise vivid distinction between earth and heaven. The break between this world and the next was less frightening than it was in Augustine's Christianity.[18]

His periods of time, very carefully computed, are described below:

<u>Age of the Father</u>
Knowledge of good and evil
Submission of slaves
Suffering
Fear
Starlight

<u>Age of the Son</u>
Power of wisdom
Obedience of sons
Action
Faith
Dawn

<u>Age of the Spirit</u>
Fullness of knowledge
Freedom
Contemplation
Love
Broad daylight

The distinctions between the three stages suggested an evolution within the divine trinity itself, which may account for the fact that he was never made a saint. His longing for the new age and for the humans that would live in it was also an indictment of people and institutions in his own age.

In the Age of the Spirit life would be permanently changed because the state of the world would be changed so completely.[19] This was to be a world of love filled with people who cared for each other and the world around them. What made this possible was the infusion of the Holy Spirit and the communism of goods. Loving equalled sharing, equalled giving, equalled receiving in love. Such was the Age of the Spirit.

Many Franciscans became Joachimites as did many Dominicans, because Joachim's new age seemed to incorporate so many elements from Francis' teachings. It also universalized an ideal monastic existence that was bound especially to appeal to those already practicing much of what Joachim predicted for the new era. The number of new believers increased, and the new movement of love and communism reached its height just before 1260. The appeal of the new, classless utopia soon to come was very great. Obviously after 1260 passed and the new age did not begin, disappointment was great, and the old order quickly reestablished itself, proving that the conversions by thousands of people to an age of love had not been very deep. What remained was the continuing belief that the spiritual age was still to come, occasional critical outbursts against wealth and privilege, especially in the church, and the memory of hope tinged with frustration that the new era with its classlessness and absence of hierarchy had not materialized.

Both the Franciscans and the Joachimists continued for many years, and their message was taken up and widely preached by others. This was a spiritual communism that articulated a deep sense of Christian piety and a strong awareness of the human need to belong to a social whole; a heaven on earth or an earth in heaven that ended poverty and wealth, powerlessness and privilege. Yet, however much is made of the spiritual content of their communism, the implementation of their ideas would have dramatically moved **secular** society into a communist era. Neither Francis nor Joachim called for their followers to put up with a world that did not at all match their ideas, as it seems early Christians were urged to do. Neither reformer called for an inner classlessness compatible with external class servitude, as early Christians spoke of inner freedom compatible with their external bondage. Both Francis and Joachim expected the inner to be matched by the outer, along with real changes in society and its institutions. So did others, centuries later.

Liberation Theology

The theology of liberation that developed in Latin America and the Philippines in the 1970s and 80s and in Haiti in the 1990s was similar to these ideas from so long ago. Those who called themselves part of the liberation theology movement broke with the idea that Christ's message of hoping, loving, and sharing had to be deferred to a heavenly future. They recalled that Jesus had told listeners that they would not die before **seeing** the Kingdom of Heaven. The Kingdom was supposed to be earthly perhaps more than it was to be heavenly.

To some extent this was a position wandered into, rather than self-consciously sought. Once bishops, priests, and nuns began identifying with their congregations rather than with the political or religious elites a curious thing happened. Giving material assistance to impoverished parishioners led to asking **why** the poor seemed so permanently miserable. Rev. Vic Hummert wrote that Bishop Dom Helder Camara of Brazil had said one time that when he gave bread to the poor, people would say that he was a saint but when he asked why the people did not have bread he was called a communist.[20] That question had never been a popular one because its answer exposed the hypocrisy of the ruling class. George B. Shaw knew this when he wrote the Preface to *The Irrational Knot*.

It is the secret of all our governing classes, Shaw wrote, which consist finally of people who, though perfectly prepared to be generous, humane, cultured, philanthropic, public spirited and personally charming are nonetheless unalterably resolved to have money enough for a handsome and delicate life. In pursuit of that money, they will batter in the doors of their fellow-men, sell them up, sweat them in fetid dens, shoot, stab, hang, imprison, sink, burn and destroy them in the name of law and order. And all this, he cynically added, shows their fundamental sanity and rightmindedness; for a sufficient income is indispensable to the practice of virtue.[21] This is hypocritical nonsense accepted only by those already converted.

Liberation theologians wearied of weak answers as to **why** one small set of people had it all while the large set of people had so little. What they wanted to see was what they thought the gospels had been all about--a reversal of the accepted hierarchical order, and a more equitable distribution of wealth. Although many liberation theologians became partners with atheistic Marxist revolutionaries in Latin America and elsewhere, the economic revolution anticipated was a social revolution grounded in the sovereignty of God over all creation. This would begin when God's mercy was acknowledged and shared on earth as it was in heaven. Compassion, not dollars or ability to pay, would redefine the nature of the socio-economic world.[22]

Liberation theology opened up Christianity to urge an actual **practicing** of what was often preached. Sin was redefined to focus attention on sin as failure to love one's neighbors and therefore one's God. And the sin being described was called a breach, a break, an alienation in friendship with God and with others that was considered the ultimate cause of poverty, injustice, and oppression. To move against sin had long been the church's preoccupation; redefined, however, it meant that the church should, as part of the move against sin, move *toward* a love of one's neighbors and God, as well as *against* poverty, injustice, and oppression that resulted from sin. This broadened the church's message and placed it alongside the oppressed, against the oppressor, in solidarity with the poor.[23] Occasionally this has meant that a priest or nun joined the revolutionary struggle of Marxists against the establishment. An example of this was Father Camilo Torres of Columbia who resigned from the priesthood, joined the armed struggle, and was killed by government troops on February 15, 1966.[24] For Father Torres there was no other way to express his Christianity than to rise in opposition to an exploitative, hierarchical order even though that structure was supported by his own church. His church was not fighting the Christian fight, according to his beliefs, but the Marxist revolutionaries were. In order to implement his Christianity, he felt he had to leave the priesthood and join the revolutionaries. He wrote that the revolution was a means of obtaining a government that would feed the hungry, clothe the naked, teach the uneducated, perform works of charity, and love its neighbors not merely in a transitory and occasional way, nor merely love some neighbors, but the majority. For this reason the revolution was not only permissible, but obligatory for all Christians who see in such activity the one effective and complete way to create love for all.[25]

Although he felt that he could not become a communist, he could fight alongside them to bring about the needed social revolution that would liberate the masses of people and open the door to the spiritual goal. Communism in this instance was an important step on the way to the Kingdom of Heaven. This was called "relativizing" communism, and it is what allowed these very spiritual people to fight alongside allegedly atheistic Marxists. It very simply argued that the communist goal would have not only a beginning but also a middle and an end, after which would come the Kingdom. Marx had similarly "relativized" capitalism by showing that capitalism was a limited mode of production to be superseded by socialism and communism. Radical Christianity could relativize communism and then go well beyond it, they thought, by insisting on the radical transcendency of God's Kingdom. The revolutionary dynamic would thus not end until the process had reached the Kingdom of God. The future communist society that represented the final goal for Marxists would for these Christians be the means to the Kingdom of Heaven on earth.[26] The revolution would not be the end of the struggle, but only the beginning that should properly have occurred centuries before. Meanwhile, liberation theology would benefit from revolutionary activity but not be trapped by it.

Unanswered, of course, is the begged question: Can violence in the name of love and caring ever be justified? These people who were *right there* said a resounding "yes" -- violence *could* serve the interests of love without being contaminated by it. Other answers are theoretically possible, but considering the frustrations arising from dealing with these nearly intractable problems, the affirmative answer is understandable.

In many ways the Christianity of liberation theology and the revolutionary message of Marxists in Nicaragua during the 1970s, for example, were nearly identical. This can be illustrated by the words of Father Ernesto Cardenal, describing the authorship of the Gospel commentary/dialogue called *The Gospel in Solentiname*. He wrote that the authors of the commentaries were not the people in the community who contributed various parts of the book. The true author, he wrote, was the Spirit that inspired the commentaries. He wrote that the Solentiname *campesinos* knew very well that it was the Spirit who made them speak, and that it was the Spirit who inspired the Gospels. By this he meant the Holy Spirit who was the spirit of God instilled in the community whom Oscar called the spirit of community unity, and Alejandro called the spirit of service to others, while Elvis called it the spirit of the society of the future. Felipe called it the spirit of the proletarian struggle, while Julio said it was the spirit of equality and the community of wealth, and Laureano the spirit of the Revolution. To

Rebecca it was the spirit of love.[27] This is understanding God as a verb rather than an abstract noun.

The articulators of the theology of liberation were more explicit than Francis or Joachim, perhaps because a revolution was going on in their countries as they wrote. Identification with Marxist revolutionaries was not easy, but it was far simpler than identifying with the existing establishment fighting the Marxists, for it was that self-same establishment that was oppressing the people for whom liberation theologians spoke, an oppression which involved both the state and the official church, at times to the point of a church participation in torture and murder.[28] Above, Father Cardenal identified the third person of the trinity as the spirit of community, of service, of the future society, of the workers' struggle, of equality and the community of wealth, of revolution, and of love. If all this were part of God, then fighting for them is certainly fighting for God and against evil, an evil enshrined in the institutions of property, wealth, and privilege.

Like Francis of Assisi and Joachim of Fiora, however, liberation theologians failed to bring about the revolutionary changes that were sought. Because of the tenacity of the opposition, the power of patrons of the status quo outside their countries like the Vatican and the United States, the liberation theologians, like Francis and Joachim, gradually faded from the scene as a new and interesting phenomena, but the force of their argument continued. This was visible in 1994 if one cut through the turmoil of Haitian immigration to see what the military dictatorship in Haiti feared from the liberal wing of the Haitian Roman Catholic church: liberation theology.

In Haiti the movement was known as the *Ti Legliz* or Little Church to distinguish it from the larger church under the control of the more complacent church bureaucracy able to coexist with the evils of poverty and destitution. The Little Church was a grass roots movement that resisted the military government that had ousted the elected president, Father Aristide. Liberation theology in Haiti called for the complete transformation of Haitian society and an "option in favor of the poor."

For example, the Rev. Jean-Yves Urfié, a priest born in France, was active both in the movement and in publishing the weekly newspaper called *Libète*. His Christian radicalism was based on the idea that in Haiti a cancer was growing that had to be removed. That cancer he called the Tonton Macoutes, the paramilitary criminal force organized during the dictatorship of François Duvalier, but still active on the side of the radical right.[29]

Leaders of the military government saw the Roman Catholic church as its only institutional rival, and over the years army leaders have tried to control the clergy by co-opting them into powerful positions or by intimidating them. In September 1993 the intimidation increased to the point where an associate of exiled President Aristide named Antoine Izmery was pulled out of a memorial Mass and shot dead in the street, delivering the mafia-type message that no one in Haiti had sanctuary.

For three years the principal target of the Haitian government's effort to erase the Little Church from Haiti was not important people such as priests whose deaths made headlines, but little people who usually pass unnoticed. Hostility was directed at the small local parishes, led by lay people, who met regularly to discuss the Bible and its application to daily life. These little groups, generally made up of strong Aristide supporters, functioned as a grass-roots movement called ecclesiastical-base communities. After Father Jean Paul Aristide was ousted in September 1991, these communities became the target for attacks by both the military government and the Roman Catholic hierarchy; one with guns and terror, the other with proclamations from the pulpit.

The resulting repression turned the base communities into an underground refuge for victims of political repression. An estimated 300,000 Haitians were reportedly living in internal exile.[30] The base communities provided sanctuary and hiding places for people, and exiled people could move from one base community to the other. Some people did this for two years or more. As a result of this continuing defiance, the homes of priests and nuns were irregularly inspected by the authorities, often at odd hours, and there was a strong effort by the government to rid Haiti of foreign born priests.

The church hierarchy in Haiti was led by Archbishop François-Wolff Ligondé who had strong ties to the dictator Duvalier. Opposition to Aristide was strong. Ligondé had condemned Father Aristide's election from the pulpit, and Aristide's own superiors in the Alesian order expelled him for inciting hatred and violence and a class struggle. Doing the same thing on behalf of the privileged was of course quite all right with the church leaders.

Of Haiti's 11 bishops, only Willy Romélus of Jérémie has consistently supported the work of the Little Church. He has twice been the victim of an attempt to kill him and he is isolated by the rest of the church leadership. Another possible exception is Bishop Emmanuel Constant of Gonaïves, normally a conservative, who has spoken against violations of human rights committed by paramilitary groups, even though the largest of these is led by his own nephew.

Despite the apparent odds against the Little Church, Father Urfié could say in 1994 that "the popular church here is still alive, even though a lot of leaders have been killed, because we believe that the blood of the martyrs is the seed for Christians. The more you persecute a religion, the more you give it strength."[31]

History says that Father Urfié is correct. In the meantime, however, repression and suffering characterize the rows of narrow concrete-block shacks that make up the slums of Cité Soleil and La Saline where Aristide's supporters live. People painted his symbol, a tiny red rooster on their homes, but that became dangerous after the military coup. In 1991 when Aristide was deposed, soldiers rode through the slums in pickup trucks, firing their weapons into the homes at random.[32]

Among his strongest supporters, Father Aristide became more of a historical legend, or a saint, than a real person who might come back to improve things in Haiti. Things were not expected to get better; drinking water still came from dirty ditches that also carried raw sewage, babies still went hungry, and there was still no electricity. Things were expected to improve in heaven but not on earth--at least not in Haiti and particularly not in the slums of Cité Soleil.

And then the conflict tightened. The Rev. Jean-Marie Vincent, a forty-nine year old priest who was a close friend of Aristide was killed. Father Vincent had been active in helping peasants in the northwest of Haiti, teaching them to read and trying to change the laws so that peasants could own their own land. People who knew him said that he never considered his work political, but evangelical.[33]

Fear intensified in Haiti after the assassination of Father Vincent, but there had already been sufficient reason for terror. Random attacks on innocent people, specific attacks on spokespersons for democratic rights were common. For the family of Robert Jean, who had been in hiding for almost three years because of his public statements in favor of democracy, the situation worsened considerably in June 1994. His nineteen year old daughter was repeatedly raped by five armed men. Her seventeen year old brother was beaten with batons, handcuffed, and forced to watch. Their nine year old sister was beaten to the floor. Robert Jean was not at home to protect them that night, but, in truth, the poor were without protection for a long time in Haiti.

This fact seemed finally to sink into the consciousness of American leaders and in the fall of 1994 U.S. troops paved the way for President Aristide's return. With enormous difficulties ahead, the theology of liberation had a new chance to demonstrate a different kind of politics, a Christian politics attuned to the needs of the weak rather than the strong. The dream of equality, a dream shared by real religion, seemed a little closer. But the spiritual revolution need not be Christian, nor any other recognizable religion that relies on words to express its meaning. It only needs to be spiritual.

Dorothy Bryant's *The Kin of Ata Are Waiting for You*

The final example of sharing that is part of a spiritual revolution is not a real event but a fictional island in Dorothy Bryant's novel *The Kin of Ata are Waiting for You.* It is an unusual book. The hero is a criminal who has murdered his girlfriend after an argument. Both were stoned on wine and pot, and he was driven to the edge by recurrent nightmares, but those were variables not excuses. At 4:15am, the killer, himself an author of novels, dressed and drove away, stupidly leaving his girlfriend's body in his own house for others to find when the daylight came. His lawyer, he thought, would get him out of this scrape as he had before. His psychiatrist would help along the plea of temporary insanity by testifying about his nightmares. No remorse was visible about the life he had taken from Connie; yes, he had remembered her name while driving away. He thought only of escape, of how his reading public might react to the scandal, of how he might excuse his behavior and not be punished. Like many others he was self-centered in the childish, totally selfish way that people have who believe that the universe revolves around them. A less likely hero would be difficult to imagine, and a strong temptation to put down the book is balanced by the realization that one is only on page 4. Surely something must improve? It does, but in an improbable way that moves the reader, without any awareness of such movement, from a consideration of nightmares to dreams, from selfishness to service.

The "hero" drove down the expressway and turned up a mountain road that climbed and climbed. At a curve his car went off the road, over the mountainside, flying and bouncing to the bottom. At some point he felt thrown out of the car and knew that his death would be a permanent plunge into his nightmare. He heard himself scream in the horror of knowing what was to happen.[34]

But he did not die. Instead, with many painful injuries, he came back to an awareness of vague shapes taking care of him, giving him water to drink. He could not see them, but he sensed their presence. He thought he was in a hospital, groggy from the accident, but he wasn't. He was on an island, in the midst of an apparently primitive people called the Ata.

They spoke a language he could not understand, but when they moved him he realized he had been in a kind of cave. He realized that he wasn't blind, it had been too dark in the cave to see. Plato used a similar example in *The Republic*, and the book suddenly becomes intriguing. Would he see the light? What was the light? Would he see what the light illumined?

The answers come slowly. When he awoke in a tent, he was aware that his injuries were being treated by some wet leaves, but he had no idea where he was or who these people were. He ate some pink mush on a leaf, and wondered if he had fallen into an Indian reservation or some kind of rural commune filled with back-to-nature people. A black woman, whose name he later learned was Augustine, came into the tent and fed him, and a boy and a dog came in to treat his injuries. Then eleven others came into the tent to sleep, arranging themselves like spokes in a wheel with feet at the hub. They awoke with the dawn and when two people had arisen they stood speaking to each other for a while, total gibberish at first, but then he discovered that each was telling the other one the dreams they had experienced the night before. Then they washed and went to work for the day.

After a few weeks the bored "hero" was allowed to go outside the tent, but there was nothing to see except a low wall on which people would place shells, leaves, fruit, and jugs of water. But he could watch and count the people as they passed by him.

He calculated that the Ata were a small group; less than 150 people had walked past him, including babies carried by others. They all dressed alike, walked alike, and had the look of people listening to far off music. There were all kinds of races and mixtures, like Augustine's blue eyes or a blond boy with oriental eyes. They all seemed so much alike that gender was often difficult to determine, especially since there didn't appear to be sexual rôles. Everyone took turns doing everything.

They ate in a common room, a dining tent, but they had the strange habit of feeding each other with lots of smiling and laughing. They were **nourishing** each other. Only very small children who had not yet learned proper habits fed themselves. When he got the idea he did it too. He began to feed Augustine and then others in the circle. They all seemed pleased that he had caught on; as though he had moved from being a very small child to a child who had learned something. There didn't appear to be much food, he thought, but being fed in this inefficient way took so much time and was so enjoyable that everyone, including himself, acted as though they'd had enough. The lesson without words was that helping others had fulfilling side effects. When people fed others rather than themselves, there was always enough food.

Realizing that he could not return to his former life without a good deal of assistance, he gradually acclimated to the people on the island. He and Augustine formed a sexual relationship that began as a form of rape and slowly became a shared nurturing as he grew into the group. Part of his difficulty in fitting in was language. They spoke a funny language, he thought, and it wasn't used as much as he thought a language should be used. It was funny in that it was a vague language, the word for food meant anything edible, and all animals had one name. The language had no past or future tenses, everything was NOW. It also lacked any sense of the singular, because when they spoke the subject would always be plural, another quiet lesson without words. For example, animals and plants could be masculine and feminine (not neuter), but people were unaccountably gender neutral. One pronoun fit the whole human race. He could not understand how they communicated with a language of such poverty. But that was the catch--the language was not used much. They didn't communicate much with words. Whenever they had a choice they used gestures. Words were the last resort rather than the first resort that he was used to. The Ata felt that if one talked too much it was "donagdeo," the negative opposite of "nagdeo." The word "nagdeo" was used to convey a good morning or a good day feeling as well as the positive ethical feeling-- sort of a sincere God be with you. "Donagdeo" was the opposite and referred to activities that other cultures called "sin;" movements away from one's God. Ata who "sinned" were pitied rather than punished. If one felt donagdeo, the response was to isolate oneself quickly in one of the island's small caves until "purified" or "cleansed" and back on the right way again.[35] The only reason for isolation, therefore, was to remove the barriers to social living.

The essence of the culture was spiritual, which connoted the social, sharing life of the Ata. The opposite was also true. The sharing facilitated the spiritual life of the individual. The goal of life was to return to the sun from which all had originally fallen, and the people yearned to know the way back. The story that the old people told was that the sun took pity on the people who wanted to find the way, and when they fell asleep, the sun shone through the sleep and showed them the way. In the silent light of sleep the people saw that as there was a law of gravity there was also a law of light and that the law of light was stronger than the law of gravity. The light would gradually fill them until they would rise up to meet the sun.[36]

The light of sleep was the dream, carefully recounted to another as soon as they awakened. This dream was the light that they kept within them both waking and sleeping until they became the light, gravity was overcome, and they returned to the sun.   Dreams thus were communications between God and the individual. Sharing the dream made it a part of the social consciousness. What the "hero" didn't realize was that the dream was much more important than the words in the language, and that words distort the dream.

Dreams were not only more real than actions, but they showed the way back to the sun. Following the way gave people peace (nagdeo); disturbance of the way brought the disharmony called dis-ease (donagdeo); needing the quiet isolation of the cave to cure. The way was virtue, the same feeling that Mary Ansell and Sarah Scott had, a feeling and a life that brought one closer to one's God.

The "hero" and the reader are being weaned from a dependence on words to a dependence on feelings and dreams as more reliable sources of ethical guidance. Until the full truth struck him, the "hero" felt that the Ata were hiding something from him and that the "something" involved a community treasure that he could steal so that he could get off the island and back to civilization. The reader at this point is ahead of the "hero" and realizes that the treasure is not gold at all, but a world of dreams that builds a solid world of nagdeo.

He searched for the treasure and recruited young people to help him look. When he finally communicated what he was looking for an old man smiled in amusement. Irritated, the "hero" hit him, and the old man fell down and died. Once more a murderer, he ran away again, but no one followed him. For three days he stayed hidden, then he decided to face the people who must want revengefully to kill him. He came down from the hill and found forgiveness rather than revenge. The Ata asked **him** to forgive **them** for wanting to harm him in retaliation. He confessed his other murder and described himself as an empty man. He was accepted back into the group. From this point on his desire to leave the island faded as he identified with the larger whole, the social unit.

But this is not the end of the story, even as it was not enough in Plato's cave analogy for the individual to climb out of the cave, grow used to the light, and see Agathon. The individual in Plato's example had to go back to the cave, to bring the light to the people in darkness. Our hero also had to go back and try to bring the light of the Ata with him. He began to listen to his dreams and to what other people said, discovering in the process that the desire for good dreams regulated the activities of the community as each person sought the best daytime rhythm for her or his body. The well-tuned body had the best dreams, it was widely believed. So one stopped work or slowed down when tired, ate when hungry, slept when sleepy, etc., and the result was a balance between mind and body that the Greeks would have envied.

Children were not possessions of their parents but belonged to the whole community. No one, Augustine said, belonged to anyone else. Did she then belong to herself? She didn't understand the question. Did she belong to the group? It was clear that the verb "belong" was what was confusing Augustine. The Ata did not have that conception and simply did without it. Possession was not known. What was treasured was not something that could be possessed. In a sense it did not exist. Augustine said that the treasure was what was most real and precious, but it could not be seen or touched.[37] Nor could it be expressed in words. Words, Augustine said, get between us and the meaning we seek to convey. Only when one experiences the meaning is the meaning known.[38] The lesson is simple but profound: live virtue rather than talk about it.

The "hero" could now face his various selves in his dreams until only two were left--a woman who became increasingly black and the man who had given up trying to control his life. Augustine entered his dream and showed him what to do. He couldn't describe what had happened because words failed this former writer. "A rational man is not equipped to ask the right question about a non-rational event."[39] He now knew that the Ata were not a primitive people but far ahead of anything he had ever known. Illness did not exist because they avoided donagdeo that would result in imbalance and disease and harm their ability to return to the sun. They did not avoid writing and words because they were primitive but because THEY KNEW (as many supposedly advanced cultures did not) that words froze the dream and caused people to mistake the word for the unknown behind it. The word, therefore, instead of expressing the unknown became a thing between the people and the unknown that it was supposed to symbolize. Spoken words were okay, they rose like smoke and disappeared; it was the written ones that were donagdeo because they caused people to stop dreaming.[40]

These people, he came to understand, were sustainers, spiritually altruistic people who took on the pain of others and who tried by their good actions to balance the bad actions of others. They were people who tried to maintain the balance of this insane world, "...until it would, of its own choice and from its own realization of necessity, come back to Ata."[41]

The sharing on Ata was a part of the spiritual revolution that moved people to a sense of "us," reminding the reader of what Victor Ferkiss pointed to years ago, that a belief in individualism is **socially** grounded.   Actually, he wrote, notions of discrete individualism discontinuous with society are *lies* designed to prevent social action. Ferkiss correctly argued that if we realized the extent to which our "individualism" is already shaped by society we would use that consciousness to make the shaping process more fully reciprocal, less one-sided. In so doing we would not only mold society, but through that remolding reshape ourselves.[42]

That was the story of the Ata, an experience that awaits the reader. It is the spirit of the early Christians, of St. Francis, Joachim, and the liberation theologians. It is the spirit of community, the Holy Spirit, the spirit of sharing and loving.

Endnotes
Chapter Three

1. John Dominic Crossan, *The Historical Jesus: The Life of a Mediterranean Jewish Peasant* (San Francisco: Harper Collins, 1992), pp. xi. Also see pp. 228, 229. For a discussion of the kingdom of the destitute or beggars see pp. 272-274.

2. Ibid., pp. 262-263.

3. Ibid., p. 298.

4. Ibid., p. 422.

5. Acts 2:44

6. Acts 4:32

7. Acts 4:34

8. Acts 4:35. The verse actually specifies distribution to every *man* according to *his* need. Probably language sexism.

9. Acts 5:1-11.

10. Frank E. and Fritzie P. Manuel, *Utopian Thought in the Western World* (Cambridge: Harvard University Press, 1979), p. 181.

11. Matthew 10:7-10.

12. Mulford Sibley, *Political Ideas and Ideologies* (New York: Harper & Row, 1970), pp. 257-258.

13. Taken from a postcard sized handout titled *Prayer for Peace* with a subtitle reading "The Prayer of St. Francis."

14. Delno C. West and Sandra Zimdars-Swartz, *Joachim of Fiore: A Study in Spiritual Perception and History* (Bloomington, IN: Indiana University Press, 1983), pp. 1-2.

15. Ibid., p. 3.

16. Ibid., p. 4.

14. Ibid., pp. 103-104.

18. Manuel & Manuel, *op. cit.*, p. 57.

19. Ibid., p. 58.

20.   Rev. Vic Hummert, "Liberation and Payoffs" (Letters to the Editor), *The New York Times*, January 17, 1994, p. 10.

21.   George B. Shaw, Preface to *The Irrational Knot*, vol 2, xvi-xvii, *The Works of Bernard Shaw* (London: Constable & Co, 1930-38), cited in Paul A Hummert, *Bernard Shaw's Marxian Romance* (Lincoln: NB, University of Nebraska Press, 1973), p. 10.

22.   Richard Batey, *Jesus and the Poor* (New York: Harper & Row, 1972), p. 21.

23.   Gustavo Gutierrez, *A Theology of Liberation: History, Politics, and Salvation*, Sister Caridad Inda and John Eagleson, trans. and eds. (Maryknoll, NY: Orbis Books, 1973), pp. 35, 301.

24.   Father Camilo Torres, *Revolutionary Writings* (New York: Harper Colophon Book, 1972), p. 356.

22.   Ibid., pp. 314-315.

26.   Rosemary Radford Ruether, *The Radical Kingdom: The Western Experience of Messianic Hope* (New York: Harper & Row, 1970), p. 193.

27.   Ernesto Cardenal, *The Gospel in Solentiname* (Maryknoll, NY: Orbis Books, 1982), pp. ix-x.

28.   "Bishop Assails Church Role in 'Dirty War,'" *The New York Times*, April 29, 1995, p. 5.   An Argentine Bishop, Jorge Novak, admitted church collaboration with the Argentine government during the 1970s when some 4,000 people were killed and 10,000 "disappeared."

29. Larry Rohter, "Liberal Wing of Haiti's Catholic Church Resists Military," *The New York Times*, July 24, 1994, p. 3.

30. Ibid.

31. Ibid.

32. Rick Bragg, "Haiti's Poor Love Aristide but Don't Expect Him," *The New York Times*, August 16, 1994, p. 6.

33. Rick Bragg, "Haitian Priest, Who Had Aided Aristide, Is Killed by Gunmen," *The New York Times*, August 30, 1994, pp. 1, 2.

34. Dorothy Bryant, *The Kin of Ata Are Waiting For You* (Berkley: Moon Books/Random House, 1971), p. 5. Formerly published as *The Comforter*.

35. This blend of theology and philosophy from Christian and non-Christian sources is an example of the fascinating fact that over the millennia of human history people's theologies are basically similar. Differences, often thought quite important, actually detract from the beauty created by the blending.

36. Dorothy Bryant, *op. cit.*, p. 64. A Christian church with stained glass windows can depict Jesus with a halo around his head. On a bright day the halo appears to be the sun, with Jesus showing the way.

37. Ibid., p. 112.

38. Ibid., pp. 117-118.

39. Ibid., p. 133.

40. Ibid., p. 201.

41. Ibid., p. 204.

42. Victor Ferkiss, *The Future of Technological Civilization* (New York: Braziller, 1974), pp. 151-152.

Chapter Four

Communal Sharing
as an
Ideal Social Alternative

Thomas More Utopia
Thomas Spence Spensonia
Étienne Cabet Journey to Icaria
Marge Piercy Woman on the Edge of Time

Communism can be advocated in a spiritual form as a corrective to an evil society. It can also be the main characteristic of an imaginative society described as existing on a fictional island[1] against which one's own society can be compared and judged. The idea that paradise was an inaccessible island was a very popular idea in the medieval period. At one point Ceylon was thought to be a spot from which paradise could be seen. Dante wrote of earthly paradise as an island, and Prester John's utopia was an island. Isidore of Seville described the Happy Isles as the place which stimulated Ovid to write about the Golden Age. Isidore thought they were located "...in the ocean, left of Mauretania, close to the setting sun, and separated from each other by the sea."[2] It is not surprising that islands were involved in the chief conceptual utopias developed: those of Thomas More, Thomas Spence, Étienne Cabet, and, with a little imagination, Marge Piercy.

Utopias are ideal societies, existing only in the imagination of their authors, whose goal in articulating them was generally political and moral improvement. Those included in this chapter all stress a high degree of communal sharing, although some utopias do not.[3] Beginning with Thomas More is to begin with perhaps the model for most other utopian authors, even more so than Plato.

Thomas More, *Utopia*

Thomas More was born in London in 1478 to a family headed by a London lawyer, Sir John More. Thomas lost his mother at age six and experienced three stepmothers. According to Erasmus, More was an affable and sweet young man, and he loved jokes and farces.[4]

In his twenties he suffered periods of deep depression, balanced by times of spiritual joy. Most of the time he believed that life was a vale of tears only mitigated by the search for that union or oneness with God that spelled salvation.

He belonged to an era when educated intellectuals were influenced by Plato who was the central figure in the fifteenth century rediscovery of Greek literature. The *Utopia* that More wrote was influenced by Plato's *Republic*. More wrote as though he were proposing a better ideal society than that created by Plato, based on moral rather than on metaphysical grounds.

During 1492-1494 More studied at Canterbury Hall, now Christchurch, Oxford, and in 1494 was a law student in Lincoln's Inn. At age 21 he won a seat in Parliament and quickly distinguished himself by a rousing attack on a new subsidy demanded by King Henry VII. After being admitted to the bar, More earned a reputation as a strong pleader of causes, and he quickly became a luminary in the court of Henry VIII. He was knighted in 1514. In 1516 he accompanied the commissioners sent to review an alliance between Henry VIII and Charles of Austria. As a well educated and well travelled man with a sense of honesty and humor he became internationally known among the small number of humanist intellectuals associated with the renaissance and with Erasmus.

He wrote *Utopia* in 1518 when he was forty years old, still in the king's favor, still with seventeen years to go before he would be executed for his religious opposition to Henry VIII's oath of supremacy that the king wanted all his officials to sign. This oath acknowledged the king rather than the pope as the head of the church. Thomas More refused to acknowledge Henry's leadership of the church, was arrested, held in the Tower of London, and indicted on grounds of treason, which was what disobeying the king was called. He was found guilty, and sentenced to death by beheading. Before his own troubles with the king, More had been instrumental in the king's service in sending many Protestants to their deaths for their religious beliefs, and, ironically, he joined them in 1535. Four hundred years later he was declared a saint by a slowly grateful Roman Catholic church.

The book *Utopia* is composed of two parts: Book One described and validated the messenger who brought the news about the island of communal sharing to Europe and encouraged the reader to consider concepts and precepts that differed from the usual. For example, More wanted his readers to consider English society from a different perspective, one that disallowed private property. He wrote, for example, that as long as private property exists, as long as money is the measure of all things, a nation cannot be governed justly or happily. Justice cannot exist where the best things are held by the worst people. No one can be happy where property is limited to a few. The few are always uneasy and the many are always wretched.[5] Plato, that wisest of men, knew that the one and only road to the welfare of all lies thorough the absolute equality of goods.[6] When that equality of goods is not present, More argued, the result is two sets of people whose fortunes ought to be interchanged. Unless private property is done away with, the distribution of goods cannot be fair and the society cannot be happily governed.[7] Through the eyes of the traveler, a man named Hythloday, More created a willingness on the part of the reader to consider something quite different. That was the island of Utopia, described in Book Two.

Almost immediately one perceives that a price has been paid for the equality. There is an astonishing amount of regimentation and a woeful lack of spontaneity on the island. Perhaps More simply did not like spontaneous things. Some people don't. On Utopia, for example, there were fifty-four cities not less than twenty-four miles apart to provide enough room for farm lands in between. Rural households were staffed by people sent from the cities in two year service terms, staggered so that some experienced people were always on hand. More food was grown than was needed by these farmers, so the excess food was shared with those in the city. Seasonal need for extra labor was met by people from the cities. Food for people in the cities seemed provided by happy accident rather than by careful planning. Why does More apparently leave such a **basic** element to chance and minutely plan for trivia? He seemed to take food for granted as might a person who had never gone hungry.

The fifty-four cities were all similar to each other. The cities had walls, ditches, and moats, and the streets were all twenty feet wide, suggested by Robert M. Adams as commodious by European standards at that time.[8] Every house had a front door as well as a back door to the garden, neither of which was ever locked; the absence of private property removed any reason to steal. There seemed little desire for privacy. Anyone who desired to enter could. Every ten years people changed houses, but since the houses were all similar, i.e., three stories high with fronts faced with stone and with flat roofs, the purpose of the move every decade must have been to prevent people from becoming attached to any particular location, somewhat reminiscent of Plato's desire to prevent private attachments in the Republic.[9]

The government of Utopia was as democratic as a person like More could be in 1516. The distrust of the masses still evident in the framers of the American experiment in 1776, particularly the indirect election of Senate and President, was reflected in More's earlier description of government in Utopia. Officials of the society were elected by the people every year, and these elected officials then elected a prince by secret ballot from among four applicants nominated by the people of the city--evidently the capital city Amaurot. The prince would hold office for life unless impeached for moving toward tyranny. Officials at the top level met regularly with the prince but no decision of any import was permitted unless it was discussed for three days in the senate or popular assembly. As a matter of fact it was a capital offense to discuss public business outside of the senate or popular assembly. Yet three sentences later More described how the members of the popular assembly should discuss matters with the households they represent. Such discussions were needed to protect the citizenry from tyranny. So that the society could run on the most democratic of lines, everything of any import was discussed with every household. While the indirect elections suggested distrust, other provisions, such as discussing important things with every household, made More's democracy seem quite radical even for the late twentieth century. Moreover, the size of the island's population made some of More's prescriptions easier to implement than they would be for societies whose populations numbered in the millions.

Occupationally, the Utopians were mainly farmers. They were given theory in the classroom and encouraged to practice their agricultural skills during field trips to the country. Besides the farm work, people also learned a second trade. This included women as well as men, but because women, according to More, were not as strong as men, their crafts would be somewhat lighter than those assigned to men, perhaps wool-working rather than masonry, or linen-making rather than metal-work.

Usually a son was trained to his father's craft. Daughters were not mentioned here as following the craft of their mother, for example. Gender equality did not seem to be a priority for More. This was quite visible in what followed. If the son felt attracted to another line of work than that of his father, he was transferred by adoption into a different family that practiced that particular trade. Both that son's father and the authorities made sure that the young man was assigned to a grave and responsible householder. All this thinking about the future of the young man should, one imagines, stimulate similar thinking about young ladies, particularly since More had just indicated gender equality in the preceding sentences of the same paragraph.[10] But young ladies were not mentioned except to indicate that they would be assigned to one of the lighter trades.

One of the occupations of the officials was to make sure that no one sat around in idleness and that everyone worked hard at their trade. This did not sound so good, but More sweetened the pot by adding that the work day was only six hours long. People worked three hours in the morning before dinner, they rested a couple of hours after dinner, then they worked for another three hours. They had another meal called supper, and at eight o'clock they went to bed and slept for eight hours.

This appeared quite regimented because leisure hours were also expected to be busy about some occupation that pleased the individual. More could not leave it at this vague level, however. It was as though a reader might find something to criticize in these idle hours, so More first stated that they are left to the individual to fill, and then filled them for the individual. For example, there were public lectures before daybreak, and compulsory attendance was only for those who had permission to be in a learning module, while many others, both men and women, attended them voluntarily. After the evening meal, an hour was spent in recreation in one's garden during warm weather and in the common halls during the winter, playing games or just conversing. Their games did not involve gambling with dice, which to More was a foolish and ruinous game. One game was a battle of numbers in which one number captured another, and another was a game in which virtue battled various vices either in combination or by themselves. If this sounds like about as much fun as a Sunday School outing in the pastor's back yard, that's because More was a highly moral and virtuous man who described his own character as he described the people of Utopia.[11]

Workers on the island produced in six hours a sufficiency for everyone. More than enough, Thomas More said, of both the necessities and conveniences of life. This might seem strange, More felt, since the people did not work very hard, but remember that almost all of the people worked. Many people in European societies did not work; most women, for example, did not work outside the home, but they did in Utopia. Additionally, there was in the European idle group a lazy gang of priests as well as the rich, especially landlords and their retainers whom More considered swaggering bullies. Then More suggested that the reader recall that in Europe people produced for the market rather than for consumption, which involved a great deal of waste. In other words, when production was organized so that almost all people participated, **and** people produced for use rather than for trade, the amount of time each must spend working became quite low.

One class of people were exempt from working; these were the intellectuals who needed time to devote to study. This too was a reminder of the influence of Plato. This exempt group was not self selected, so lazy individuals would not gravitate toward this group. Individuals desiring to enter this group must have the recommendation of the priests and the support by secret ballot of the elected officials. If the scholar disappointed the recommenders, he (or she?) became a worker again, but for the successful the rewards were rather significant. Ambassadors, priests, officials, and the prince himself were chosen from this group of scholars who seemed to be the source for the philosopher-rulers so important to Plato.

Housing lasted a long time because people took care of it rather than abused it as More thought was done elsewhere. Clothing also lasted a long time because the main garment was a loose sort of robe made of leather, which lasted seven years. When they went out in public, people covered their leather garment with a cloak, but everywhere on Utopia the cloak colors were the same--the color of natural wool. Although elsewhere, people might want a variety of colors and materials in their clothing, on Utopia people were content to wear the same cloak through both seasons on top of the loose leather garment that lasted seven years. So far less need for new construction or repair, and far less need for the manufacture of clothing or its raw materials.[12]

There was considerable equality on Utopia, but there seemed to be far less freedom. Sexual freedom was not part of the island either. Both bride and groom were expected to be virgins at marriage. Nonetheless they would have seen each other naked prior to the marriage ceremony so that blemishes came as no surprise. While divorce for adultery or intolerable behavior was possible, remarriage for the guilty party was not. In some cases divorce would be allowed by the Senate after careful deliberation if new partners had already been selected to replace the incompatible partners. Women did not marry until they were eighteen, and men not until they were twenty-two.

Despite his own passionate nature, More determined that on Utopia premarital intercourse was not only forbidden but severely punished. The reason was because, in More's belief, no one would marry if they could have promiscuous sex.[13]

Each city had 6,000 households. If a household had too many adults in it, the excess would be moved to a household that had too few. If there were too many households, some must move to a different, less populated city. If the whole island became overpopulated, the excess number was required to establish a colony on the mainland, where they functioned as sort of a people reserve in case population went down below the optimum number. In that case they would be brought back from the colony.

Each city had four districts, and in the midst of each district was a "commodities market" to which heads of households brought their produce or products for exchange. Food markets were nearby as well for breads, fruits, vegetables and meats. Animals would have been slaughtered outside of the city.

Meals would be eaten in common in large halls constructed so that fifteen people were on a side, thirty people to each dining hall. One could pick up food from the market and prepare and eat it at home, but it was not thought proper and was therefore very seldom done. In the dining hall the men were to sit with their backs to the wall while the women were seated on the inside by the aisle, so that if the woman had a sudden pain she could get up and leave with less annoyance to others. More's knowledge of women may have been limited despite his two marriages.

Lactating females were separated along with the young children from the other adults, but this separation benefitted only the children under five years of age. In the other room cradles, clean water, and a warm fire made it simpler to care for them. Older children, up to the age of marriage either waited on tables or stood in absolute silence along the walls, eating whatever was handed them by those seated at the tables.

Oddly enough, although More was describing a society of equality, Utopia had slaves! These very unequal people were prisoners of war, former citizens guilty of some crime, or men from foreign lands who had been condemned to death in their own countries. Slaves did the dirty work of the society, like slaughtering the animals. Some in foreign lands volunteered to be slaves on Utopia because they would live so much better as slaves on Utopia than they would free in their own countries. These volunteers could leave when they wished, but others were fettered for life.

There is a great deal of scholarly speculation as to why Thomas More wrote *Utopia*. Was it purely a joke? Did he intend to suggest communism for England and for Europe? A lively discussion can develop over these and related questions, but the point here is that this is the first major attempt to spell out in some detail what the future society might look like. Utopia was not a golden age where people did not have to work for their food; not a place where the land grew the wheat by itself. Utopians were not living in some Garden of Eden, nor were the circumstances similar to the heaven of golden streets and songs of praise. The communism was for nearly every citizen, unlike Plato's, and even touched the lives of the slaves. It was a bit less spiritual than the society apparently desired by Francis or Joachim. Thomas More took people as he found them in sixteenth century England and placed them in a distant, isolated society where liberty and freedom were sacrificed for equality and regulated behavior.

Thomas Spence, *Spensonia*

In the late 18th century, a London stationer named Thomas Spence (1750-1814) had a little shop from which he published bits of philosophy, which he called "Pig's Meat." One of his philosophies in print was an idea he published in 1795 for a utopia of his own, which he named after himself. The title of his essay was *A Description of Spensonia*.

After an interval of six years, he returned to these thoughts and published in 1801 *The Constitution of Spensonia: A Country in Fairyland situated between Utopia and Oceana; brought from thence by Captain Swallow*. The purpose of all this writing activity was to suggest the adoption of Spensonia's form of society which he felt people had unwisely left earlier in their history.[14]

Thomas Spence described the beginnings of Spensonia in a parable about a father who had many sons and who wanted to provide for them all. Normally the father's possessions would pass to the eldest son with the other sons forced to look for different careers; perhaps as an officer in the military or as part of the church hierarchy. The father in Spence's parable solved his dilemma by building a ship named Spensonia that his sons could use for trade. In order to achieve his purpose of providing for all his sons, the father insisted that the profits of the ship were to be shared in common among them.

The ship carrying the sons on their commercial voyage was wrecked on an island, and the sons were forced to transfer their rules for society from the ship to the island. One of the first things that they did was to insist that the communism that had applied on the ship would also be in force on the island and apply to whatever landed property they seized. All property on the island, therefore, became the property of them all collectively, and whatever profits there were would be shared with everyone.

The island was named Spensonia after the ship, and officers of the island were quickly chosen who could distribute the parcels of land that each person or family wished to occupy, collecting a rent for the public use according to the value of the land. The value, one imagines, was conceived in much the same way as in other societies; i.e., distance from market, proximity to water, quality of soil, etc. Monies collected were used to cover public costs or were divided among the people as a dividend, whichever seemed proper. At rent time a dividend would always be distributed, even though public demands were great. This dividend was to be a reminder of their past rights. When one paid rent, in other words, one got something back.

The sons further decreed that all additional land inhabited would also be governed in the same fashion. The inhabitants of a territory would together own the land, and the people of that parish would enjoy the rent from the land and control the police. A National Assembly or Congress, subsidized by a small tax on each parish, would legislate on national matters.

The most visible public work was always done by the parish. Home building, road construction, or the planting of trees, for example, would all be done for the parish by the local citizens. In other words, the people in that parish would be organized for whatever purpose by a parish official, and that is how the necessary work would be done.

Spensonia's decentralization of activity reduced the amount of regimentation that More found necessary on his island of Utopia. There would be far less central direction on Spensonia and more of the independence and self-help characteristic of rural communities. Unlike More whose motives in writing *Utopia* will always be unclear, Spence meant his utopia to be the necessary criticism of existing English society that would begin revolutionary change.

Spence knew that his utopia would not last unless he could keep it free from those who enjoyed the fruits of other people's labor and contributed none of their own. Two methods of safeguarding the new society were developed: the vote by ballot and the universal right to bear arms. Voting by ballot would ensure secret, honest voting, and the right to bear arms would mean that each could defend themselves and the society from invaders.

Thomas Spence felt uncomfortable with superficial demands for political change that did not include the common ownership of land and goods. He wrote that thousands of abortive schemes were daily proposed for redressing grievances and mending the constitution. But where the shoes were so ill-made at first, and so worn, rotten, and already patched, they are not worth the trouble or expense to repair, but ought to be thrown to the dunghill. A new pair of shoes should be made, neat, tight, and easy for the foot of one that loves freedom and ease. Then would all the controversies about this and the other way of cobbling that continually agitate society be removed; and people would walk along the rugged and dirty path of life easy and dry-shod.[15]

In other words, stop trying to repair the society. Throw that society away, and correct the root of the problem; the unequal distribution and ownership of property.

Étienne Cabet, *Journey to Icaria*

Étienne Cabet (1788-1856) also felt that the root of the problem was the unequal distribution and ownership of property, but he came to this position gradually. Cabet was born in Dijon, France in 1788, so he was of the post-revolutionary generation. For the first forty years of his life he was an idealist with Jacobin sympathies, but his speeches and his writings were so inflammatory and critical of the government that he was condemned to either a two year prison sentence or five years in exile. He chose the latter and spent most of his exile in England where he was influenced by Sir Thomas More's *Utopia*, as well as the ideas of social reform taught by a contemporary in Britain named Robert Owen, a socialist-industrialist generally considered to be the father of British socialism.

Cabet began to believe that he had found the cause and remedy for historical disorders and calamities: the cause was bad social organization while the remedy was a better one. The better one was achieved first by destroying aristocracy in favor of democracy, then abolishing opulence and poverty in democracy by means of a community of property. Communism, he felt, was workable, would solve all social problems and increase both savings and production while assuring abundance and happiness for all people.[16] The purpose of the Icarian community was "...not alone the interest and happiness of its members but also that of humanity as a whole."[17]   There was a Manichean duality in Cabet's conception of the difference between the old ways linked to darkness and Satan and the new, tied to light and the reign of God,[18] but the new when it gradually appeared would benefit the whole of the human race.

In the general amnesty of 1839, when Cabet felt free enough to return to France, he returned as a communist with a dream of equality. In 1840 he published what he imagined was an updated version of Thomas More's *Utopia*, calling it *Voyages et aventures de lord Carisdall en Icarie* (*Voyage to Icaria*) in which he elaborated his scheme for equality. It was more of a critique of existing society than a plan for the future, but it did include Cabet's version of Thomas More's ideas updated with the later contributions of Robert Owen.

Robert Owen (1771-1859) was born in Scotland but by the age of ten he was alone, searching for work in London. He began as a poor boy and he made it big, but he never forgot his humble origins. At the age of nineteen, he had risen to the position of superintendent of a major cotton mill.[19]

He came to see that decent treatment of workers and their families could result in higher production. More than that, however, he came to believe that a proper environment and education could so lead to the perfection of the human race as to make it nearly unrecognizable in the sense of social justice and human happiness. He purchased New Lanark, a factory village located near his mill and became a benevolent dictator; boarding up the saloons, cleaning up the streets, and sending inspectors to people's homes to make sure that things were kept clean there as well. He built a school for the workers' children and insisted that they attend. He built a community center where dances, concerts, and lectures could be held. The working day was reduced to ten hours. Owen created an environment that encouraged people to be happy.

Although the people initially objected to this highhanded treatment, they soon grew to adore their autocratic leader. Their village became the envy of Britain, and every year some two thousand visitors came to see the marvels at New Lanark mills. But Owen's hope that his ideas would spread to other areas was disappointed. Other capitalists found self-serving reasons not to listen to Owen or to take New Lanark as a model for the future. Out of frustration, Robert Owen moved from being a liberal capitalist to becoming a communist in the sense of calling for the abolition of private property and the establishment of communes where people could live in equality. He was full of plans for model communities arranged in quadrangles that would put cooperation in the place of competition. Luxuries would become commonplace as they were made available to everyone.

For a time it really seemed as though Robert Owen's ideas would spark a new age, for tiring of the lackluster reception he received in Britain, he took his ideas to the New World where he was lionized. He was entertained by Thomas Jefferson and James Madison, and spoke twice before joint sessions of Congress with President Monroe, the entire cabinet, and Supreme Court Justices in attendance.[20]

With this kind of enthusiasm, it was no wonder that other people who felt much the same way would become disciples and either try to push Owen's ideas or develop related notions of their own. This is where Cabet fits--he was influenced by More and by Owen to create his own island of perfection called Icaria.

The Voyage to Icaria became a best-seller much to his surprise and it seemed as though every literate radical working person and every intellectual was soon familiar with the book's content. The book used the same device utilized by More, that is, describing Icaria through the eyes of a traveller who had been there. In this case it is a man named Lord William Carisdall whom Cabet allegedly met at the home of General Lafayette in Paris, and met again in London in 1834. Carisdall was described as a very rich man, a fine man, pleasing to look upon, with a character and manners that suggested nobility and amiability. Even so Carisdall deserved the reader's pity because he had been orphaned since infancy and had spent most of his young life travelling and studying the lands and peoples he encountered. This paragon of virtue, Cabet's literary creation, stated emphatically in the very beginning that he had found people unhappy everywhere on earth even where nature seemed to conspire to make things easy. Carisdall also found unpleasant "...the vices of the social organization in England as elsewhere."[21]

Lord Carisdall came across a grammar book and dictionary for the Icarian language. His extensive travels had made him a connoisseur of languages and so his immediate response was approval because the Icarian language struck him as so rational, so regular, so simple. It was so superior a language, he began to believe, that it could function as a universal language. "Yes, I have no doubt of it, all people will adopt it sooner or later, by replacing their language with it or by joining it with their own, and that the Icarian language will someday be the language of the whole world. "[22]

His interest in the language sparked his curiosity about the people who spoke it, and he discovered that Icaria was a place of pleasure, peace, joy, and happiness. Icaria, he learned was truly a second promised land, an eden, an elysium, or a new earthly paradise.[23] He determined to visit it, to see for himself this wonder that had magnificent roads, rivers, and canals, delightful countryside, enchanting gardens, fine looking homes, charming villages, superb towns, and classical monuments. Its industry surpassed England's and its arts surpassed those of France. People travelled about in balloons. Children were charming, men were handsome, and the women were enchanting and divine. All the social and political institutions were rational, just, and wise. Crime was unknown.[24] He determined to visit Icaria to see these wonders for himself. To help him later recollect his observations he kept careful notes in his journal.

His trip supported the idyllic description he had been given; even the Icarian ship that took him there was unusually safe and comfortable. Everything was hyperbole.

Icaria was divided into a hundred provinces and was a very organized machine that ran quite smoothly. Each of the provinces was divided into ten communes. Capital cities were, of course, in the center of each province, because everything was symmetrical and as tightly organized as books in the local library. The streets of Icaria were straight and wide, lined with beautiful gardens. Each block had 15 houses, all the same size and appearance. Everything was very sanitary, the city saw to it. Dust was collected by machines and sidewalks were enclosed with glass to protect people from the rain.[25]

As the appearance of the city was carefully regulated by the state, so was the daily life of the citizen. Utopian authors generally had a low appreciation of spontaneity because they were too full of their prescription for the future. They tended to overlegislate. Breakfast **for everyone** was at 6am and was prepared according to scientific standards. The work day was expected to be seven hours long in the summer and less in the winter. All the large industries, farms, home building, etc., were owned and run by the state. All the citizens could do was to elect the officers, but during the tenure of those officers the citizens had very little to say; once elected the officers became technician-dictators; for the good of the citizens, of course.[26]

Every male wore the same kind of clothing. All women and all children dressed alike as well although some variation was permitted in color. The courtship period was specified at six months, and was followed by marriage to one partner for life. Divorce was possible, but the expartners were expected to marry others. Singleness or celibacy was actively discouraged.[27] Children were educated in public schools from age five to eighteen for males and from five to seventeen for females. At the age of leaving school individuals were slotted into the work for which they appeared best suited. Everyone could retire at age 65.[28]

Newspapers in the usual sense were not permitted because of the frequent lying and contradictions to be found in the press. On Icaria there would be no hostile press, but rather a single communal newspaper for each Commune, a single provincial paper for each Province, and a single national press for the entire Nation. The editorial staffs would be elected officials, supposedly disinterested, temporary, and revocable. The papers would print only reports and facts without any editorial opinion.[29] Art and literature were encouraged, even though books had to be submitted to the state for approval before being published. Inhabitants would have a progressive income tax, no inheritance rights, state regulation of wages, and national workshops.[30]

Although this sounds far too regimented to be attractive, approaching the gulag life of Ivan Denisovich, Solzhenitzyn's hero, *Voyage to Icaria* did forge new communist ground. On the cover of the book was the old slogan that Karl Marx would later make more famous: "To each according to his needs." It is hard to see how the need for freedom was to be met, but at the time this was not an important consideration-- equality was too important to compromise in any way. So private property and every form of social inequality had to be eradicated from the imaginary utopia. All citizens gave their labor to the state and then withdrew what they needed from the common store.

Between the genders there was also supposed to be equality, but since the family was retained as the basic unit and the father recognized as its head, the gender equality may not have been very real.[31] If one wished to be kind, one could say that gender equality on Icaria was better than normal 19th century perceptions of sexual equality--women were educated, for example, and could freely choose their marriage partner--but the equality was not as good as it could have been. For example, only adult males were citizens.[32] Females were not even Associates in the community. Article 2 of Chapter II of the Icarian Constitution specified that the Society included "...all who are or will be definitely admitted, with their wives and children."[33] Women were to have a consultive political voice rather than an active one. They advise the males, or contribute to the discussion whenever the issue concerns them.[34]

Nonetheless, women were treated well in Icaria. The impression given is that women were loved, adored, idolized, treated with respect and consideration by the males, but not made equal. Cabet wrote in italics: *The Icarian People are the Brothers of all other People.*[35] Icarian women were freed from conjugal despotism and the law proclaimed equality between husband and wife **but** only the husband's voice was preponderant.[36] To paraphrase George Orwell, all the people were equal but some of the people were more equal than others.

The position of "savage tribes" carefully colonized by Icarians suggests another area of inequality, although this is not clear at all. The Icarians decided that they might be overpopulated in the future and so decided to colonize neighboring lands that were fertile but only minimally populated by savage tribes. A gradual program of civilization for the savages was begun. It was a very different program from that performed by Europeans on American Indians who were massacred or African tribespeople who were enslaved. The Icarians were gentle and gradual and slowly civilized others through persuasion and example. The result was that "...these savages adore us almost as beneficent Deities, and beseech us to establish ourselves in their midst in order to bestow on them more benefits."[37]

There was to be a comprehensive system of public services, and the community would each year draw up a production plan based on estimated needs. The work would then be divided among the citizens with the capital equipment and raw materials being supplied by the state. There would be no army.

Although sounding quite austere the idea of Icaria was enormously popular. The book had many imaginative parts. For example, Cabet described the raising and lowering of railway cars by powerful machines just as lock-keepers raise and lower boats. Or the idea of transporting coal to cellers without even soiling the sidewalks. Or dumbwaiters; rainwater collected in cisterns; soft music played in hospitals from invisible sources; indoor plumbing with hot and cold running water; sewage removal to a central processing machine; fireproof fabrics; and prefabricated housing.[38] Even his ideas of regenerated Christianity were imaginative and increased his appeal. He wrote of this in his 1846 *Le Vrai Christianisme*, and he meant following the example of Jesus and the early communist Christian church. Cabet's communism **was** his Christianity. All great thinkers, including Christ, Cabet argued, thought communism the best system. Icarian Communism in Cabet's mind was the **same thing** as properly understood Christianity.[39] Jesus Christ ranked first in humanity by virtue of his devotion to the happiness of the human species and by his proclamation of the principle of equality, fraternity, and community.[40] "We repeat it, Icarians are *true Christians*, disciples, imitators and workers of Jesus Christ, applying His Gospel and Teachings while working to realize His Kingdom of God, His new City, and His Paradise on earth."[41]

Like Rousseau, Cabet developed a universal religion that was both rational and a common denominator of all religious beliefs. To him that meant that the Icarian religion was a system of morality and philosophy that had only one function: to bring people to love each other while giving them rules of conduct that encompass everything: Love neighbors as yourself, do **not** do to others what you would not want done to you, and **do** do to others all the good you would desire for yourself. Sounds simple, but it's profound as an expression of the essence of Christianity.

Similarly, Cabet's description of the deity suggested that he had read Aristotle and St. Thomas as well as Immanuel Kant's *Critique of Pure Reason*. The divinity, he wrote, is the first cause of which I see the effects, to whom I attribute a human form in order better to comprehend it and to be able to speak more easily of it, but of whom, with my restricted senses and my imperfect organization, I cannot perceive and know either in form or essence.[42] One reason for the popularity of the book could have been the depth of meaning with reference to religion; another may have been the futuristic, imaginative side of Cabet's thinking. Although *Journey to Icaria* is not well known, it rewards careful reading for more reasons than its support of communism and equality.

By 1847 it has been estimated that Cabet had a very large following; from two hundred to four hundred thousand, all evidently eager to put Icarian ideas into practice.[43] These numbers suggested to Cabet that a great many Icarian communities were in the offing. The size of the commune population, he felt, should not exceed the number of males who can meet in a single Assembly; about one to two thousand men with their wives and children. This would create a ceiling for the total commune population somewhere between four and five thousand.[44]

Cabet felt that the New World, America, would be the place to implement his ideas. Establishing working models would silence his critics, he thought, and so he arranged for a large grant of land in Texas. When his followers landed in New Orleans, however, they discovered that they had been cheated. The land was much smaller in size than described and was distant from any river or settlement. When Cabet himself came the following year, the commune was moved to Nauvoo, Illinois on the site of a former Mormon settlement where already existing buildings and roads made the initial settlement far easier.

The Nauvoo Icaria was never much like the imaginary one, however. The number involved was small: actually only about fifteen hundred participated. And he just could not get them to act in harmony. He had to make serious compromises; individual property holding was permitted, mixed with elements of common living and collective discipline and although it did last for several decades, dissent finally brought it to its knees. Kenneth Rexroth argues that in no other communist community did one see such violent conflict. Factions stopped speaking to each other, ate in different parts of the dining room, had separate social activities, stopped working together in the fields and mills, and even broke out in fistfights in the streets. Children took the adult arguments to school and fought with each other. Since the board of directors no longer supported Cabet, they insisted that those who did not work should also not eat. Cabet petitioned the state legislature to revoke the community's charter. The majority responded by expelling Cabet and his followers, and a few weeks later Cabet had died.[45]

After his death in 1856 Cabet began to be remembered more kindly by followers who felt guilty about driving him out of the community. They forgot how cranky and dictatorial he could be, and Cabet became a kind of culture hero who had founded a new civilization, and sections of his writings were read in church as though they were a new gospel.[46] This new reverence for Cabet did not, however, erase the problem that arose between authoritarian and democratic followers. The same kind of split and dissention arose again, demonstrating that it was the ideas that were in conflict, not simply personalities. Cabet's attempts to reach communalism had succeeded only briefly in creating something new and different.

More, Spence, and Cabet described ideal social alternatives that pushed toward an absolute equality achieved through an excess of regimentation. Although ideal islands were conceived, they did not attain full equality. Although Cabet did not have More's slaves, women were definitely second class citizens. A world without slaves may have been beyond even More's imagination. Similarly, full gender equality may never even have occurred to Cabet. It certainly occurred to the last example of ideal alternatives.

Marge Piercy, *Woman on the Edge of Time*

Marge Piercy's story[47] is about a sharing, loving community in the future, but it is also the story of despair and hope, about the helplessness/strength of the female, and about potential futures that depend on individual action. The heroine is Connie Ramos, a Chicana with a Mayan cast to her face; a small chin, a sensuous nose, and almond eyes. She was in her mid-thirties and lived in New York City, at or near the bottom of the social scale. She had been born dirt poor in Texas, and had moved to Chicago as a child, and then had run away to New York as a young woman. She was abandoned by her lover when he made her pregnant, then met and married a man named Martin, a lovely man who acknowledged the child, Angelina, as his own, but who died far too soon. Later Connie partnered with a blind, black, saxophone player who was a pickpocket on the side, and for a while she felt like the three of them were a family. Unfortunately Claud was arrested and imprisoned. While in jail he participated in a volunteer medical experiment, contracted hepatitis and died.

Connie tried to make a living by working for her brother, a self-centered, arrogant man who owned a nursery some distance away. Making minimum wages, fighting public transport to and from work, worrying about the pesticide ambience in which she had to work, and trying to find a few minutes to be with eight year old Angelina were the mile markers of her life. Quality time was difficult to find. One day, tired and hungover from a bad evening, she lashed out at Angelina, bruising her and breaking her wrist. Instantly contrite she took Angelina to a hospital where Social Services took over once they discovered that Connie had abused her daughter. Angelina was taken away and put in a foster home, while Connie was sent to Bellevue for mental evaluation. When she was released, her child remained in foster care while welfare ladies regularly came to visit to determine whether Connie was looking for work, was clean, or whether she was living with a man. Things did not look good.

Connie, in the midst of this despair, began to discover that she was tuned into the future. After her initial disbelief, she discovered that she was communicating with a person in the year 2137. She became a woman on the edge of time; in the midst of misery, betrayal, and the loss of her daughter she became aware of not just one but two potential futures. The first is a world where love, equality, and self-dignity were paramount in the communal, nonsexist, and nonracist society. This so very good future was, however, only a possible one. A darker potential also existed: environmentally insane, mindlessly and soullessly technocratic, exploitative, racist, sexist, and authoritarian.

These possibilities intertwined with Connie's own life. While her life went from bad to worse as a friend lied to the authorities about her and Connie became an involuntary mental patient, it paradoxically seemed as though which future would actually take place depended on something Connie could do. Considering where Connie was and how much medication she received, to imagine that she was the key to the future took an extraordinary amount of faith.

But she wanted to bring about the good future if she could. By the time the reader is aware of Connie's importance, the reader wants the good future as well. The future revealed by Luciente, the woman from 2137, was ecologically sensible and seemed aware of the interconnectedness of all living things. Private property did not exist, nor did buying and selling. They used genderless pronouns like "per" for both "her" and "his." When Connie finally was able to space-travel mentally with Luciente, she was disappointed--the future villages made her think of her own past and the poor village she had come from. In this future society the villages held about 600 people and population levels were strictly enforced by the people themselves. A new baby was always a deliberate replacement of a person who had died.

Connie saw a river, some little buildings, and a few strange structures that looked like long-legged birds with sails that turned in the wind, a few large terra-cotta, yellow buildings and one blue dome. None of the buildings was bigger than the supermarket in her own neighborhood. The bird objects were the tallest things around and they were scarcely higher than some of the visible pine trees. There were a few lumpy free-form structures overrun with green vines, but no skyscrapers, no spaceports, no traffic jam in the sky. Are you sure we went into the future, she asked? Would it be more modern if we went to a city?

Luciente responded that **big** cities didn't work, which made the situation even more unreal to Connie. Most buildings were small and randomly scattered among trees and shrubbery and gardens, made of scavenged old wood, old bricks and stones and cement blocks. Some were wildly decorated and overgrown with vines. People were visible on bicycles and on foot. Clothes were hanging on lines near a long building--shirts flapping on wash lines! In the distance beyond the blue dome, cows were grazing, ordinary black and white and brown and white cows chewing ordinary grass past a stone fence. Intensive plots of vegetables lay between the huts and stretched into the distance. On a nearby raised bed a dark-skinned old man was puttering around what looked like spinach plants.

The roofs of the huts--that's all she could call them--were strange looking because they contained rainwater catchers and solar energy equipment. The housing was above ground because the water table was close to the surface. A gaudy chicken strutted across the path, followed by another. The path was made of stone fitted against stone in a pattern of subdued natural color, with mustard-yellow flowers alongside. Low-growing tulips looked like bright stars on the ground.

Connie was disappointed when she saw the goats, because it reminded her of her Uncle Manuel's ranch in Texas which she had thought of as a place for wet-back refugees. All that this futuristic scene lacked, as far as Connie was concerned, was a couple of old cars up on blocks in the yard. What had happened, she wondered, that big war with atomic bombs people were always predicting?

Luciente's response was clear. We like it this way![48]

The village to which Luciente took Connie raised chickens, ducks, pheasants, partridges, turkeys, guinea hens, geese, goats, cows, rabbits, turtles, and pigs. Luciente stated that the village of Mattapoisett was famous for turtles and geese. Every region, she said, tried to be "ownfed," or as self-sufficient as possible in proteins, but you're right, Connie, we're peasants. We're all peasants. Connie responded sadly that it seemed to her that a lot of striving and struggling had gone on only to end up in the same old past, stuck back home on the farm; a peon again with ten chickens and a goat, just like the old grandparents.[49]

What they had done, Luciente responded, was build on what good there was in the past before the white men came, and on the good that was brought from Europe. It just took a long time to put the old good with the new good.

Just as on More's island of Utopia, the door of Luciente's house was unlocked. It didn't even have a lock, merely a catch on the inside. Windows on two sides. Big desk, worktable, bed, lots of colors.

Wood floor with rugs. This was Luciente's space. She lived with two males; one pillow friend (Jackrabbit) and one hand friend (Bee). They each had their nearby space. Everyone had their private space, but many places could be linked together for families. For greater privacy you shut your door with a sign on it indicating that you did not wish to be disturbed. Luciente said that people behind such doors could be meditating, coupling, sleeping, or just pouting. It didn't matter. What did matter was that privacy was available when a person wanted it.

In the nearby village of Cranberry, the homes had courtyards sunk into the earth to the level of an ample story, surrounded by dense, often thorny hedges. Neither kids nor animals could get through. On ground level there were lots of trees, gardens, paths, swings for kids hung from trees, and people either trotted or biked by as goats and cows grazed, and chickens pecked. The surface was studded by solar heat collectors and intakes for rain-water cisterns.[50]

At first Connie was disappointed again. This did not look like an improvement over her time. What was worse, if this future were true, it killed the dream people had for their children that things would get better for them than it had been for you. This way, if Angelina had a child, and then her child had a child through five generations, this village life that resembled Connie's grandparent's life was what awaited them.[51] Later in the book this point is underscored when Luciente commented that her society was more evolved than was Connie's. Connie's response was that things had devolved rather than evolved, away from cities and high-tech life to village life that she associated with her grandparents in Mexico. But Luciente could not agree. We plan cooperatively, she said, we have limited resources and can afford to waste nothing. We see ourselves as partners with water, air, birds, fish, and trees. We learned a lot, she said, from so called primitive societies that were primitive technically but were socially sophisticated. We learned from cultures that dealt well with handling conflict, promoting cooperation, coming of age, developing a sense of community, handling sickness, aging, going mad, and dying.

Yeah but, Connie argued, you still go crazy, get sick, grow old, and die. I thought that by your time some of these problems would be solved. What she didn't realized was that some problems are solved only if one stops being a human being and becomes instead a metal and plastic robot. Not even dying was a problem if it were accepted as part of being human.[52]

Luciente's future society was carefully and thoughtfully put together out of the best that the recent and distant past had to offer. Although

Connie's surprise was because the society had not changed enough, it had changed dramatically. There were no fathers, for example, because the distinctions between the genders was absent. What had been "women's work" was now work willingly done by all people whether male or female. The concept of fathers was so foreign to Luciente she had to ask her wrist communicator for a definition. When Connie said "male parent" Luciente assumed she was talking about a male co-mother.[53]

When a person died there was no funeral. Mourners stayed up all night talking about the dead person, and at dawn they dug a grave, laid the body in the grave, and planted a tree in the grave with the body. The tree then functioned as a living memorial to the person. On the way home from this service, Luciente said, we stop at the brooder to signal the intent to begin a baby. In a week or so when caught up on work and sleep people would discuss into whose family the baby would enter, and who would be the mothers.[54] Three were chosen and they are the co-mothers. The co-mother can be male, and if two are male one must agree to nurse along with the female co-mother so that the baby has two nurses.

Connie was flabbergasted and disgusted to see a 45 year old man with a red beard nurse an infant. He had breasts like a flat-chested woman, she thought, temporarily swollen with milk. Connie felt angry. How dare men share that pleasure formerly reserved for women alone? These women thought they had reached some sort of victory, but it seemed more like surrender to Connie. They had given to men the last refuge of women. There was nothing special about being a woman anymore. Women had let men steal the last remnants of ancient female power, sealed in blood and milk.[55]

The brooder was where the genetic material was stored, and where the embryos grew for the sixteen villages of the township. When people entered the building, they were disinfected. Inside, the brooder looked like a big aquarium, with blue carpet, and strange but pleasing music playing. There were tanks and machines and closed compartments. Something that beat like a heart was over against the wall. In the brooder embryos grew until almost ready for birth, a gestation period of 42 or 43 weeks being considered normal. Connie could see babies bobbing in the nutrient liquid, with their eyes closed. One dark female was kicking, while a pink male with an oversized penis was crying.[56]

The planning or grand council decided which proportion of what skin colors to breed and mixed the genes well throughout the population. Luciente felt that they had broken the bond between genes and culture to end racism for all time even though separate cultural identities were maintained. We don't want the melting pot where everybody ends up with thin gruel, she said. We wanted diversity because strangeness breeds richness. The result was something like black Irishmen, or black Chinese. All mixed up. There was no genetic connection between the co-mothers, the family, and the child.

Connie expressed dismay, but Luciente said that this was part of women's long revolution. Breaking all the old hierarchies, we discovered that it wasn't all taking, there was one thing women had to give up too, the only power they ever had--the power to give birth. As long as women were biologically enchained, she said, we would never be equal and males could never be humanized to be loving and tender. So we all became mothers. Every child has three to break the nuclear bonding.[57]

Although there were strong emotional connections between the mothers and the child, the children spent a good deal of their time gaining a practical education while living in the children's house. This practical approach included sex education, in an era when AIDS was presumably remembered as an ancient plague. While touring the children's house, they came on a boy and a girl about six or seven seriously trying to have sex with each other. Connie was horrified, wanted to pull them apart and give them a good lecture. Her guides pulled her back, laughing. This was how children learned about sex, they explained. Not from books, or from earnest discussions with adults, but by experimenting with each other. One of the guides, the head of the children's house, said that Connie's reaction was interesting. Our ideas of evil, she said, center around power and greed; taking from other people, their food, their liberty, their health, their land, their customs, their pride. We don't think of this as legal but deplorable, we think of it as evil. We don't find coupling bad unless it involves pain or is not invited.[58]

Connie commented on the lack of toys in the children's house, and the guides suggested that when children weren't kept out of the real work, they don't have the same need for imitation things.[59]

At puberty, the individual child faced a survival test and earned a new name after successfully passing this test. New guardians took over and this set the children free from the co-mothers to increase independence. The whole community was involved in the puberty rites, so that what was really happening was that the level of overt loving and belonging became community wide.

There were no bosses. People volunteered to do the necessary things on a temporary basis. If a person had an important job for a period per next job would be one of the less appealing ones just so that an individual did not begin to feel more important than or indispensable to the community. Lazy people were not tolerated long because other people had to do their work. Eventually such people were asked to leave, and they wandered from village to village getting more sour and more self-pitying as they went.[60] Some evidently do not want to do military service or be a mother, either, and, however important, it was not forced on them. An unwilling soldier was dangerous to per comrades, and an unwilling mother would presumably not sufficiently love the baby.

But they did produce, and without working hard all of the time. The area known as Mouth-of-Mattapoisett exported protein in flounder, herring, alewives, turtles, geese, ducks, and blue cheese. Goose-down jackets, comforters and pillows were manufactured in automated factories. The area was the plant-breeding center for this whole sector in squash, cucumbers, beans, and corn. They manufactured jizers (guns), diving equipment, and the best nets on the Cape. Aesthetic exports were beautiful poems, art work, holies [glass pictures], rituals, and a new style of cooking turtle soups and stews.

People did not seem in a hurry to Connie, and the kids always seemed underfoot. People stood around talking a lot. This seemed like wasting time to Connie, but she was told that everything got done; the brooder was cared for, food was brought to and cooked in the fooder, the animals were cared for, and basic routines were followed for cleaning, politicking, and meetings. That left lots of time for talking, studying, playing, loving, or just enjoying the river. During the spring planting, or harvest time, or during crises caused by storms, work was very hard indeed. But most of the time it was easy. After bosses' and bankers' jobs were eliminated there were plenty of people to do the work on a part time basis. And we feed everybody without hurting the soil.[61]

Luxuries still existed. Rare and expensive things circulated through the libraries, so that a person could have a rare painting hanging on their wall for a month, then the pleasure was passed on to someone else.[62]

Government was a township planning council made up of people chosen by lot and representing six villages. Members of the council served 1 year terms: three months with the old representative, six months alone, and three months with the new person chosen. The chair rotated. The council also contained a representative chosen to be the Earth Advocate who spoke for the rights of the total environment and an Animal Advocate representing animal rights. The EA and the AA were people chosen by lot from among those who believed they were called to those positions.

The planning council fit the needs of each village into the scarce resources available, trying to do this justly. Next level up was regional planning with representatives chosen from the township level. If a dispute arose it was settled by arguments, or circumvented by barter. There was no final authority, the issue was just argued until consensus, then the winner had to treat the loser to a good meal and presents.

But there weren't any police. When Connie asked them about police they all had to check with the wrist communicators, but even that did not help. They comprehended government--the planning councils--but they never did understand the concept of police. But there was crime. It was simply handled differently. If a person was a thief the society gave per things, believing that stealing came from deprivation. There wasn't much private property. For killing or assault? Society worked with the individual either to heal the sickness or to atone for the crime. A second crime by the same individual resulted in execution.[63]

Meals were taken in the fooder, a large room filled with big tables seating at least fifteen. A child was climbing onto a bench to tell a story and across the room a man was weeping openly into his soup and others at his table were comforting him. Other people were arguing, telling jokes, and a child was singing nearby. The sound was muted, and people let it all hang out. Connie felt buffeted, but the room felt positive. Luciente said that the fooder, where everyone ate, was a warm spot, a home to all of us.[64]

Suddenly it was time for Connie to return to her own time, and the warm fuzzy of the fooder was contrasted with the bare seclusion room on the ward where she awakened. She promptly fell asleep on the urine-stained mattress, waiting for her release from the room. She had plenty to think about. Luciente's world was not the only potential world. She and her other friends in the future were not fully sure of all the events between the twentieth century and 2137 that had led up to them. Connie was made very aware that the desirable future she was seeing was *not* inevitable. All things interlock, she was told, and the communal future was but one possibility. One of the men in that future said that they had to fight to remain in existence and they had reached back through time to Connie to see if she would help.[65]

The alternative, undesirable future became much more real to Connie one day when she threw herself forward, but instead of meeting Luciente or one of her new friends, Connie found herself face to face with a strange woman in her bedroom. This woman was a contract girl, named Gildina, on a two year lease to a man named Cash. Her sense of who she was came only from Cash. When her contract ran out, she might, if very good, be renewed for two years, or perhaps one year. If not she was demoted to week-ends or one-nighters, and when that no longer worked out, the knockshop.

Only selected females could bear children. It had to be a part of the contract. Normally babies were born to females "cored" to be nothing but mothers. The verb "core" implied a removal of individual incentive or will like a lobotomy.

People on this middle level were old at age 40 and were soon eased out after that age. The contract girl had been born on the surface, born coughing because of the pollution. She always thought the sky was yellow until she got the contract to the middle level. Now she understood that the sky was grey blue.

The rich people lived on space platforms to get away from the pollution. They lived about 200 years, married and had children in the old style. They naturally had to have many organ transplants.

The duds were the poor people living on the land surface where the pollution was so heavy it was not possible to see very far--like an oldtime London fog seeping up from the Thames. Another name for the duds was organ-bank, but they were often diseased. Some duds were "pithed" to work in very polluted areas. The verb pithed similarly suggests a coring or a removal of the human essence, making a human into a robot.

Everything one wore or ate was unnatural. Food was made from coal and algae or wood by-products. It all came from big factory farms owned by the multi-nationals where it was mined and delivered every week.

Connie soon learned that what she was fearing would happen to her in the hospital, when the doctors operated on her brain and inserted neurotransmitters to control her behavior, was old history to this alternative future. Such "scientific" ways of controlling human behavior were no longer experimental or restricted to mental hospital patients with a history of violence. It was by this time, in this alternative future, standard practice. The result was that people no longer acted like humans, but like robots.

Gildina said that her man, Cash, had been SCd. Connie asked what 2that meant. Gildina replied that it meant sharpened control. He could turn off fear and pain and fatigue and sleep like flipping a switch. He's almost a Cybo, she said proudly. He could control the fibers in his spinal cord, and control his body temperature. He's as good a fighting machine as you can get without genetic engineering or organ replacement, really improved. He has those superneurotransmitters ready to be released in his brain, she said, that almost turns him into an Assassin.[66]

People in this future were monitored all the time by Securcenter to ensure the absence of subversive actions or talk. If pulled in, the sensors could determine what a person was thinking by measuring the electrical signals in the brain.

When Cash entered the apartment, he knew Connie was there because the sensors had told him. He tried to take Connie prisoner with a lot of loud, nasty words, but he discovered a strange thing, inexplicable to him. Connie was not afraid. He sensed anger but not fear--one of the keys to this story. To escape Connie willed herself back to the hospital with the conviction that this was Luciente's war. She had met the enemy and was enlisting on Luciente's side.[67]

And yet what could Connie do? She was a prisoner, a mental patient who couldn't even carry a book of matches or keep her own money. If Luciente's future needed a savior, Connie thought, they sure picked the wrong one. But the powerful don't make revolutions, she was told, people do. The people who figured out the labor- and land-intensive farming, who changed how people bought food, raised children, went to school. Who made new unions, withheld rent, refused to go to wars, wrote, educated, and made speeches. The result of all these people doing their thing was a thirty year war that ended in a revolution that set up Luciente's society. Or else there wasn't a people's rebellion, no thirty year war, and the alternative, nasty future was the only one possible.[68]

Connie determined to do something to help because Luciente's society, she has come to believe, was so good compared to her own and so very good compared to the robot technology of the alternative. The basic reason for the very positive feeling in her mind was that, as Connie said, I ask you about I and you tell me about we. Luciente said "Connie, we are born screaming Ow and I! The gift is in growing to care, to connect, to cooperate. Everything we learn aims to make us feel strong in ourselves, connected to all living. At home."[69]

How can Connie help bring about the better future? One of her future friends tells her that there's always a thing you can deny an oppressor, if only your allegiance, belief, cooperation. Even when one is up against very powerful forces, an opening to fight can be found. Find a way to fight and eventually that becomes a power.

With the dialytrode implanted she acted as oddly as possible and was unconscious for long periods while she was mentally in the future. The doctors decided to remove the implant. At this shaky stage of the brain-implant technology the doctors were feeling their way. Success for their therapy would bring more money for new projects and the bad alternative future looked very possible. Defeating the project when it was still a hardly recognized baby would defeat it for a long, long time, maybe forever.

So after the dialytrode was removed she became a model patient and played up to the staff, communicating to them that without the dialytrode in her head she was real good. Inside her consciousness she was fighting Luciente's war with coldblooded determination. She fought to get a pass to go to her brother's house for Thanksgiving, and the only way she could get her brother to invite her was to offer her services as maid and cook. She had a horrible time getting him to agree, and when there, she was indeed a servant. This was the brother who owned a nursery, for whom she had worked before the hospitalization.

She went with him to visit the nursery, to pick out plants for a party to be given at his house. While there she snuck into the poison room, and stole some very potent Parathion. She filled a small bottle with the poison and snuck it back to the hospital by putting a herbal shampoo label on the little bottle. She hardened herself to succeed in her war. The poison was her weapon.

So, after they told her they were going to operate on her brain again, she snuck into the doctor's lounge, where she made a new pot of coffee, mixing in the Parathion. The six people that were killed were the main persons in the experimental project that involved these brain operations that so figured in the alternative future.[70]

Connie, as hard as this was to believe, was in a key place at the right time, when influencing the future was possible. She struck her blow for the good future, the ideal social alternative. The rest was (would be) herstory.

Endnotes
Chapter Four

1. In Cabet's novel it appears that Icaria is not an island, but a peninsula isolated from its connections with a land mass by high mountains. However, there really is an island called *Ikaria*, a rather large Greek island, part of the Dodecanese, off the coast of Samos in the Aegean Sea. No one knows for certain, but Cabet may have noticed this island and fictionalized it as a peninsula. Marge Piercy's utopia placed in the year 2137 is easily thought of as an island in time and space.

2. Isidore, *Etymologiae (Patrologia latina* 82/2:514), cited in Jean Delumeau, *History of Paradise: The Garden of Eden in Myth and Tradition* (New York: Continuum, 1995), p. 99.

3. James Harrington's utopia, for example, is not communistic. It is cited at some length in Chapter Ten and can be found in James Harrington, *The Political Writings*, Chas. Blitzer, ed. (New York: Liberal Arts Press, Inc., 1955).

4. Frank E. and Fritzie P. Manuel, *Utopian Thought in the Western World* (Cambridge: Harvard University Press, 1979), p. 117.

5. Ibid., pp. 30-31.

6. Ibid., p. 31.

7. Ibid.

8. Ibid., p. 38, note 6

9. Ibid., note 7

10. Ibid., p. 40.

11. Ibid., p. 41.

12. Ibid., p. 43.

13. Ibid., pp. 65-66.

14. Lewis Mumford, *The Story of Utopias* (Gloucester, MA: Peter Smith, 1959), pp. 134-135. Original copyright 1922.

15. Ibid., p. 137.

16. Étienne Cabet, *History and Constitution of the Icarian Community*, Thomas Teakle, trans. (Iowa City, IA: State Historical Society of Iowa, 1917), pp. 214-215.

17. Ibid., p. 215.

18. Ibid., p. 252. The dichotomies, somewhat reminiscent of Augustine, are described in the Preamble to the Constitution. On the old side were Satan, evil, spiritual death,darkness, routine/prejudice, error, ignorance, injustice, and domination/servitude. On the new side were the reign of God or Good, resurrection, regeneration/life, light, experience of centuries, truth, knowledge/learning, justice, and enfranchisement/liberty.

19. Alfred Apsler, *Communes Through the Ages: The Search for Utopia* (New York: Julian Messner, 1974), pp. 92-93.

20. Ibid., p. 97.

21. Étienne Cabet, *Travels and Adventures of Lord Carisdall in Icaria*, which first appeared in 1839 under the title *Voyage et Adventures de lord William Carisdall en Icarie, traduit de l'anglaise de Fracis Adams*. The translator was Th. Dufruit who wrote the Introduction to the first edition. The second edition's Preface was written by Cabet in February 1842, and this French version of the book was translated back into English by Robert P. Sutton and published as a photoduplication entitled *Travels in Icaria* by Western Illinois University, Macomb Illinois in 1985.

22. *Travels in Icaria*, ibid., p. 2.

23. Ibid., p. 3.

24. Ibid.

25. Harry W. Laidler, *History of Socialism: A Comparative Survey of Socialism, Communism, Trade Unionism, Cooperation, Utopianism, and Other Systems of Reform and Reconstruction* (New York: Thomas Y. Crowell Co., 1968), p. 48.

26. Ibid.

27. Cabet, *History and Constitution, op. cit.*, p. 243.

28. Ibid., p. 49.

29. Cabet, *Travels in Icaria, op. cit.*, p. 270, which makes it sound as though there would be at least three newspapers. Edmund Wilson wrote that there would be a single state newspaper in Icaria. See Edmund Wilson, *To the Finland Station: A Study in the Writing and Acting of History* (Garden City: Doubleday Anchor, 1953), p. 105. If the three mentioned by Cabet all had the same information in them, Wilson would be correct if slightly misleading.

30. Ibid.

31. George Lichtheim, *The Origins of Socialism* (New York: Frederick A. Praeger, 1969), pp. 29-30.

32. Étienne Cabet, *History and Constitution of the Icarian Community, op. cit.*, p. 245.

33. Ibid., p. 253.

34. Ibid., p. 264.

35. Cabet, *Travels in Icaria, op. cit.*, p. 14.

36. Ibid., pp. 405-410.

37. Ibid., p. 376.

38. Ibid., pp. 21, 87, 88, 89, 152, and 501.

39. Cabet, *History and Constitution, op. cit.*, p. 218. Dom Helder Camara said something very similar: Christians must show that "authentic socialism" is Christianity lived to the full, in basic equality and with a fair distribution of goods. See Alfred T. Hennelly, ed., *Liberation Theology: A Documentary History* (Maryknoll: Orbis, 1990), p. 53.

40. Cabet, *Travels in Icaria, op. cit.*, p. 380.

41. Cabet, *History and Constitution, op. cit.*, p. 243.

42. Cabet, *Travels in Icaria, op. cit.*, p. 228.

43. Wilson, *op. cit.*, p. 105.

44. Cabet, *History and Constitution, op. cit.*, p. 245.

45. Kenneth Rexroth, *Communalism: Fron Its Origins to the Twentieth Century* (New York: Seabury Press, 1974), p. 265.

46. Ibid., p. 266.

47. Marge Piercy, *Woman on the Edge of Time* (New York: A Fawcett Crest Ballantine Book, Random House, 1976).

48. Ibid., pp. 68-70.

49. Ibid., p. 70.

50. Ibid., p. 149.

51. Ibid., p. 73.

52. Ibid., p. 125.

53. Ibid., p. 74.

54. Ibid., p. 161.

55. Ibid., p. 134.

56. Ibid., pp. 101-102.

57. Ibid., pp. 104-105.

58. Ibid., pp. 138-139.

59. Ibid., p. 136.

60. Ibid., p. 101.

61. Ibid., pp. 128-129.

62. Ibid., p. 175.

63. Ibid., pp. 208-209.

64. Ibid., pp. 74-75.

65. Ibid., pp. 197-198.

66. Ibid., pp. 297-298.

67. Ibid., p. 299.

68. Ibid., pp. 197-198.

69. Ibid., p. 248.

70. Ibid., p. 374.

Chapter Five

Communal Sharing as the Ideology
of the Lumpen

Thomas Muntzer and German Peasants
Gerrard Winstanley and the Diggers
Abimael Guzmán and the Shining Path
The Zapatistas of Chiapas
Ursula Le Guin's The Dispossessed

One of the strongest impulses toward communism arises from the frustration attending the great difficulties of gaining equality for the lowest class in society--the lumpen who represent the dregs of the social order. This frustration is understandable when it is realized that the people for whom equality is sought in this instance are very often those considered the undeserving poor: the derelicts, the homeless, the prostitutes. These people live without hope most of their lives. The frustration is especially vivid when the difficulties facing lumpen equality are unexpected; the goal was supposed to have been achieved by an earlier, actual revolution that did not go far enough or by a future, theoretical revolution that refused to seek equality specifically enough for the lowest class. Since the lumpen represent a class of rascals or scoundrels generally considered unproductive because they are believed to be shiftless degenerates, gaining equality is extremely difficult. The frustration stimulates the feeling that the lumpen were sold out; that the people who should have been concerned with gaining their equality were either being bought off or were far wimpier than earlier imagined. If a strong push is not made quickly, it is imagined, equality would never reach the lowest class.

Such was the case with the five examples in this chapter. Over a century lies between the German peasants in 1524-25 and the Diggers in 1649-1652, and over three centuries before the Shining Path emerged in 1980 and the Zapatistas in 1994. The final example describes the dispossessed in Ursula Le Guin's futuristic novel. Although they are very different they all share that lumpen frustration.

In Thomas Muntzer's case, his frustration developed because Martin Luther's reformation of European Christianity did not secularize well. The ideas of freedom Luther insisted on for his new German church were not allowed to spread into the society of peasants and landlords. In Gerrard Winstanley's case, his frustration arose because the English civil wars failed to achieve equality for those who tilled the soil. For Abimael Guzmán, the Communist Party of Peru failed miserably as an agent of revolution, and his frustrations led him to champion a violent revolution that would elevate the status of the Incan peasants. The Zapatistas' frustration arose from the failures of the Mexican revolution to change anything of significance for the Indian peasants. The frustration in the final example arises out of the failure of the propertarians to appreciate the success already achieved by the dispossessed lumpen.

Thomas Muntzer and the German Peasants

Frank and Fritzie Manuel sum up Thomas Muntzer as a series of contradictions: a theologian of the early Reformation, a leader of bands of rabble who destroyed monasteries and castles, or a terribly inept military tactician of a horde of peasants who fell easy prey to the princes' cannons, and an author of a vision of a new life on earth.[1] This complex man lived from 1488 to 1525 when he was executed as a dangerous revolutionary leader and heretic whom Luther thought was led by the devil.

The Reverend Muntzer's inspiration came from a vision in which a spiritual society was revealed to him as part of the Christian Millennium; the thousand year reign of Christ on earth. Thus, for Thomas Muntzer, the beginnings of that millennial Kingdom of Heaven had already arrived, and, a person could either wait for God to make the next move, or get in there and fight God's enemies to bring about the next divine move sooner. Muntzer belonged to the second group.

He was a learned man both in the Scriptures and in secular literature, and an early follower of Martin Luther in breaking with the Roman Catholic church. Unlike Luther, however, Muntzer was militantly antipapist from the very beginning. Luther appointed Muntzer to the church at Zwickau, a town in the southeastern Germanic area about 25 miles from the Czech border. This was a fateful appointment because ties already existed between the clergy at Zwickau and the radical Bohemian elements (Hussites) in the nearby Czech lands. The Bohemians were staunch millenarians who actively sought church reforms, and they found allies in the old corporations of weavers in the Zwickau area. The Zwickau weavers suffered from economic depression and badly needed radical change, while the newer and richer mining interests in the town sided with the status quo.[2] In such ways spiritual hands often shake secular ones, and vice versa.

The religious struggle in the Bohemian area could not be kept within spiritual bounds (Luther's couldn't either, but that is another story) and spilled over into the secular area, exacerbating existing conflicts by providing ideological justification for movements to end discriminatory social divisions. One of the Zwickau weavers, Nikolaus Storch, was a proponent of polygamy and adult baptism (both considered serious crimes), who advocated seizing the property of the rich and the forceful overthrow of both political and church authority.

Muntzer was caught up in this revolutionary and heretical vortex not long after he arrived in Zwickau. His own violent disagreement with his father helped him to disavow his connections with his middle class heritage and to look for another group to serve as the chosen ones. His tendencies toward radical ideas, unappeased by his association with Luther, pulled him in the direction of the radical millenarian ideas associated with the poor weavers and the peasants. Muntzer began criticizing Lutherans and Luther. An uprising against the bishop of the area raised so much fear that Muntzer was expelled from his congregation and the city. As Muntzer had left Luther's intellectual direction, he now avoided Luther's geographic direction as well by travelling to Prague where he sought union with the millenarians, Anabaptists, and other radicals.

Muntzer increasingly came to believe that God spoke through **him**, giving him messages not given to other people. When Prague became difficult for him he moved to Allstedt where he married a former nun and formed a union between miners and artisans intended ultimately to embrace all of Christendom. He called on princes and lords to leave their palaces and live as Christians. Those who failed to live according to his social gospel were threatened with death. Thomas Muntzer was a learned man, but he was also a violent one who threatened the delicate stability of the early reformation Germanic area.

Muntzer believed in the imminence of the Kingdom of Heaven and in the worth of activism in order to hasten its arrival. Moreover, like other violent activists, he justified violence by arguing that salvation depended not just on words but on actions as well. He claimed to have a spiritual connection to God, and he shaped his church service around such spiritual communion, but he preached violence and death to those practicing any other form of divine communion.

Nonetheless he stood for something with which the other religious rebels only toyed. Muntzer insisted on a social interpretation of the Gospel that developed a physical, earthly interpretation of what most Christians had interpreted only spiritually. Muntzer believed that the power of the heavens would be given to the people of God who followed **him**. He took the Age of the Spirit as it was articulated by Joachim of Fiore and secularized it. He argued that authority should be vested in the common people who should rise up against the petty tyrants that kept them in bondage. Otherwise the pure word of God would be undone.[3]

Muntzer argued that God's will needed human activity in order to be realized, a concept that Hegel later picked up and used, although with different words. The will of God depended on human activity, and the nature of that activity was revealed to God's prophet, Thomas Muntzer. Anyone who got in the way of this will should, of course, be summarily pushed aside as an enemy of God. The narrowness of vision that normally accompanies such a distrust of other beliefs was belied in Muntzer's case by a religious universalism that argued indifference to a person's religious background so long as the Holy Spirit was visibly present.

What was needed was the establishment of a Christian Union made up of common people. This organized union of common folk would achieve a heavenly life on earth by the whole community's proper use of the sword, the seeking of virtue, and understanding the poor.

This was a Kingdom of Heaven for the lower class achieved by violent means. A covenant bound the people together without all the prating of learned theologians. A strong anti-intellectual strain was evident in Muntzer's new world, as it would be in others. The revolutionary generally receives little or no help from resident intellectuals who sing the song of the establishment patron who feeds them. Intellectuals quickly become the enemy. Virtue in this case was found in the ignorant poor rather than in the comfortable learned. This virtue found in poverty, of course, is rarely discernable to the poor individual.

Muntzer's new society was for the honest but poor laborer, the true elect, because only those who had nothing could free themselves from pride and self-seeking. He may have been totally against private property, but no documentary evidence supports this. He certainly was against the rich and for the poor. He certainly believed that people ought to act like brothers and sisters. He stood for a redistribution of property that fundamentally equalized it, and this redistribution occurred in the context of the Kingdom of Heaven. Even so, he may have left private property in some sort of equalized state rather than totally abolished. The revolution of the elect, by the sword, ushered in the new age so enthusiastically foretold by Muntzer in his sermons and letters.

Muntzer was vague about that new age, but as Eduard Bernstein pointed out much later, that very vagueness was itself productive of utopia-making. All things were to be held in common by brothers and sisters possessed of the Holy Spirit, with goods and services distributed so as to satisfy need. Although this may sound like Joachim's Third Age, the means of becoming elect were decidedly unJoachim: the elect chose themselves by fighting through to God, and the line running between the elect and the non-elect was very much the line that ran between the rich and the poor.[4]

Muntzer led his forces against those of the Princes who followed Luther's appeals, fully expecting God to lead his forces to victory. Legend has it that he told his troops that he would personally catch cannon balls in the sleeves of his cloak and throw them back at the enemy. This miracle did not occur, unfortunately for Muntzer's forces. Superior weapons rather than superior goals won the day, and the Muntzer forces were destroyed. The dream of communal equality, however, remained alive and well, waiting for another set of people to raise its banner at a later day.

Gerrard Winstanley and the Diggers

After the seventeenth century civil wars in England were ended, quiet should have returned to the countryside. The political and religious atmosphere, however, was anything but quiet. Christopher Hill, the British historian, called this period the time when the world was upside down.[5] Manuel and Manuel referred to it as a topsy-turvy period.[6] Everything in the society, whether secular or religious, seemed to come unglued.

One of the calmest political movements of the time was the group known as the Levellers--republicans or liberals who sought a representative form of government. Three decades later, they would be the basis of the Whig party in Parliament. After the civil war they sought the enactment of liberal ideas like repealing the death penalty, extending religious toleration **even** to Roman Catholics, ending the military draft, curtailing parliamentary power, and freeing economic activity. Contrary to what their name implied, however, most Levellers were not at all interested in the sort of economic leveling that equality seems to require.

But others were. This more radical direction advocated an economic levelling that called for a communal sharing that went far beyond most liberal positions of the time. The chief example of this economic leveller tradition was the small group who followed Gerrard Winstanley (b. 1609). They were called "True Levellers" or Diggers because they tried to establish an agricultural communalism in 1649 on St. George's Hill in Surrey. The group seized this common land, seeking to fertilize, drain, and cultivate it, to provide food that could be shared communally. The Diggers hoped that their example would cause thousands of others to flock to their cause, seizing other common land and establishing a political and economic system by and for the common person based on the idea that the earth was a common treasury. Each of the workers would have a quota to fill, and production would be for the common store; ideas that would still be radical several centuries later when François Noël Babeuf articulated them just after the French Revolution. Private property was to be abolished to make room for the communal sharing deemed superior.

Winstanley's ideas came from a vision he had while he was making a living pasturing other people's cattle. Winstanley had been a small London businessman who went bankrupt in the 1640s. In 1649 when he had his major vision he probably felt he was at the bottom of the social order. Religiously speaking, prior to 1849 Winstanley was evidently a Baptist, but he also believed as many others did in a nice God who rescued all the people in Hell at the end of time. This sense of universal salvation was so strong in the 1640s that Parliament made the teaching that all were saved actionable by the Ordinance for the Punishing of Blasphemies and Heresies passed in 1648.[7] After 1649 Winstanley became a Seeker, part of a spiritualist movement that was strong on personal revelations from God. Gerrard Winstanley found that a new discipleship was revealed in his inner self. He stated that he had passed through fierce burnings and a strong sense of his own sin to a tranquility of personal awareness of God **in** himself rather than in the external letter of the law. This spirit, Winstanley believed, dwelt in every creature, but especially humans, an intuited mysticism that resembled the mysticism of George Fox, the founder of the Quakers, and foreshadowed the intuition-based categorical imperative of Immanuel Kant. Winstanley heard the voice of God speaking within himself, a voice that commanded him to preach: "Work together, eat bread together," which he interpreted as a divine endorsement of communal working and sharing. He immediately organized the St. George's Hill expedition in Surrey because in his view he had a mission from God. It did not have to make sense politically or economically; indeed, it may have appeared more visionary if it did not make a great deal of initial sense.

What he urged on the English peasantry was the continuation of the revolution already begun in England, a revolution that would have cosmic significance as England's revolution was replicated elsewhere. Winstanley and those who followed him looked for the literal realization of the Kingdom of God on earth. He believed that a life of Christian love would transform the economic and political organization of society and that human nature would be completely transformed by the workings of the Spirit **within** the individual.

His vision revealed the attractions of communal sharing as a spiritual response to the unequal distribution of property in society. In Winstanley's mind the principles of mutual aid and cooperation did continual battle against the aggressive, acquisitive, and competitive tendencies in human nature. Only by extending mutual aid and cooperation from the family to the whole society could Winstanley imagine creating a system of democratic ideals of equity and reason. Winstanley could not understand how a free political system could still have poverty because, in his view, poverty arose from the exploitation of property by the few. So when he thought about a free political system it *did not include* private property. He did not learn this from reading a book or attending a school; his communal sharing ideas arose out of his religious experience.

The focus of his endeavor was the Digger activity on St. George's Hill in 1649, a variety of pamphlets he wrote, and his book *The Law of Freedom* published in 1652. A political and religious evolution is visible in his works, but he never lost the sense that an inner revelation from God had propelled him on his mission to bring about both economic and political sharing. However, he tried to implement his communal ideas at a bad time. These were years of bad harvests, high food prices and taxes, with discharged soldiers from the civil wars swelling the ranks of the increasingly unhappy poor. There was a good deal of local anarchy, troop rebellions, and mutinies that the army normally put down. Conservatives resisting the ideas of the Diggers in 1649 thought of the military as a means of removing the Digger problem quickly. The egalitarian ideas were perceived as being more widespread than they actually were, and the Digger community on St. George's Hill was seen as the tip of a dangerous iceberg.

Unfortunately for Gerrard Winstanley, these feelings were more the result of conservative fear than fact. The number of poor men who met at St. George's Hill was but six. Even though they did increase, it was not by much. They never did attract a sufficient number to be the sort of threat imagined by the conservatives. The small band, nonetheless, began to dig the ground, preparing the soil for parsnips, carrots, and beans. The area is now a prosperous, treed suburban development, but then it was a barren heath considered common ground; unenclosed and belonging to no one. The group continued its agricultural activity and invited others to join them under the slogan: work together, eat bread together. Perhaps without realizing it, Winstanley was urging both producer and consumer cooperatives as a result of his vision in which God told him that the common people were to manure and work the common lands.

Because of his hostility to private property, Winstanley sought common ownership of the world's resources as the birthright of every person. In addition to being a political radical he became a religious one as well. He decided to call God by another name because the word "God" too much connoted a being external to the individual. The name he chose was Reason, a word that Hegel would later use as well, for much the same purpose: to indicate divine activity **within** rather than outside the individual.

The life of virtue was following the light of Reason within oneself. In a pamphlet dated January 16, 1648, Winstanley wrote that to walk righteously in the sight of Reason meant to live a life of love for one's fellow creatures; and that meant feeding the hungry, clothing the naked, relieving the oppressed, and seeking the preservation of others as well as oneself. The righteous person would also act with consideration toward all other creatures, seeing the deity in other creatures, so that the whole of creation would be knit together with love, tenderness, and unity.[8]

More than a year later *The True Levellers Standard Advanced* was published. An address to the reader that prefaced it, signed by someone named John Taylor, was dated April 20, 1649. The title page was signed by Winstanley and fourteen others and began with a clear statement of purpose. In the beginning, he wrote, the Creator, Reason, had made the earth a common treasury with humans to rule over the beasts, birds, and fish. Winstanley pointed out, however, that not one word was spoken in the beginning about one set of people ruling over another set. The cause of this division was selfish behavior that killed the spirit of human unity and brought some people into bondage to others.

The result, he continued, was a dishonoring of the Creator. Private property and enclosures and fences turned the earth, which was the common store-house for all in the beginning, into commodities bought and sold by the few to the impoverishment of the many.[9]

In June of 1649, some forty five people, including Winstanley, signed the pamphlet entitled: *A Declaration from the Poor Oppressed People of England.* The wording of the pamphlet was more belligerent than the others, suggesting the probability of multiple authorship. Writing to the lords and ladies who controlled the property of 17th Century England, the pamphlet argued that the earth was not made purposely for you to be lords and we to be slaves, it was to be a common livelihood for all. Your buying and selling of land and its fruits is a cursed thing, brought in by war, theft, and murder. It has caused divisions between peoples. It cannot be justified. The bloody and thieving power of the haves must be rooted out of the land.[10]

The reason for this "rooting out" in Winstanley's mind was because the title to land belonged to the poor person as well as the rich one. True freedom, he argued, lay in the free enjoyment of the earth. In a letter to the Lord Fairfax, Winstanley argued that if the common people in England have no more freedom than to live among their elder brothers as hirelings, they have less freedom in England than in Turkey or France,[11] something no English citizen would like to hear. Where is the freedom for which we fought in the civil wars, he argued, the freedom we thought we were wresting from the grasping hands of a decaying royalty? It was not enough, he argued, to cut off the king's head. The act of regicide was only a beginning, not the end. The revolution was not complete; yet the revolutionaries were being seduced into putting down their arms and submitting once again to the landed gentry whom Winstanley called the Elder Brother.

All laws, he argued, that were not grounded upon equity and reason, that did not give a universal freedom to all but showed favoritism to some, ought to be cut off as the king's head had been in 1649. While this kingly power had reigned, he wrote, in one man called Charles, and all sorts of people complained of oppression and the gentry, the Elder Brothers, assembled in Parliament, called upon the poor common people to come and help. Well, he wrote, we did that, and the top bough, King Charles, was lopped off the tree of tyranny. The kingly power in that one particular was cast out. But oppression was a great tree still, and kept the sun of freedom from the poor commons.[12]

Therefore, he insisted, you army of England's Commonwealth: Look to it! The enemy couldn't beat you in the field but you will lose your victory if you are not very careful. You must "stick close" to see common freedom established. Otherwise King Charles has conquered you even though you have cut off his head.[13]

In *A New-Yeers Gift* he wrote that the Great Leveller was Christ **in us**, and that this possession of the King of righteousness would cause people to beat swords into plowshares, spears into pruning hooks, and nations would no longer war with each other. Everyone, in contrast, would delight in allowing others to enjoy the earth's pleasures. There would be no more bondage.[14]

This anticipation of everyone delighting in the future did not, however, make him tolerant of different ideas of how to get to that future happiness.[15] This narrowness reflected the intolerance of his age as well as his own intolerance for different versions of the truth, but it is nonetheless sobering to realize that people like Winstanley and others who speak of universal benefits for humanity are often so very particular about how to get there.

He also did not seek an armed insurrection, even though some of his writing seems angry enough to lean in that direction. He wrote in *Fire in the Bush* around 1650, for example, "...woe, woe, woe to the Inhabitants of the Earth when Christ rises in power, and begins to come in glory with his Saints."[16] These words need to be balanced with others that insisted that the sword of Christ was the sword of love, patience, and truth, that Christ came not to destroy but to save. Since this was so, he argued, the reader should "...come out of Babylon, ...come into truth, Light, and Liberty, and be at peace."[17]

Although he remained religious, he was against the traditional church as much as he was against the new state after the civil wars because, as the liberation theologians discovered, the traditional church is often one of the largest property holders in a property-based state. Winstanley wrote that a subtle Clergy charms the people with what he called their divining Doctrine. They tell people that the unequal distribution of property is the will of God and if people object they will go to Hell.

So the poor people, or the younger brothers as Winstanley calls them, are terrified and let go of their hold in the earth, submitting as a slave to one's brother for fear of eternal damnation and in hopes of eternal bliss in heaven. So, he argued, the younger brother's "...eyes are put out and his Reason is blinded."[18]

Winstanley believed that these so called agents of God could be ignored. God's presence and power were not possessed by the clergy but were **inside** the individual person. One's savior was a power within. The outward Christ, he wrote, or the outward God, as he put it, were but men Saviors who cause confusion. The God whom people all too often served was the covetousness that flowed out of what he called Imagination which in turn resulted from the Tree of the Knowledge of Good and Evil. Counterpoised to this Imagination, however, was Universal Love which came from the Tree of Life. Needless to say, Winstanley's group followed Universal Love, while Imagination still ensnared lords, knights, gentlemen, and especially landlords.

He argued that there were two great sins in the world. The first was locking up the treasures of the world to rust and decay while those to whom it really belonged starved for want of it. This was a great sin against universal love. The second great sin occurred when those whose murdering swords took the earth's treasures to begin with created laws making it a capital offense for someone in need to take from those who are hoarding the treasures.

The religious experience he had himself was what he read onto the whole world. The knowledge of God was progressive for him, and it was evolutionary for the world as well, just as it was for Joachim and later for Hegel. The world movement of God's spirit among the poor, although it may seem small in the beginning, he believed, would definitely increase over time.[19]

In the sense that the end of a war period has always been a good time to begin a revolution, Winstanley picked a good time. There was widespread unemployment, and in 1649 conditions in many parts of England bordered on famine. The poor were so miserable that frequent rioting occurred. But in another sense this was a bad time for Winstanley to begin his struggle. Too many people after any prolonged struggle only want to get things back to normal. Winstanley's economic and religious ideas not only seemed strange to most people, but it also seemed that he wanted to prolong a struggle most people were glad to see ended. And, although many might have supported

Winstanley's notions in the abstract, having these squatters in one's own neighborhood was not seen as desirable. The people around St. George's Hill came and forced the Diggers into a church, from which the authorities released them. They were then shut up again in Kingston about eight miles to the northeast. There they were judged not to have committed a crime and were again released. Protests were officially filed by others in the neighborhood, and the army was called in; but again, no threat was seen from the few squatters and they were left alone. By April 20th, nearly three weeks after the experiment began, there were some fifteen signers of a Winstanley pamphlet *The True Levellers Standard Advanced* which tied their movement to Winstanley's divine revelation.

The notion of a divine revelation was not the only motivating factor. There was also the idea that Winstanley and the Diggers represented the chosen people of God whose job it was to convince Parliament by example and by word to remove the Norman yoke (landlords) from England and restore to the ancient community the enjoyment of the fruits of the earth.

Although they had begun with the apparently simple idea of only communizing commons property for their communal, agricultural living, the harassment of the Diggers continued, particularly after they prevented local landlords from cutting wood on the common land. The Diggers felt kindly only to others like themselves. Winstanley wrote that well-meaning people who joined the community in God's way, protesting against the Norman yoke, and who were desirous of manuring, digging, and planting in the waste grounds and Commons would not be troubled or molested by the Diggers, but helped instead. All others, of course, were the enemy.

In the autumn of 1649, however, they left behind the notion of simply digging on waste or common land. Instead they moved to Cobham Manor where they squatted **on John Platt's property,** not on common land as they had earlier. While on common land, the Diggers might enjoy the sympathy of a good many people, liberals perhaps, who were decidedly not communist but had a sense of the rightness of combining the produce from waste lands with the needs of the poor. But when the Diggers squatted on private property, their support shrank considerably. Opposition to them mounted.

Their numbers were still only about fifty at this point. By April 1650 Winstanley stated that the group had about eleven acres of grain growing and some six or seven houses. The movement gathered some small momentum, and altogether some 34 separate groups tried to farm land in common and share the produce.   Legal action against them intensified not simply because their numbers grew, but because in many instances in 1650 they were **trespassing** on other's property rather than settling common land that no one was using.   Winstanley did not recognize the legitimacy of other people's property. Harassment of the Diggers became destructive and was often overlooked by authorities. Digger cattle were turned into the grain, houses were torched, and families were turned out onto the heath. In frustration Digger demands became more shrill, demanding a confiscation of crown and former monastery lands on behalf of the poor. Both liberals and conservatives now joined together to put the movement down, and it did not survive 1650.

Winstanley had written in the Preface to his *New Law of Righteousness* that the poor were the despised of the world, but the blessing of God was in them, and through them would spread forth to fill the world. In the new society production and distribution would be under the control of the authorities, so that goods could get to the various storehouses from which people would extract as needed and to prevent the buying and selling of commodities which was strictly forbidden. Winstanley, like More and others, had perhaps too many rules for his unlaunched commonwealth, but, if one allows for Winstanley's religious preoccupation, the rules seem for the most part quite sensible. He would exclude from the franchise all those who had supported the King in the Civil War, which was understandable if not tolerant.   Some rules were downright liberal, and would be for centuries: his rules on marriage and sex, for example. People could marry whom they love, because neither birth nor portion would any longer be a factor. If a man lay with a maid and she became pregnant, he married her. Period. Rapists were put to death, so long as there were two witnesses, because rape was robbery of a woman's bodily freedom.   When one reads *The Law of Freedom* it might appear as though there were more laws than freedoms, but this was probably due to the fact that the laws were all presented at once. There might even be more regimentation than was consistent with Winstanley's liberal beginning, but he probably felt at the time that he had to distinguish his movement from contemporary groups who advocated no social rules at all.   With a naiveté reminiscent of the innocents in the Garden, Winstanley tried to create a commonwealth peopled by commoners like himself, a society by and for the very poor, without lords, princes, priests, or landlords.

Abimael Guzmán and the Shining Path

The Shining Path movement in Peru was a twentieth century phenomenon. Its full name was the Peruvian Communist Party in the Shining Path of José Carlos Mariátegui, and it came to be known as *Sendero Luminoso* or Shining Path. The founder of this movement was Abimael Guzmán Reynoso (b. 1934), a former professor of philosophy at the University of San Cristóbal de Huamanga in Ayachucho. Professor Guzmán received his PhD and a second degree in law from the San Agustin National University in Arequipa.

Guzmán was a member of the Communist Party of Peru until 1964 when he broke away to form a pro-Chinese faction of the party. He was protesting the decided lack of revolutionary enthusiasm in the Peruvian communist party that was following the peaceful coexistence line from Moscow. Within a few years, however, even the pro-Chinese faction seemed too tame and insufficiently oriented toward the peasantry. He broke away and began his own movement: the Shining Path.

Because he was the university personnel director, Guzmán could use his position to recruit like-minded faculty and students. During the 1970s, assisted by his wife, Guzmán secretly built his radical organization. The Shining Path surfaced in May 1980 during the presidential election in Peru.[20]

What emerged from the secrecy of the 1970s was a radical Maoist organization dedicated to the notion of revolution by and for the countryside against all that was represented by the cities. This position reflected the anti-urban attitudes of Mao Zedong, and was similar to the Khmer Rouge position implemented in Cambodia at about the same time (1975-1978). However, the Shining Path ideology did not suggest linkage with the Khmer Rouge despite this similarity. *Sendero* was so parochial and had such an uncompromising ideology that even links with ideologically close leftists in Peru were not allowed. Guzmán once described Cuba's revolutionary hero, Ché Guevara, as a "choir girl," condemned the Soviet Union as having a corrupt and treasonist ideology, and reviled Chinese leaders for betraying Mao Zedong. The only international contact was with Albania in the mid-1970s but even that link snapped a short time later.[21] The Shining Path stressed instead a connection to the founder of Peruvian socialism, José Carlos

Mariátegui (1894-1930). Carlos believed that the original basis for Peruvian socialism lay in the pre-Columbian peasant community destroyed by Spanish conquerors centuries before. The descendants of this proud people, the Quechua-speaking peasants of today, live in Peru but also in Argentina, Bolivia, Chile, Ecuador, and in Columbia. In attempting to bring about a communism by and for peasants, Guzmán was looking at Peru with its extensive Indian population but also to the entire western side of South America.

Abimael Guzmán became known as the Fourth Sword of Marxism following Marx, Lenin, and Mao Zedong, but the major thrust of Guzmán's ideology was derived from Mao's orientation to the peasantry of China. He sought to destroy everything that, in his judgment, wasn't or shouldn't be a part of peasant life; things like the national market economy, industry, the banking system, foreign trade, currency, and ownership of land beyond a plot less than five acres. In place of all this would be communal villages and barter exchanges oriented to peasant needs.

The method chosen by Guzmán to reach this vague egalitarian goal was violence directed against the cities; blowing up power lines, bridges, and office buildings, and violence against public officials, village administrators, and large landowners.   Its weapons were dynamite stolen from Peruvian mining companies and rifles stolen from the police. It received no outside assistance and financed its operations by robbing banks, taxing peasants, and taking a cut of the profits from the growing of coca in the areas it controlled.

For a time the Shining Path seemed indestructible and a growing menace to Peruvian society. It established several front organizations and even had a newspaper for a time. It so infiltrated the schools that many school children believed that Guzmán was the president of Peru. In 1992, the Shining Path had established what were called popular schools in which children were taught Maoist ideology, slogans, and hymns from the *Sendero* movement. One reporter alleged in 1992 that approximately 60 percent of Peru's school children were affected by the Shining Path influence, even in regular state schools.[22]

In one sense it seemed more like a populist cult with Guzmán as guru than a revolutionary communist group, and in another sense *Sendero* seemed more inclined to the racial supremacy of darker-skinned peasants than a communal society in which lighter-hued city folk might be welcome.   Reports that Shining Path members from Quechua speaking communities of the highlands forced their language on an

Ashaninka ethnic group from the Amazon lowlands confirmed an impression of ethnic violence that had less to do with communism and more to do with dominance.

On the other hand, the Shining Path organization, for all that it was focused on Guzmán the leader, was also far ahead of the rest of Latin America in that it was open to female participation at the highest levels. These women did much more than make the coffee or warm the beds of the revolutionaries in the evenings. The number two position was always a woman, and in 1992 eight of the nineteen members of the Central Committee were women. The literature of the group stated that some 40 percent of the guerrillas were women, and this might have been true. A strong reason for women to seek membership could have been the misogynist Latin American machismo culture, but it also may have been because a woman's place in Peruvian society was often unpleasant, uneasy, and undesirable. Until 1980 she could not vote if she were illiterate. If she were raped the criminal was rarely punished. If her skin were dark, things were even worse because of the entrenched racism against Indian groups. For uneducated women of darker skin color it was nearly impossible to break out of the cycle of poverty, continual childbearing, excessive physical labor, and early aging. Although it was not surprising, therefore, that Peruvian women joined the Shining Path, it was surprising that so many attained leadership positions. Most became hardened guerrilla fighters, often standing out in the five thousand member force for being more ruthless by far than the males.[23]

The existence of the group and the efforts to suppress it cost over 27,000 deaths in the thirteen years of its active existence, and some $25 billion dollars in damages. The battle was fought by the Peruvian government without success for twelve years, but in September 1992 Abimael Guzmán and several other leaders were captured by the police. With their arrest and the successful incarceration of Guzmán, the heart seemed to go out of the movement. Morale slipped, other leaders left the movement, thousands of guerrillas turned themselves in during an amnesty program, and the Shining Path seemed to dim to a faint glow that would not survive the loss of the *caudillo*.[24]

This remains true even though new attacks occurred in February and March 1995, suggesting that the Shining Path guerrillas could still be considered a potent force and a threat to the security of Peru even though its top leadership had been removed for over 2 years. The Shining Path goal remains the destabilization of Peruvian society,[25] but they are expected to continue their decline in membership and morale.

Like the Muntzer and Winstanley movements, Guzmán's search for communism and equality was opposed by a powerful establishment. Unlike the groups led by Muntzer and Winstanley, however, it appeared for a time in the early 1990s that the Shining Path might be successful in overturning the government in Lima and developing some sort of peasant-oriented society. That dream died in 1992, however, with the capture of the leader, and the movement faded as others had.

Even so, the dream of equality refused to die. Contemporary evidence of the recurring dream came from the uprising in southern Mexico in 1994.

The Zapatistas of Chiapas

As though intended as a reminder that the dream of equality is by no means dead, a new set of have-nots sought redress for past and present grievances. The ancient human quest reappeared on January 1, 1994 in Chiapas, the southeastern corner of Mexico when the Zapatistas emerged with guns and discipline. Towns were captured in Chiapas, very close to Guatemala, by peasants calling themselves the Zapatista Army of National Liberation. The reasons for the rising of about two thousand combatants were described by a young guerrilla named Jesús: there was no work, no land, no education, and no way to change that through elections. Their name was chosen to honor Emiliano Zapata (1877-1919), the peasant hero of the 1911 Revolution.[26]

Chiapas, where this rebellion emerged, ranks last among Mexican states in households with electricity (66.9%), last in the number of children under 14 years of age who attend school (71.3%), and last in the number of people over 14 who can read (69.6%). It is fourth from the bottom in the percentage of households with access to sewers (41.2%) or running water (58.4%). In addition Chiapas has consistently earned one of Mexico's worst records of human rights' abuse. Advocates of Indian rights have long claimed that the government uses torture in handling the Indians. In their proclamation of war, the Zapatista army claimed that their struggle was for work, land, housing, food, health care, education, independence, freedom, democracy, justice, and peace.[27]

What should have been clear right from the start was that the Zapatista ideology of socialism was more of an afterthought than an engine of the uprising--the struggle is for people to have a better life.[28] And because the struggle is relatively new the socialism sought is fairly vague. They sought a better life through defeating the political party in power, not through any absolute transformation of Mexico. If the problems in Chiapas continue to go unalleviated for a long enough time Zapatista demands will become more absolute and more difficult to achieve. The result would then be more authoritarianism.

Continuing events in Mexico suggest that the Zapatista struggle will be a long one, with the government promising changes, not following through, the rebels threatening to take up arms again, government military moves against the rebels, then more official promises that no one intends to honor, as the situation steadily worsens. Much of what the Zapatistas seek has been sought many times before in Mexico. Previous failures only intensify the new frustrations when the dream is again denied.

Ursula Le Guin's *The Dispossessed*

The novel opens with a description of the wall around the spaceport on the moon named Anarres. This wall is to keep foreigners who landed at the spaceport away from the people of Anarres, and to keep the people away from the spaceport. The notion of a wall is repeated later when the hero of the story, a man named Shevek, is describing the people on the parallel planet called Urras. The walls on Anarres keep out foreigners and keep Anarresti in--it's a bad thing, but not as bad as the walls on Urras, individual walls that **separated** people by denying the social nature of the human.

The moon colony, Anarres, had been founded some 170 years previously by a wise woman named Odo on the principle of the abolition of private property. That it had lasted so long was a tribute to Odo's principles of equality and sharing, especially since Anarres was arid and bleak. Life on this moon was difficult, but some of the difficulties were created by the Anarres people themselves. They were beginning to move beyond the spaceport wall; other walls based on fear were emerging. Anarresti were beginning to see any difference as dangerous, and to accept pressure for social conformity as desirable.

For the most part Ursula Le Guin tells the story in alternate chapters. First the reader is on Urras, then Anarres, then Urras again. The hero of the story, Shevek, a rather anarchistic individualist, was a native of Anarres who was visiting Urras. Alternative chapters flashed back to show how Shevek got to where he was.

Shevek was a research physicist who had run into the problem that even on Anarres knowledge was not easily shared. As a matter of fact some knowledge was guarded by those that possessed it. Shevek had picked up some books from his mentor, Sabul, and had turned to go when Sabul told him that those books were not for general consumption. Shevek didn't understand. Sabul said "Don't let anyone else read them!" Treat them as though they were a pack of explosive caps you had found in the street. Would you share these dangerous things with passersby? These books, he said, are explosive.[29]

If the sharing did not go far enough in one direction, it went too far in another. Shevek's work could only be published if it were presented as mainly Sabul's work and not his own. When scientists on Urras, the propertied and class-divided other world from which the Anarres settlers had come, invited Shevek to Urras to receive a physics prize for his work, no one expected him to go because people did not leave Anarres unless they were traitors who would not be allowed back.

Shevek decided to go, however, because it was obvious that people who fear contact with the enemy demanded a conformity that increasingly isolated Anarres. That conformity was their safety. Shevek, however, wanted freedom rather than safety. Too much equality, he thought, hampers liberty and stifles the spirit, and this can happen even in a society dedicated to sharing.

If everyone must agree, or all work together, or not work at all we're no better than a machine. If an individual can't work in solidarity with his fellows, it's his duty and his right to work alone. But, Shevek said, we have been denying people that right, saying, more and more often, that they must work with the others, and accept the rule of the majority. Such rules are a tyranny because only if the individual accepts no rules and is a responsible self-initiator will the society live, and change, and adapt, and survive. "The Revolution is in the individual spirit, or it is nowhere. It is for all, or it is nothing. If it is seen as having any end, it will never truly begin."[30]

Shevek believed that life on Anarres was better than anywhere else, but that it fell far short of the ideal. Liberty was being ignored. A need for group consensus was robbing the individual spirit of its vitality. The weight of the State was allowed to stifle initiative. Part of the problem was the aridity of the planet and the poverty of their beginnings, but when Shevek was talking Anarres had existed for 170 years.

Work assignments, or postings, were not always pleasant either. If you were partnered with a significant other, one of you might get a post far from the other. The work itself was not always pleasant even though people did take turns. When Shevek's wife Takver nursed his daughter Sadik until she was three she was accused by her group of being "propertarian" about her child. Group conformity was put in the way of individual pleasure in loving another.

There were limits on artistic expression. The story was told of a man named Bedap who wrote a satirical play when he was twenty years old about a Urrasti who stowed away on a moon freighter, came to propertyless Anarres and tried to buy and sell things. He couldn't even enjoy sex without having to pay for it first. He amassed gold which no one wanted. The play met with criticism and censorship and this destroyed the young author. The entire brotherhood seemed against him. Shevek blamed bureaucratic rigidity, an unwillingness to change or to see another point of view, as well as an internalization of the need for group support. The result was that the group conscience dominated the individual conscience. "We fear our neighbor's opinion more than we respect our own freedom of choice."[31]

Although Anarres was not an ideal society, it was much better than any other. Better by far than Urras. One of the ways that it was better was in the gender equality experienced by women on Anarres. Women were thoroughly integrated into the intellectual, or academic, or scientific society. Half of the scientific positions were held by women. On Urras females were excluded from such society, justifying their exclusion on the basis of tired arguments about women's lack of ability in math and science, the proper place of a woman, etc. Shortly after arriving on Urras Shevek noted that all the scientists who came to see him were males. So he asked, are all the scientists here men? Of course they are, was the response. Females are not very good with math or abstract thought. "Of course, there are always a few exceptions, God-awful brainy women with vaginal atrophy."[32]

Women with brains were not real women; a vicious example of a different kind of group-think brought on by superficially accepting idiotic notions of "women's work" and "men's work" and assuming gender capabilities from the acceptance of gender rôles.

Shevek was surprised to be given a private room of his own. On Anarres, a private room was only for copulating, or so that a child could be punished for having egoized. Solitude equated with selfishness and disgrace. Everyone had the workshop, laboratory, studio, barn, or office that he or she needed for work, certainly. One could be as private or as public as one chose in the baths. Sexual privacy was freely available and socially expected, but beyond that privacy was not functional. It was wasteful excess. Society could not afford to pander to excessive individualism.[33]

What about the individualist who did not wish to share or to agree with the rules of the society on Anarres? A person whose nature was genuinely unsociable had to get away from society and look after him/herself and was completely free to do so. The individualist could build a house wherever desired. If the house blocked a good view for others or took up a fertile bit of land he/she would probably discover heavy pressure from neighbors to move elsewhere. When people won't cooperate they move on. Other people get tired of the noncooperation and make fun of the individual, perhaps get a bit rough, take the person's name off the meal lists so that he/she has to cook individually. All this is humiliating, and so these people move on. Nonetheless there were a good many solitaries, pretending that they were not members of a social species.[34]

Education on Anarres was practical, teaching students the basics but also farming, carpentry, sewage reclamation, printing, plumbing, roadmending, playwriting, and so forth. The curriculum on Anarres, just like curricula elsewhere, tended to guide students into becoming adults who fit into an existing, sharing society. No one was ever punished for anything.

What kept people in order was internal rather than external, the desire to share rather than the desire to gather privately more than someone else. Besides, Shevek argued, no one on Anarres had anything worth robbing. And, as for violence, the threat of punishment never deters it anyway.

The dirty work was done by everyone at regular intervals. People took turns doing the less desirable work. The committee could ask you for one day in each ten day period, and that generally was sufficient. This was not very efficient because it meant that unskilled people would continually be doing the work, but the alternative was to ask someone to spend their working life doing that dirty job, perhaps one that would cripple or harm the worker if the exposure were prolonged. So people taking turns made more sense, and people accepted these odd jobs because they were done together and because they put variety into their work life. Shevek said that here on Urras the only incentive to work was financial, but on Anarres where there was no money the motives for work were clearer. People liked to do things and they liked to do them well. They took pride in doing difficult, dangerous jobs, because they could show off to the weaker ones. Work was done not for money but for the work's sake--it was the lasting pleasure of life. The private conscience understood that and so did the social conscience. So the only reward on Anarres was one's own pleasure and the respect of one's fellows.[35]

People on Anarres worked five to seven hours per day, with two to four days off each ten days. The details of which days off, time to come to work, etc., were worked out between the individual and his work crew or gang or syndicate.[36]

Who did the dirty work on Urras? Poor people did. What was their incentive? High wages? No, actually. They got rather low pay. Why then did they do the dirty work? Because low pay was better than no pay.

On Anarres, the work was not always pleasant but with everyone taking their turn it was difficult to become angry. It was not a job into which a person was forced due to economic circumstances. Eating took place in the commons, a big room with many tables, several cooks and servers, and others who just washed up afterward. Children, after infancy, stayed in children's dormitories. Parents could pick their children up each day after school, if they were in the area, go to the baths together, eat dinner *en familie* at the commons, and then, an hour or two after dinner take the child back to the dorm. The adults lived in big dormitories with 200 rooms, holding perhaps 400 to 500 people. The society was governed by what were called executive meetings, in Shevek's opinion a lot of talk and very little action. Several people spoke at once, nobody at great length, a good deal of sarcasm, a great deal left unsaid, emotional tones very often fiercely personal, and although an end to the meeting was reached, there was seldom a conclusion.

The longer Shevek stayed on Urras, the brighter and better his own society of Anarres seemed even with its faults. He argued, after drinking a bit too much at a party, that although Anarres was dry, poor, bleak, and difficult, it was a society **for humans**. You have a beautiful planet here on Urras, he said, but the faces on Urras are not beautiful. On Anarres nothing is beautiful but the faces of people, of men and women who have nothing but each other. On Urras you can see jewels, on Anarres you see the eyes, and in those eyes you can see the splendor of the human spirit because our men and women are free. They possess nothing but they are free. You, the possessors are the possessed. "You are all in jail. Each alone, solitary, with a heap of what he owns. You live in prison, die in prison. It is all I can see in your eyes--the wall, the wall!"[37]

It was difficult to impress anything on the Urrans because they

thought in such different terms. Earlier in the book a scientist had said
that there was a lot to admire on Anarres, but the biggest problem was
that citizens were not taught to discriminate, which, he felt, was the
best thing civilization could teach. He didn't want to hear notions of
brotherhood and mutualism and common humanity and leagues of all
the worlds. He wanted only to hear about the law of existence--the law
of struggle, of competition--the elimination of the weak--the ruthless
war for survival. The best to him were the survivors.[38] This man
thought mutual aid was something that pampered the weak; a source
of weakness rather than strength.

Later, a lady at a party suggested that Shevek's society on Anarres
had no morality. She seemed shocked but titillated by the idea. Shevek
did not know what she meant. To him she was not speaking sense. To
hurt a person there, he said, was the same as here on Urras. She was
disappointed. You mean, she said, implying backwardness, that you
have all the same old rules? She believed that morality was a
superstition like religion that had to be thrown out.

Shevek was puzzled. My society, he said, is an attempt to reach
morality, not to preach it. I agree that people should throw out the
moralizing, yes--the rules, the laws, the punishments--so that people can
face good and evil squarely and choose between them. This assumed
that people have that ability. On Urras the assumption was that people
did not have this ability, and even the question was obscured by the
context of property values and hatred of the weak.

Still trying to get his point across, Shevek said that Anarresti follow
one law, the law of human evolution. The Urran woman responded
that the law of evolution meant that the strongest survived!--thinking
that she had made a telling point.

Yes, Shevek argued, and the strongest in the existence of any social
species are those who are the most social, the most ethical. You see,
he said, we have neither prey nor enemy on Anarres. We have only
one another, and there is no strength to be gained from hurting one
another--just weakness.[39]

Urran society, on the other hand, was one where the strongest was
the person who stepped on the most people to get higher than the rest.
On Anarres the strongest was the most social, the kindest person. As
a result Urras was a society where no one trusted another, and where
the basic moral assumption was not mutual aid but mutual aggression.
Shevek was frightened to be on his own.[40]

On Anarres because nothing was owned and private property did not
really exist, a child free from the guilt of ownership and the burden of

economic competition would grow up with the will to do what needed doing and the capacity for joy in doing it. It was useless work, Shevek thought, that darkened the heart. The delight of the nursing mother, the scholar, the successful hunter, the good cook, the skillful maker--the delight of anyone doing needed work and doing it well--this durable joy was perhaps the deepest source of human affection and sociability as a whole.[41]

Adversity on Anarres brought people together. During one prolonged drought they found that they worked harder, voluntarily. They pulled together much better under the lash of adversity. Their solidarity was a bond worth having. This did not mean that everyone was a sweetheart. Shevek's neighbor, a lady named Bunub, wanted their double apartment and could be quite nasty about it. Bunub entertained men regularly and was quite bitter about her life while doing nothing to change it. A math colleague of Shevek's, Desar, was similarly malicious. Being secretive and possessive was psychopathic on Anarres, while on Urras it was rational behavior.[42]

A Urran servant named Efor allowed as how life on Anarres was different, that no one was ever out of work there, that no one ever went hungry while others ate. Shevek hurried to point out that there were hungry times on Anarres, but if there was hunger everyone shared it. Efor understood. What made the biggest impression on him was that on Anarres there were no owners.[43]

Near the end of the story Shevek rebelled against the Urran society and the isolation he has been placed in by his sponsors. He escaped from his apartment at the university, and found a revolutionary leader from whom he asked assistance. Shevek needed help, he said, because the state wanted his scientific theories and he did not want the state to have them. So he couldn't stay in his apartment, and there was no way he could get back to Anarres on his own. The opposition leader, a man named Maedda, said they would willingly help him, because the society on Anarres had meant so much to them for the past century and a half. Just to know that it exists, that there is a society without government, police, economic exploitation! They can never again say that it's just a mirage or an idealist's dream. You, yourself, Dr. Shevek, are a revolutionary idea in the flesh. A dangerous idea made flesh.[44]

And in that instant the revolutionaries realized that they had a very effective leader in Shevek, and Shevek decided to write for their paper and give a speech in which he spoke to the minds of thousands of listeners. He said that the bond uniting them was not love but their shared suffering, that brotherhood arose from the understanding that there is no help for us but from one another. And the hand you hold out to help is empty because you possess nothing, you own nothing, and you are free. All you have is what you are and what you give-- yourself in brotherhood and sisterhood.

We on Anarres, he said, have no law but the single principle of mutual aid between individuals, no government but the single principle of free association. We have no states, nations, presidents, premiers, chiefs, generals, bosses, bankers, landlords, wages, charity, police, soldiers, wars, nor do we have much else. We are not rich; we are poor, and none of us is powerful. If you join us you become wholly dependent on other people for your life.

You cannot make or buy the Revolution, he concluded. You "...can only be the Revolution. It is in your spirit, or it is nowhere."[45]

The power of the Urran state put down this general strike and revolt in the normal violent manner, but Shevek was rescued by the Terran Embassy which granted him political asylum--protection from the Urran authorities who were searching for him.

Shevek's discussion with the Terran Ambassador indicated she also had a strong identification with the lumpen on Anarres and an enlightening perspective for Shevek to think about. Shevek had just argued that there was nothing on Urras that anyone from Anarres could ever need. We left Urras, he said, with empty hands, a hundred and seventy years ago, and we were right. We took nothing because there was nothing here but States and their weapons, the rich and their lies, and the poor and their misery. On Urras there was no way to act rightly, with a clear heart, nothing you can do that is not affected by profit or fear of loss, or the wish for power. In saying "good morning" a person on Urras knows which is superior and which inferior. Acting like a brother or a sister is impossible. People here manipulate each other, or command them, or obey them, or trick them. There is no freedom. Urras is a beautifully wrapped box, blue skies, green meadows, great cities. But if one moves beyond the superficial, and opens the box, all that is inside it is a dusty black cellar containing a dead man whose hand was shot off because he held it out to others. "I have been in Hell at last," Shevek said. "Desar was right; it is Urras; Hell is Urras."[46]

But the Terran Ambassador, while accepting the negative assessment of Urras, told Shevek that from her perspective Urras was paradise, not hell. Urras was an enchanted planet because her world, Earth, was a ruin, a planet spoiled by the human species who had multiplied, gobbled, and fought until there was little left. Then, she said, we died.

We destroyed ourselves, but we destroyed the planet first: no forests, the air and sky are grey, and it is always hot. There were nine billion people, but now there are not even 500 million. It was still habitable, but not like Urras. Anarresti chose a desert to build a new, sharing society, she said sadly, but Terrans made a desert out of a beautiful planet. The old cities were still visible everywhere partly as dust and bones, but we failed as a species, as a social species. So, she argued, Urras looks splendid and vital compared to Earth.

If Urras is a paradise, Shevek said, what then is Anarres to you? Nothing, she replied, it's beyond a dream. We forfeited our chance for Anarres before it ever came into being.[47] But, Shevek asked, don't you believe in change, in chance, in evolution? Would you destroy us, he asked in bewilderment, rather than admit our reality, rather than admit that there is hope for the future? She responded that she was trying to be realistic. How can you be realistic, he said, if you don't know what hope is?[48]

As though everything important had been said, Shevek was allowed to return home to Anarres and his family and friends. The different positions occupied by the lowest class suggested that the future held several potential directions. Things could go very wrong and people could destroy the earth. Things could remain about the same and we would continue to shuffle along believing that misery and poverty were sent by God. Or we could hope and reach for brotherhood and sisterhood, stretching our essence to reach the higher plateau; not ideal, not perfection, just a great deal better.

As Shevek said, only individuals can make choices. A healthy society was what he wanted, one that would let him exercise that optimum function--whatever he did best, freely, and in the coordination of all such functions finding its adaptability and strength. The society on Anarres might fall short of the ideal, but his responsibility only increased. When the myth of the state was out of the way, the real mutuality and reciprocity of society and individual became very clear. Society might give security and stability, but only an individual had the power of moral choice, the power of change, the essential function of life.[49]

Endnotes
Chapter Five

1. Frank E. and Fritzie P. Manuel, *Utopian Thought in the Western World* (Cambridge: Harvard University Press, 1979), p. 183.

2. Ibid., p. 185.

3. Ibid., p. 188.

4. Ibid., pp. 195-196.

5. Christopher Hill, *The World Turned Upside Down: Radical Ideas During the English Revolution* (New York: Viking Press, 1972).

6. Manuel & Manuel, *op. cit.*, pp. 332-366. The phrase is a part of the title of Chapter 13: "Topsy-turvey in the English Civil War."

7. W. K. Jordan, *The Development of Religious Toleration in England: Attainment of the Theory and Accommodations, 1640-1660* (Cambridge: Harvard University Press, 1940), pp. 90ff.

8. Gerrard Winstanley, *The Works of Gerrard Winstanley with an Appendix of Documents Relating to the Digger Movement*, edited and introduced by George H. Sabine (Ithaca, NY: Cornell University Press, 1941), p. 111.

9. Ibid., pp. 251-252.

10. Ibid., p. 269.

11. Ibid., p. 288.

12. Ibid., p. 357.

13. Ibid., pp. 573-574.

14. Ibid., p. 391.

15. Manuel and Manuel, *op. cit.*, p. 350.

16. Winstanley, *op. cit.*, pp. 470-471.

17. Ibid.

18. Ibid., p. 569.

19. Manuel & Manuel, *op. cit.*, p. 351.

20. Gordon H. McCormick, "The Shining Path and Peruvian Terrorism," a Rand Paper (Santa Monica: The Rand Corporation, 1987), pp. 1, 2, 5, and 9.

21. Ibid., pp. 18-19.

22. James Brooke, "Shining Path Rebels Infiltrate Schools, Making Them a 'Decisive Battlefield' in Peru," *The New York Times*, August 30,. 1992, p. 6.

23. Nathaniel C. Nash, "Shining Path Women: So Many and So Ferocious," *The New York Times*, September 22, 1992, p. 4.

24. James Brooke, "Leader's New Image Saps Shining Path's Strength," *The New York Times*, November 27, 1993, p. 3.

25. Calvin Sims, "A Stepped-Up Terror Campaign in Peru Shows the Shining Path 'Is Not Dead Yet,'" *The New York Times*, March 20, 1995, p. 5.

26. Tim Golden, "Rebels Determined 'to Build Socialism' in Mexico," *The New York Times*, January 4, 1994, p. 3.

27. Ibid.

28. Tim Golden, "Left Behind, Mexico's Indians Fight the Future," *The New York Times*, January 9, 1994, pp. 1E, 6E.

29. Ursula K. Le Guin, *The Dispossessed* (New York: Avon Books, 1974), p. 85.

30. Ibid., pp. 288-289. The author may be referring to problems experienced by the Soviet Union during its seven decades of existence, and depicting them as needing solution on Anarres. Her anarchistic resistance to group-think, however, reminds one either of George Orwell or Ayn Rand.

31. Ibid., pp. 262-263, 265.

32. Ibid., p. 59.

33. Ibid., pp. 89-90.

34. Ibid., pp. 89-90, 121.

35. Ibid., pp. 120-121.

36. Ibid., p. 151.

37. Ibid., p. 184.

38. Ibid., p. 115.

39. Ibid., pp. 176-177.

40. Ibid., p. 167.

41. Ibid., p. 199.

42. Ibid., p. 223.

43. Ibid., p. 229.

44. Ibid., p. 237.

45. Ibid., pp. 241-242.

46. Ibid., p. 278.

47. Ibid., pp. 279-280.

48. Ibid., pp. 281-282.

49. Ibid., p. 267.

Chapter Six

Communal Sharing
The Basis of Religious Collectives

Anabaptists in Middle Europe
Perfectionists in Oneida
Ann Lee and the Shakers
Kibbutzniks in Palestine and Israel

In his book on communities, George Melnyk wrote that Christianity was the religion of occidental communalism and that it could be divided into the Roman Catholic monastic movement and Protestant utopian communities for men, women, and children.[1] What is being described in this chapter, then, should be Protestant utopian communities in rural areas.

They were all religious, but not all Protestant or even Christian. The Anabaptists of sixteenth century Europe were, of course, Protestant Christians. So also were the people who aspired to perfection in Oneida, New York, and the followers of Mother Ann who were called Shakers. They would each have argued, perhaps, that they had a superior brand of Protestant Christianity, but they would still fall into Melnyk's categories. The Kibbutzniks, however, escape those categories entirely because they were neither Catholic nor Protestant. Kibbutzim were (are) examples of Jewish rural communism that began in 19th century Palestine and became, after 1948, a significant part of the state of Israel.

Anabaptists in Middle Europe

Anabaptists were early Protestants who strongly believed in the necessity of being rebaptized as adults. They came out of the Zwingli group of Swiss reformers that had begun, as had Luther's, by representing almost all levels of people. Over a short period of time, however, it became obvious that the universalism could not be maintained; class interests broke up the Protestant groups whether they were Lutheran or Zwinglian.

In the Zwingli case, the breakaway group probably began in 1521 but it did not become visible until the spring of 1522. This very small but reforming element in Zwinglian protestantism that became known as the Brethren remained for a time as part of the Zwingli congregation at Zurich, but not for long.   They were evolving out of religious reformism into positions that made it impossible for them to remain as simply a distinct part of Zwinglian Protestantism.

The main issue dividing the Brethren from Zwingli was the issue of social reform, which the Brethren could easily have picked up from the Taborites of the century before.   They could also have arrived at their radical position from their own reading of the Bible.   The issue of social reform has often troubled religious people because their religion calls for equality, but the believers' daily lives are lived in gross inequality.   There is, therefore, a strong temptation to create the kind of social reform that will lead to the desired equality.   Either revolutionary developments result or people take refuge behind platitudes of inner freedoms compatible with external bondage.   It is not a comfortable issue now and it wasn't in 1523.   What added fuel to this fire was the feeling the Anabaptists had that Christ had *freed* them from earthly law including the heavy church taxes levied by the Protestant controlled government.   Ironically, it was not their different religious beliefs that caused them to be expelled from Zwingli's group but the issue of money the state collected on behalf of the church.   When the Brethren demanded an end to punitive church taxation, the Zurich town council and Zwingli parted company with them.

The response of the Brethren was to call for Zwingli to separate his church from the state.   Zwingli was forced to decide, as was Luther during the Peasant Wars, between the egalitarians who wanted a church separate from the state and the powerful friends who wanted a state church.   Both men chose the latter.   Both men's churches became state churches, giving the new Protestant churches the power of the state with which to persecute those who disagreed, like the Brethren.

Although there was a general sense of sharing among the Anabaptists, there was no unanimity on even such a fundamental point as the issue of private property.   Some Anabaptists advocated a fairly strict equality, others a looser variety, and some advocated hardly any sharing at all. Naturally one group could not tolerate the others despite their otherwise great similarity.[2]

A small number of Anabaptists believed that the community of things should extend to a community of persons.   Franck wrote that this group wished, together with all things else, to have their wives in common. Perhaps they were driven by lust rather than by the principles that had motivated Plato; that was often said of communists by their critics. At any rate they were soon suppressed by other Brethren in the community and driven out.[3]

Some Anabaptists argued that because Christ had said that publicans and harlots should enter the Kingdom of Heaven before the righteous, women should become harlots in order to receive a higher place in the Kingdom. Some felt that because they were rebaptized, they could not sin no matter what they did. Women who had sex with Baptists did not sin, they were told, because the act of sex with a Baptist constituted a spiritual marriage.[4]

Despite these real differences, their overwhelming similarity was their decision to rebaptize as adults because they believed that their original baptism was insufficient. The trouble was that rebaptizing was a capital crime and had been since the Code of Justinian was promulgated in 529AD. Originally aimed at curtailing allegedly heretical practices of the Donatists in northern Africa who rebaptized because they felt the original baptizers were impious, the death penalty for rebaptism proved to be a useful device by which Christians with the power of the state behind them could kill fellow Christians who believed in adult baptism.

So there was Anabaptist separateness on the basis of adult baptism, surely, but also because of their fundamental disagreement with Luther whom they considered along with the Roman Catholic church to be the anti-Christ, because of their desire to separate physically from the world, and their literal interpretation of the Bible. During the excitement of the Peasant Wars (1524-1525), the Brethren spread easily, but after the peasants were defeated by the Princes in 1525, persecutions against the Brethren grew much stronger. They were banished or arrested, and the persecution increased in severity. A pamphlet published in 1528 warned authorities that anyone teaching communism was only trying to excite the poor against the rich, subjects against the divinely sanctioned rulers.[5] In 1529 the Reichstag of Speir ratified the Imperial Edict of January 4th, which advocated hunting down the Anabaptists like beasts. They were to be killed as soon as captured without a judge or a judicial inquiry. Some captured Anabaptists were racked and pulled apart; others were burnt to ashes and dust; some were roasted or torn with redhot pincers; still others were hanged, beheaded, or drowned; while others were starved or rotted in dungeons. Men, women, and children, it made no difference.[6]

The persecution did not suppress the Anabaptists; as sometimes happens it seemed to cause their increase. Perhaps the reason was that the Brethren who were captured and executed died as martyrs, faithful to their beliefs despite the horrible nature of their deaths. The persecutions also made them very close to each other, and this closeness attracted others and intensified their communism.

Although the persecutions made Anabaptists in general outcasts from traditional society, persecution was not uniform throughout the European area. In some areas the Brethren were allowed to function without interference in their communal societies because they were simple farmers who worked hard as a demonstration of their religious beliefs. Their agricultural communities were extremely productive; and so for some officials the persecution against the Brethren didn't make economic sense. Anabaptist women were often in demand by the outside community as wet-nurses and child tenders, and the Anabaptist schools were so superior to outside schools that persons of other faiths gladly sent their children to them.[7]

Among the Moravian Baptists particularly, the group sometimes called Hutterites, the ideas of communal sharing remained strong. Their communities were well organized by Jacob Hutter (Jacob the Hatter) whom William Kephart called a "brilliant organizer." Hutter was probably born between 1475 and 1500 and was martyred for his religious beliefs in 1536, three years after becoming the leader of the Moravian Brethren.[8]

The Hutterites did not have a community of wives. They thought adultery a very serious sin. In addition, sex was thought to be a serious matter; i.e., not something that could be fun. Couples did not marry for love; pairings were the responsibility of the elders, rather like Plato's handling of that issue in *The Republic* or like other religious communities such as the Perfectionists at Oneida, New York. However, the woman's role in the marriage was made easier by the community of housekeeping and the education of children in common.[9]

The communities were made up of households scattered over Moravia with very large houses surrounded by outbuildings. At their peak there were seventy, each of which might hold from four hundred to six hundred people; the largest one had some two thousand individuals.[10] A household had one kitchen, one bakehouse, one brewhouse, one school, one room that was a maternity room, one room in which mothers and children could be together, one eating room, and one room for the sick who were cared for by appointed females. In each of these households where everyone lived there would be a host and householder who controlled the distribution of the money and goods among the members, and supervised the needs of all in the house. The elderly were apart in slightly larger facilities, but basically all were together with these single accommodations. They **really** were a community; they lived together so closely they could not avoid it.

Food for the Brethren in these households seemed quite adequate. Meat was served daily at the evening meal, while vegetables sufficed at other meals. Bread was generally available, but any special baking had to wait for a major religious holiday. Wine was served at least twice daily, and before evening prayers a drink was served. Everyone received according to their needs and according to the common wealth. If there was more in the social pot there would be a greater distribution; however in famine times the distribution would be more like rationing.[11]

Children were kept with their mothers for the first eighteen months, and then they would be removed to the educational institution. This idea probably came from Plato, since many of the intellectuals in the early Anabaptist movement knew Plato well and discussed *The Republic* in the light of their religious communism.[12] The schools were staffed with numerous individuals under a school-mother with titles like school masters, school-sisters, childrens' maids, etc.

Physical health was important and investigated thoroughly before a child was admitted to the school. Punishment for misbehaving was limited, and, in general, avoided in an age that otherwise appeared to cherish it. Even for severe transgressions such as thieving or lying, the degree of the penalty was determined only after consultation with a Brother and even then was not allowed to be a blow to the head or mouth.

Upon leaving school the young man or woman would join part of the industrial or agricultural work force or work in the household itself. The industries as well as the farms supplied the needs of the community first and only then might the goods be sold outside the community. The men were noted for their horse breeding, mills, and brewing skills while the women were known for their fine weaving.

Because they did not seek to convert the outside world with their ideas and because they became a productive part of the local area, these Anabaptists were not persecuted for many years. Everything was shared. If one worked for outsiders away from the community, all of one's wages and tips were presented to the community. What they represented (and sometimes still represent) in those areas where they lived, were communist islands in a sea of agricultural capitalism, teaching by example that there was a more egalitarian way to live. Production was cooperative and organized by the community itself. Care was taken to insure that involvement with the outside world was the least possible and that whatever work was necessary was done by the Brethren themselves. Although there were many rules developed to organize production properly, a nonproductive bureaucracy did not evolve; as a matter of fact the productivity of the Brethren was envied by others. The jealousy exhibited by outside farmers and merchants was one of the factors in causing the Moravian rulers to exile them from their lands. Karl Kautsky, himself a German socialist, considered this proof that communism was a sound economic principle.[13]

Political life was democratic, but it was a republican sort of democracy in the sense that leaders were not all elected directly and the authority deemed vested in the whole people was represented by a Council of Elders. The top leader was called Bishop. He was selected by other leaders who cast lots to see who the new Bishop might be, but the new choice could not take office until the selection was ratified by a vote of the people. This was a democratic tint to an otherwise republican government. Leaders below the Bishop, who consulted with the Council of Elders, were both clerical and secular: the clerical being responsible for the moral life of the community and for recruiting new members, while the secular leaders called Servants of Need were the purchasers, the foremen, the householders, and the stewards.[14]

When this organized community was forced to disband some moved to Hungary and Russia, while others emigrated to Canada and elsewhere. The Hutterite communities in Moravia had come to an end. They had been a success and became an important part of the Moravian economy. During the Thirty Years' War the Bohemian and Moravian nobles were defeated, and their defeat marked the loss of the Anabaptists' protection. Expulsion orders were issued by the victors and the Anabaptists were forced either to convert to Catholicism or move to other areas.[15]

Not all Anabaptist communist communities, however, left a positive memory. The dreadful experience at Münster under John of Leiden was, like the Pol Pot regime in Cambodia, a communist disaster of many different dimensions.

In 1532 Münster was a Lutheran, rather democratic city in Westphalia. In 1532 and particularly 1533, it was swamped with Anabaptist refugees from less tolerant areas. Many of the refugees came from the Catholic Netherlands, led by a man named Melchior Hoffman who claimed that Jesus Christ was going to return to earth in

1533, allegedly fifteen centuries after his death.   Melchior used different mathematics than Joachim of Fiora did, but just as Joachim taught, Melchior Hoffman stated that when this second coming occurred, a new age would begin.

The Melchiorites, as they were called, had earlier split into two groups.   Both believed in the imminence of the new age or the New Jerusalem, but one side also believed that God needed help to bring the new age about: a violent suppression of Anabaptism's enemies.   The other group believed that the new age would come about on its own by some sort of miracle.   Karl Marx, centuries later, also believed in an inevitable revolution, but he too felt that the revolutionary date might be hastened by human activity against the enemies of the proletariat. In both cases the desire for human intervention directed against the perceived enemy reflected the strong frustrations of the people waiting for the desired event.

So Melchior Hoffman's arrival in Münster created great excitement. Preparing for the New Jerusalem caused many Münsterites to shrug off their Lutheranism and become communists, and like the early church, wait for Christ's arrival.   Since it was expected so soon, violence against non-Anabaptists to further Münster's likeness to the New Jerusalem was not really considered.   Many Münsterites gave up their possessions and shared them with the whole community, and news of the existence of such a visible, loving, communist community drew other people from all over Europe, just as Joachim's prophecies had drawn people in 1260.

Christ did not return in 1533, however, and Melchior Hoffman was imprisoned in a cage hung from a tower.   Feelings ran quite high in Münster for weeks.   Into this excited depression came a young man who was caught up in the more militant branch of Anabaptism then active in the Netherlands, the people who argued the need of a righteous war against their enemies.   The man's name was John of Leiden, or Jan Bockelson.   His mother was a tradeswoman from the general Münster area who had been a servant to the mayor of nearby Soevenhagen, a man named Bockel.   She bore him a son in January 1509 and married him after she had purchased her freedom.   That son, Jan Bockelson, was twenty-five years old when he came to Münster from the Netherlands.

He quickly galvanized the city, pulling inhabitants into the new militant spirit he had brought with him.   In this kind of "we have to do it ourselves" to bring about God's kingdom, Münster rather self-consciously began to look like a New Jerusalem.   Anyone who did not agree with the new concepts was expelled from the city. Many people were severely beaten in the name of this militant Christianity. A similar misery happened in Cambodia in 1975 when the Red Khmer, in the name of a militant anti-urban sort of communism, did not care if maltreated refugees were male or female, pregnant, old, sick, or well. Humanism, Christian or secular, can at times be brutally inhumane. All those considered Anabaptist enemies were pushed out of Münster. They could take neither food nor belongings with them, and the resulting seizure of food and property swelled the wealth of those remaining in the city.

Münsterites were told to hand in all gold, silver, and other precious possessions to the central authority so that the wealth could be shared in common. Except for the Bible, all books were burned; a definite anti-intellectual component. Non-Anabaptist churches were destroyed and the Bishop of Münster was killed.

Stories of atrocities within Münster alarmed the neighboring communities and they attacked the walled city so as to free it from the Anabaptists. The people inside the city walls, however, wanted to remain, and they courageously withstood the siege for over a year. They came to see, though, that their success in holding off the attackers was a very mixed blessing because the siege cut off all supplies to the city. The people of Münster were forced to make do with what food and medical supplies they could find within the walls. As males fell victim to the various military attacks, the female population became three times the male. Polygamy and a sort of free love was authorized and practiced by Bockelson who declared himself to be the king of this New Zion, giving a strange new meaning to the word "euphemism." "Apostles" were sent out from Münster to carry the good news of the New Zion to others who might want to join. Jan Bockelson's aspirations were worldwide.

"King Jan," the supposed messenger from God, allegedly maintained a lavish court surrounded by impoverished Müsterites who were forced to eat pets, rodents, grass, and even the bodies of dead comrades in order to stay alive. As people in this New Zion complained, terror became common and executions frequent. This altogether unpleasant place was finally overrun by attacking forces in 1535 who promptly killed almost the entire population of the city, silencing witnesses as to what had really gone on in the city. Gossip and the bias of anabaptist enemies, may have made the Münster example far worse than it was.[16]

Jan Bockelson was arrested and led through various towns and cities on a chain like a mad dog. He was executed in 1536, amid the terrible stories about what had happened in Münster. Even though the stories were based on very slender evidence, they revealed how even the search for the dream of equality can result in an undesirable and very unequal nightmare. The Jonestown community disaster in November 1978 in which nearly a thousand men, women, and children died either in a mass suicide or mass murder was a similar negative example.

Perfectionists in Oneida

The membership of this group was almost entirely American. Their founder, John Humphrey Noyes, was born in Brattleboro, Vermont in 1811. He was a college graduate, studied a little law, then theology. At New Haven in 1834 a revival preacher convinced him of a different kind of salvation, which he called Perfectionism. Back in Putney, Vermont he began to preach his new ideas and in short order gathered a number of disciples and married one of his converts.

The number of members in the group grew to about forty in his own congregation plus others who loosely affiliated from other states. By 1845 Noyes' spiritual views led him to communism and in 1846 the small group of new communists began a small experiment in communal living. Word quickly spread about strange sexual practices in the community and people in the surrounding area rose up in arms. The Perfectionists were forced to leave. In 1848 they joined others of like mind and formed a communal settlement in upstate New York at Oneida. Small communities also developed in Brooklyn and Wallingford, Connecticut. Gradually the Brooklyn group joined the Oneida group, but the Wallingford group flourished on its own.[17]

The early people were mostly New England farmers and at first they were quite poor. It seemed to them that a way out of poverty was to move beyond farming and to diversify into various industries which might be profitable. They developed a good saw mill, for example, and a blacksmith shop, and they began to make traps by hand. Like the Anabaptists in Moravia, the communists at Oneida quickly gained a reputation for good workmanship. By January 1857 the group discovered that they were worth about $67,000 and this growth in annual earnings continued with only a few exceptions. In 1864, for example, they had their best year in terms of net earnings: they made almost as much money in one year, $61,382, as their entire net worth seven years before. This prosperity was not to last at that level, but the Oneida and Wallingford communities did prosper. By 1874 they numbered 283 persons; 131 males and 152 females.[18]

Originally they insisted that all employees in their farms or industries be from the community. Then, as they grew wealthier, they began to hire workers from the outside. These outside workers were treated well and paid a good wage. They were not hired to take advantage of cheap labor, but to do things the Perfectionists themselves did not want to do.

They published a newspaper called the *Circular* that came out several times a week. They sold this newspaper but they also gave it away to anyone who wanted to read it. This was stated clearly in the paper itself, which created three categories of readers: those who could afford to pay the two dollar cost per issue and make a contribution besides, those who could only afford to pay the two dollars, and those who could not even afford that and should receive the paper free. This, stated the paper, was the law of Communism. Enforcement had to be by the honor system. "We have no means of enforcing it, and no wish to do so, except by stating it and leaving it to the good sense of those concerned.[19]

Their name came from their perfectionist theology. They believed that the second coming of Christ had already occurred in 70AD when the temple in Jerusalem was destroyed by the Romans. At that time, Noyes wrote, there was a **primary** resurrection and judgment and the final kingdom of God began then in the heavens. Since that time all was ready for the eventual perfection of this earthly life, but the Christian church lost this vision shortly after the first generation of Christians left the scene. Noyes' church considered itself a successor to the true primitive church rather than to the later church that strayed from the right path.

Noyes taught that a real, spiritual awareness of Christ in one's soul brought an **inner** perfection that a full Christian life would gradually balance with **outward** perfection. So when Noyes taught perfectibility, he did not mean immediate sinlessness so much as the possibility of working for that goal in this life. One who was perfectly holy, he said, was not necessarily released from all infirmity. He meant by perfect holiness that purity of heart which gave a person a good conscience. This primary state was attainable by mere faith in the resurrection of Christ. It was in fact the communication of the purity and good conscience of Christ and may therefore be received instantaneously, existing in us antecedently to all external improvement or good works.[20]

Perfectionism implied the possibility of living without sin, but that did not mean living without making mistakes; just living without sin.

And what was perfect under 1855 circumstances was not necessarily still perfect under the circumstances of 1860. The times evolved as did people.

Another way in which the religion of the Oneida Community differed was that virtue was equated with happiness. Noyes argued that the way of salvation was pleasurable, and that the happiest man was most virtuous and did the most good.[21] Eventually when the Kingdom of God was on earth, even death would be eliminated.

If his ideas had been accepted by other churches he probably would never have started his communist community. But when he realized that his ideas, particularly his ideas about marriage, would never be accepted, he developed a community in which his perfecting people could live. Since he was trying to emulate the early church, he insisted that Christ commanded communism. The communist settlements at Oneida, New York and Wallingford, Connecticut were established in the hope that they could attain sinlessness when selfishness was removed from their hearts by God.

All this was made easier by living in communism, a communism that Noyes taught was not only commanded by Jesus, but that was also **the social state of the resurrection**. For this reason the communism at Oneida and Wallingford was never simply an economic doctrine, but a vital part of their religion that extended beyond property to the persons in the community.

They did not have marriage as it is commonly known, where a man and a woman agree to spend their lives together, because they believed that the Scriptures taught differently: "For in the resurrection they neither marry, nor are given in marriage, but are as the angels of God in heaven." (Matthew 22:30) Since Noyes taught that the primary resurrection had occurred in 70AD, the Christian church should not have recognized monogamous marriages.

But that did not mean an **absence** of marriages. It meant ideal marriages, or what they sometimes called complex marriages, which were actually a combination of polygamy and polyandry. They believed that the same spirit that abolished property in things abolished it in persons as well, meaning that no one had exclusive rights to any other person. Although considerable freedom in choosing sexual partners existed, even at the beginning there was an insistence that the sexual activity had a spiritual dimension, so that one's partner was chosen with that in mind. Perhaps an older, holier sex partner would be suggested rather than a younger, less pure individual. The request for sexual coupling generally came from the male through a third party such as, perhaps, an older female, and the female being asked had every right to say no. When outsiders argued that this was a kind of sexual orgy, Noyes responded that they were all one family whose privacy should be respected.[22]

Later on when rules became more formal a committee would decide whether to authorize a sexual union, and the goal of this greater formality was eugenic improvement of the community's human stock just as it had been for Plato. Generally the committee would sanction the sexual union but exceptions existed. Minors must not "marry" without the consent of their parents or guardians, one should not seek a "marriage" with someone outside the community, nor with one who was in rebellion against the community's authority.[23]

The deliberate use of a method of birth control and the expectation that women should enjoy sex as much as men were surprisingly advanced positions for the mid-nineteenth century. The method of birth control was called "male continence" where the male would withhold his climax even though encouraging the female to have many. This was not coitus interruptus, as that is generally understood, because the coupling sometimes went on for over an hour.[24] Additionally, young or inexperienced males would usually be coupled with postmenopausal women to avoid conception. The sexual coupling without the fear of pregnancy must have been a pleasure for both parties. Even though they were encouraged to have many sex partners, and usually did, it was also sometimes true that this system did not work because the Perfectionists would fall in love with each other.[25]

Nonetheless the birth control effectively reduced a major risk to a woman's life. In the nineteenth century before birth control became a regular practice, women had children one after the other until they wore out physically and mentally. In the nineteenth century it was widely believed that medication to relieve the pain of childbirth was against the Christian religion because women were required to bear Eve's punishment described in Genesis Two as sorrow in bearing children. The Oneida community certainly did not have a perfect system of birth control, but they seemed to move in that direction.

Life centered on a large four-story brick building with huge rear extensions and a wing containing a kitchen and dining room. A large hall on the second floor was used for community meetings. There were some six thousand volumes in the library as well as an ample collection of pamphlets and journals.[26] Family rooms were on each floor with spartan bedrooms running off the family rooms. They all lived in the same house. The community was small enough, therefore, that the communism was **real** in the sense that it was practiced before it was described.

With over two hundred people living in one house some organization was vital. The administration of the community involved a bookkeeping department, twenty-one committees and forty-eight departments. Every Sunday morning the heads of departments met in what was called a Business Board, which functioned somewhat like an executive committee. The past week was discussed, and a secretary took notes that were read to the entire community that evening. The ensuing discussion set the plan for the next week. So the Perfectionists were not only communistic, but decidedly democratic about it as well.

The members might work hard but the hours of work as on Utopia were not long. They seemed to enjoy what they were doing, because, Nordhoff reported, they put off the drudgery onto the hired labor.[27] But there still were some jobs more disagreeable than others, and those were rotated among people more often than the pleasant jobs.

Children were raised by their mothers until they were weaned and then they were put into a general nursery where they were cared for by both men and women whose occupation this would be. One nursery was for the wee ones, another for those older. The children ate their meals with the adults. Thus, although the Perfectionists never claimed to be and were not feminists (they believed women were best off subject to men), they nonetheless made significant contributions to female concerns like birth control and the enjoyment of sexual relations. Also, childrearing and housekeeping chores were often done by someone else so that the woman was free to seek out the employment of her preference in the community.

They criticized each other to help maintain the perfectionism and discovered that this criticism occasionally healed physical illnesses. Perfectionists were an interesting group of communists whose religious views created as many enemies as their attitudes on property and persons. Unfortunately secularism gradually overcame their religious views, and they lost their reason for their communism. They finally broke up in 1880-1881, over thirty years after Oneida was begun in 1848.[28]

Ann Lee and the Shakers

In the previous century a different sort of perfectionist group had come from England to America, led by a young woman named Ann Lee (1736-1784). Ann Lee was a very religious young woman who spent long hours in prayer, sometimes adversely affecting her health. She had a great dislike for the physical aspects of sex, but her father nonetheless insisted on her marriage to a man named Abraham Stanley. She had four children who all died in infancy or early childhood, and she felt that this was a punishment for allowing herself to be led away from her strong beliefs against physical sex.[29]

At the age of 23 she joined a revivalist group and quickly became their leader. She was motivated by a vision in which she saw Adam and Eve in the Garden of Eden committing the sin (sex) that led to their expulsion and plunging the rest of the human race into that bondage of sin. Ann Lee, it was revealed in the vision, was not the returned Jesus Christ as some had earlier believed, returned this time as a woman. Instead she was a successor to Jesus, the mother incarnation of the word of God to be re-given to people in this second coming of Christ. The second coming had personified in her. She felt that in her person she was the Word of God. To the group she became Mother Ann or Ann the Word.[30]

Because of persecutions in England, the group decided to carry the new faith to the new world. Eight people joined Mother Ann on the ship to take them to America, and after a miraculous passage in which they were saved from a terrible storm by supernatural actions of the waves which allegedly repaired the leaking ship (according to the Captain), her tiny group reached the shores of America just two years before the outbreak of the war of independence against England.

At first they had to separate, with everyone finding some sort of job in order to survive. They had no money and no friends in the new world. For some time it seemed that even physical survival was going to be beyond their grasp. During the next two years Ann Lee came very close to starvation. When their fortunes began to change for the better, the small group purchased a tract of wilderness land near Albany at Niskayuna, New York. For three years they survived there, building homes and workplaces, but not growing. In 1779, however, there was a revivalist movement in upstate New York, and it centered on the little community of New Lebanon. The revivalist movement stressed a revival of feeling, a greater sense of mysticism in the religion as opposed to ritualistic theology, and was very focused on the second coming of Jesus. The Shaker beliefs about Mother Ann and their strong beliefs derived from the Quakers about being **moved** by the

Holy Spirit fit right into this New Lebanon revival meeting atmosphere.

The meetings were full of noise--some people confessing their sins in public and praying aloud for mercy, some saw visions, while others danced and shouted with joy at the nearness of the Kingdom of God. When summer eased into autumn and winter and the Kingdom did not come, the revivalist movement faltered except for those who had heard of a strange people who lived above Albany who said they served God day and night and did not commit sin.[31]

At that time the small band of Shakers numbered only about a dozen adults but they received the visitors from New Lebanon with hospitality and spirit and began making converts to the new religion. But with converts came also resentment from nonconverts. Persecutions began against a set of people that would not use force even to protect themselves. In spite of (perhaps because of) the climate of intolerance the Shaker community began to organize. A missionary trip into New England by Mother Ann and a few followers lasted nearly 2½ years. Many friends now existed in the New York and New England area and organizing Shaker communities became possible.

The Shakers believed in three cardinal principles: the mother and father element of God, the perfectibility of human nature removed from the sin of sex and power and riches, and the imminence of the millennium, which had already begun to occur.[32] They were called "shakers" because of the form of religious hysteria that occurred in their meetings where people would fall to the floor in a kind of coma, or twitch violently, or move about on all fours barking like a dog. Accompanying such unusual behavior were evidently visions of such beauty that they made up for waking up with dirty clothes after the meeting. Outside their religious meetings, however, the Shakers were a sober lot who had pooled all of their resources just like in the New Testament book of Acts. They had left behind all worldly possessions as well as sin, because they believed that they could live lives of celibacy and purity. In part their need to live in their own community was to protect them from temptation, just as was the case with Plato's Philosopher Queens and Kings or religious people in monasteries and convents.

Everyone in the religious society had equal rights and privileges *according to their needs*, without any observation of how much they brought into the church at the beginning. What people earned by their labor could be used for their own support, but income beyond that was devoted to the relief of the poor and the mutual good of others. If people wished later to leave the society, then they could have back the property they relinquished in the beginning, but not the interest on that property, reminding the reader of one of Sarah Scott's provisions in her book, *Millenial Hall*. Community wealth acquired through thrift and hard work was social wealth, community property just as in the beginning they had shared community poverty.[33]

Officials in the community did not receive money for their services, reminding one of somewhat similar provisions Karl Marx and Friedrich Engels made for administering the affairs of the future communist society. The Shakers believed firmly in the mutual and equal enjoyment of all things, both spiritual and temporal. And yet this was not a democracy, but instead an aristocracy of ability headed by ministers who were the highest authority, just as they had been in Calvin's Geneva. Both women and men were equally represented in the authority structure, a gender equality that came naturally from the leadership of Ann Lee, but also more subtly from the fatherhood and motherhood or the bi-gender character of God. On the other hand, the denial of physical sex helped account for a separation of the genders that must have seemed artificial except to a strong believer. Early homes were built with two entrances, two stairways and two apartments so that gender mixing did not occur. Churches suffered the same fate, with the left side for the men and the right side for the ladies. Eating in the common dining rooms saw the two sexes in the same room at the same time but eating at different tables. Any meeting between two people of opposite sex, even elders and eldresses of the church, had to be chaperoned by someone over ten years of age. Travelling for missionary work always had to have two of each gender to avoid any trouble.[34]

The gender equality and gender separation, however, did not at all diminish the notion that some work was woman's and some was man's. Housework, cooking, butter and cheese making, and mending were woman's work. Men's work was the heavier labor, the bringing in of chopped wood, tending to the stock, feeding the fires, working in the shops, the mills, or the farms. The women served for a month at one task and then took up another. No such job rotation was available for the men.

The Shaker day would start about 4:30am and end about 9:30pm. Chores would be done for the first hour, then breakfast, then work until the noon dinner hour, then more work until the evening supper at 6:00pm. During any of the meals the eater had to finish whatever they had put on their plate. Waste was a big no-no. After the early years the fare tended more and more toward vegetarian diets. Pork, for example, was banned entirely. Evenings were times for religious meetings or diversions of an edifying nature. At 9:00 or 9:30 it was bedtime.

The Shakers wore a distinctive costume during most of the 19th century, and the uniformity of the costumes was more the result of frequent visiting from one Shaker community to another than it was due to authoritarian pronouncements from New Lebanon. They stood out for other reasons than costume, however. Their settlements were always very well built and extremely clean. The barns were as clean as the houses. They themselves were always clean and healthy looking. Mother Ann had told them that good spirits would not live where there was dirt, because there was no dirt in heaven.[35] They tended to work very hard even though they believed that they were living in an already begun millennium after Jesus' second coming. Not for them the congregated waiting that appeared to characterize the New Testament community described in Acts. Mother Ann had said that they should do everything as though they had a thousand years to live and yet live as though you had to die tomorrow.[36] The result was a high level of productivity that made them very good neighbors, and good people to have in a county.

Schools were provided for the children people brought into the community, with sisters teaching the girls and brothers teaching the boys. Discipline was seldom needed. If the child did not respond to reasonable persuasion the child did not stay in the school. Their approach to schooling, however, was that a little went a long ways. Too much schooling was unwise, it was felt, because practical skills were far more important than mental ones. To people of such simple faith it must have seemed that too much learning created rather than solved problems.

After the Civil War in the United States the steam seemed to go out of the Shaker movement. Longevity was a built-in problem for a society whose main definition of virtue was abstinence from sex. Any growth in numbers or even a maintaining of numbers meant converts from the outside rather than children from the inside. They tried to support themselves while simultaneously building the Kingdom of Heaven. For a time they were successful. In 1887 a December 27 editorial in *The New York World* commented on the centennial of the Shaker community, calling it "...the first and only successful attempt at Communism...."[37]

Their way of life was communistic in a country that feels uncomfortable around anything socialistic or communistic. But the Shakers felt no affinity whatsoever to Marxist or European socialism.[38] Their communism came out of their religious beliefs. Their theology was deistic, non-trinitarian, and humanist, and their celibacy often broke up families. Nonetheless they sought to build a utopia on earth as an earnest of the utopia in heaven. No member ever felt economic insecurity or faced unemployment. No member ever had a reason to envy another. Their idealism was practical. They didn't try to create a revolution, they simply settled apart and created their own society rather than trying to create the same society for everyone.

And they lasted over a century.

Kibbutzniks in Palestine and Israel

The word kibbutz comes from the Hebrew word *kvutzah* meaning group, but the word kibbutz left that generic meaning behind and has come to mean something specific in Jewish agricultural communities both before and after Israel received statehood in 1948. Originally the communities were established in Palestine to handle unemployed Jewish settlers who had come to Palestine and who had little if any agricultural experience. This all took place before the twentieth century. In the beginning the banding together in a group was a survival technique rather than an ideological position, somewhat like the natural communist organizations of prehistoric peoples long ago.

The first actual kibbutz was the result of a compromise solution to the problem of hiring Arab laborers who would work for lower wages than would the Jewish workers. Jewish workers went on strike over the issue. To help solve that problem and also provide employment for Jewish families, one part of a collective on the eastern shore of the Jordan was put at the disposal of the workers who could work the land as though it were their own so long as they filed a yearly work plan with the settlement society. This experiment worked so well that the first kibbutz, called Degania was formed around 1909.[39]

Like the Diggers in seventeenth century England, the number of people involved in the first kibbutz was only about six.[40] Unlike the Diggers, however, the kibbutzniks went on to provide a significant example of implemented communism in Israel.

Degania worked so well as a communal society that people from all over Palestine came to look, and, occasionally, to start a new kibbutz somewhere else.   The new groups did not become stable easily, however, in part because many kibbutzim simply had too few members even to approach self-sufficiency or attain **any** kind of efficiency. Another problem in the beginning was unanswered questions: can the commune hire labor from the outside? should everyone receive the same wage?, should all adopt the same life style? The growth in numbers was slow: by 1914 there were fourteen kibbutzim.

After World War I the number of Jewish agricultural communes continued to grow, and many new kibbutzim now paid attention to optimal size so that more services and goods could be provided by the larger number of people involved in both agriculture and light industry on the same kibbutz.   This made the kibbutz as self-sufficient as possible, rather like the later attempts in Mao's China where self-sufficiency on agricultural communes was the desired goal.

The new kibbutzniks faced the difficult questions. They decided not to hire cheap labor from outside and that all members of the group would do the same work and keep the same standard of living. Melnyk, citing Amia Lieblich, provided some examples of this concept of all doing the same work and referred to a woman who wrote educational programs for the whole country who also sat in the laundry room folding sheets or a man who taught at the kibbutz teacher college who also sorted olives twice a week on the line in the food factory.[41]

In other words, although the principal occupation and possibly the prestige of an individual was known to others, that person did the more common work of the commune as well as others who did not write educational programs or teach in the kibbutz teacher college. Lieblich's examples, moreover, were of people who held higher prestige occupations, occasionally but regularly doing the less prestigious work of the commune.   Examples going the other way, where the person whose main occupation was stoop labor but who occasionally taught or wrote books may not be available because such examples were rare or because they did not exist.   Kibbutzim were (are) not usually anti-intellectual, in the sense of overinflating the importance of the lower classes to the point of denying intellectual merit as did some other communist groups.   The important thing for the kibbutz was that the dirty work or stoop labor was not performed by outsiders who would work cheaply, rather than by commune members.   All members of the group did all of the work, within the limits of the possible, of course, and all lived in the same way as others.   No one lived better than another in the sense of finer clothing, better housing, or whatever. The kibbutzniks described themselves as a small community that is based on economic cooperation, on holding property in common, on the democratic management of work, the collective rearing of children, and the distribution of goods on an egalitarian basis.[42]

This did not mean that there were no ideological differences. There were several difficult differences to work out that took patience and long discussions to settle. Size was one differential that was allowed to divide kibbutzim from each other. Optimum was seen by some as small and by others as large. Some kibbutzniks wanted decentralization and fought against any kind of centralized authority, while others sought centralized administration and felt that the issue of decentralization was not very important.

At times in the period both before and after statehood in 1948 new kibbutzim were also used as armed settlements to expand territory under Jewish control, normally at the expense of the Arab population in the general area. In addition the new kibbutz would often be placed in a desert where the only hope for crops was widespread irrigation, or in a swampy area that required permanent drainage. In this sense the "Work Together, Eat Bread Together" of Gerrard Winstanley was implemented, because Winstanley's original idea was that the unfertilized, waste land would be cultivated by the Diggers. Over time, technological progress created more productivity on the kibbutzim and through the addition of light industry extended the range of goods produced, something Winstanley had no opportunity to see in his short-lived Digger communities.

Darin-Drabkin described the basic kibbutz principles as a voluntary society based on sharing nearly everything: property, production, labor, consumption, and living arrangements. In other words, the kibbutz community was responsible for the satisfaction of the individual's needs. "From each according to his ability, to each according to his needs" in accordance with the community's means--this principle underlay the unique socio-economic form called the kibbutz. From the beginning it was fundamentally different from other cooperative enterprises in Israel or anywhere else in the world.

The unique character of the kibbutz is reflected, first and foremost, in its complete, indeed even extreme, collectivist nature. No private property or private economic activity is allowed. Moreover, this collectivism includes the cultural, social and educational spheres, no less than the various economic aspects of kibbutz life.[43]

The fairly rigid character of the kibbutz did not arise out of a religiously held ideology of collectivism so much as out of the specific needs of Jewish settlements in Israel in a context where the people making decisions were well aware of potential benefits of collectivism in such a chaotic environment. The principles of socialism were well known to most of the settlers, and, indeed, there was a long standing attraction to collectivist ideas among Jewish intellectuals that went back to the 19th century competition in Jewish intellectual life between socialism and Zionism. In the kibbutz case Zionism and socialist principles combined together with the pragmatic need by former urban settlers to build an agricultural community **by themselves** in a forbidding environment often under extreme military threat, and under conditions where the living standard for all needed to be quickly raised.

They were often begun with great enthusiasm and a willingness to work hard for the common good according to rules that had not really been tested by time. Model rules for a 1930s kibbutz expressed the basic purpose of the community as managing and developing the collective farm, organizing the various industries, maintaining a common purse for the whole organization into which all individual earnings were put and from which all individual needs were provided. The kibbutz was also expected to assist members in raising their economic, cultural, and social levels by mutual aid and to care for their sick, support the old, the feeble, and other dependents, and to maintain and educate the children of members. Finally the kibbutz should establish and maintain public institutions and services and generally undertake all activities normally undertaken by village authorities.[44]

The collectivist property is geographically fixed in the sense that the person leaving the kibbutz cannot take it with them. For example, when joining the organization an average person instantly becomes an equal shareholder in the wealth of the commune. A wealthy person might sell former properties and turn the profits over to the commune, just like in the New Testament communism. But should a person leave the kibbutz permanently, the social wealth stays behind, and all that a person takes with them are articles of personal consumption such as clothing, books, etc. Depending on the particular kibbutz, the departing member may also receive a small cash settlement to help defray expenses while he/she looks for work, but this cash amount is fairly small and is in no way intended as an equal share of the social wealth.

The social property concept does not extend to all of Israel. Indeed, kibbutzniks never represented more than 8 percent of the total Israeli population. Their strength in Israeli life came more from the fact that kibbutzim associated themselves with political parties and labor unions right from the beginning and were always prepared to take an active role in the political life outside the kibbutz. In no way were they isolated from the capitalist world that surrounded them, except in those important areas where they had voluntarily created a communist island in the sea of capitalism.

Moreover, the collective wealth of one kibbutz did not transfer to another except under very specific conditions and terms. On the kibbutz it might appear that the individual does not have **any** property because so much is socially owned and so little is owned individually. It is fair to say that on most kibbutzim the concept of "mine" has been replaced with "ours."

Moreover, the concept of social property extends beyond the economic sphere.; The kibbutz relieves the individual family of responsibility for personal services and childhood education. Cooking, cleaning, mealtimes, buying provisions, and educating the children become social functions performed by various parts of the community.

Equality is very important. With everyone receiving according to need, there is of course an inequality in reward due to the unequal needs, due to larger or smaller families, health or strength differences, and so forth. A person with six children should receive more than a person with two, all other things being held the same. If each received an equal reward and had unequal needs then the society would only be paying lip service to equality. Rewarding according to need was the only way this problem could be surmounted. Equality was and is a very important part of kibbutz life.

The social education of the children for a time carried **public** schooling well beyond its level in the United States. Kibbutz children from very early age were placed in boarding schools where, as Darin-Drabkin said, they ate, slept, studied, and played.[45] Skilled people cared for and taught them at every level, and every child that could received at least a secondary education. Unlike the situation in Plato's communism for the philosopher kings and queens where the goal was to prevent the children from knowing parents and parents from knowing their own children, on a kibbutz strong efforts were made to pull children and parents together. Daily visits encouraged close relations, but the children did not live at home; they were reared socially or collectively. The goal was to take the drudgery of parenting away from the biological parents, leaving the pleasures of parenting intact. Such a system emancipated parents in their productive years, and underscored the social or collectivist nature of the kibbutz compared to the individual. Individual families were not given an excuse to feel different from the rest of the community. The difficulty experienced by the children was that with multiple "mothers" early childhood became a bit more complex, and, as Bettleheim wrote, the learning task took longer to develop.[46] Gradually the separation between parents and children was abandoned, however, as an unsatisfactory experiment. Although there is some variation from kibbutz to kibbutz, most children now live at home as they would in the rest of Israel.

Politically speaking, the kibbutz governs itself democratically. The principle components of the kibbutz government are the 1) General Assembly, 2) the Secretariat, 3) Committees , and 4) Circles of branch workers. The General Assembly is the meeting of all kibbutzniks. A larger kibbutz may have a council to help guide the otherwise rather large Assembly. This council will comprise perhaps 10 to 15 percent of the Assembly members. The Secretariat is similar to an executive branch of government in that the bureaucracy is housed here. The manager of the kibbutz is normally part of the Secretariat as is the treasurer. Agendas for the meetings of the General Assembly are prepared by the Secretariat. The Committees are normally important subgroups which involve more kibbutzniks in the administration of the society and are organized according to the specific functions of the committee. They report to the General Assembly. The Circles of branch workers are an important part of economic life in that almost every day branch meetings are held after work to discuss the daily work plan and talk about successes and failures. These discussions inform the elected Branch manager who can then more efficiently coordinate his or her branch of the kibbutz economy with whatever overall plan exists. This is a down to earth democracy operating in a way like a good workers' council might in a more industrial context.

Over the years kibbutz government has shown a tendency to become somewhat less democratic in the sense that the power has shifted over time from the General Assembly to the Secretariat or other executive institutions. This is a common evolution in government but it can be troublesome in a collective if the style of the democracy becomes perceptibly arbitrary or authoritarian.[47]

In summary, the kibbutz organization shows a successful use of communist principles in a specific agricultural-light industry setting, partly because of military threats or the tremendous challenges of the physical environment. Their shelf-life under conditions of peace and prosperity is less assured, suggesting that kibbutzim, like many other things in life, have but a limited utility. If kibbutzim prosper in the future, it will underscore the possibility that communist societies can coexist with capitalist societies for long periods of time. Either way, the kibbutzniks, like the Anabaptists, the Perfectionists, and the Shakers have earned a firm place in history.

Endnotes
Chapter Six

1. George Melnyk, *The Search for Community: From Utopia to a Cooperative Society* (Montreal: Black Rose Books, 1985), pp. 82, 84.

2. Karl Kautsky, *Communism in Central Europe in the Time of the Reformation* (New York: Russell & Russell, 1959), p. 164.

3. Ibid., p. 165.

4. Ibid., p. 167.

5. Ibid, p. 185. Cited in Will Durant, *The Reformation*, vol 6 of *The Story of Civilization* (New York: Simon & Schuster, 1957), p. 397. Durant cited the London, 1897 edition of Kautsky.

6. Kautsky, *op. cit.*, p. 187.

7. Ibid., p. 206.

8. William M. Kephart, *Extraordinary Groups: The Sociology of Unconventional Life-Styles*, Second Edition (New York: St. Martin's Press, 1982), pp. 280-281.

9. Karl Kautsky, *op. cit.*, p. 203.

10. Ibid.

11. Ibid., pp. 204-205.

12. Ibid., p. 205.

13. Ibid., p. 212.

14. Ibid., p. 213.

15. Ibid., pp. 213-214.

16. Ibid., pp. 242-243.

17. Charles Nordhoff, *The Communist Societies of the United States* (New York: Schocken Books, 1965), pp. 259-260. First published in 1875.

18. Ibid., pp. 262-263.

19. Ibid., p. 265.

20. John Humphrey Noyes, *The Berean: A Manual for the Help of Those who Seek the Faith of the Primitive Church* (Putney, VT: Office of the *Spiritual Magazine*, 1847), p. 170; cited in Maren Lockwood Carden, *Oneida: Utopian Community to Modern Corporation* (Baltimore: The Johns Hopkins Press, 1969), p. 13.

21. Alfred Barron and George Noyes Miller, eds., *Home Talks by John Humphrey Noyes*, vol I (Oneida, NY: Oneida Community, 1875), p. 263; cited in Carden, *op. cit.*, p. 14. Volume I was the only volume published although more were intended.

22. Alfred Apsler, *Communes Through the Ages: The Search for Utopia* (New York: Julian Messner, 1974), p. 115.

23. Constance Noyes Robertson, *Oneida Community: The Breakup 1876-1881* (Syracuse: Syracuse University Press, 1972), p. 174.

24. Apsler called this "male continence," but he made it sound like coitus interruptus. See Apsler, *op. cit.*, pp. 119-120.

25. Maren Lockwood Carden, *op. cit.*, pp. 49-58.

26. Apsler, *op. cit.*, p. 117.

27. Nordhoff, *op. cit.*, p. 281.

28. Carden, *op. cit.*, pp. 89-111.

29. Marguerite Fellows Melcher, *The Shaker Adventure* (Princeton: Princeton University Press, 1941), p. 8. Republished in 1960 by the Western Reserve Press.

30. Ibid., p. 10.

31. Ibid., p. 22.

32. Ibid., p. 87.

33. Ibid., p. 94.

34. Ibid., p. 148.

35. Henri Desroche, *The American Shakers: From Neo-Christianity to Presocialism*, John K Savacool, trans. (Amherst: University of Massachusetts Press, 1971), p. 227.

36. Melcher, *op. cit.*, p. 155.

37. *New York World*, December 27, 1887; cited in ibid., p. 284.

38. Henri Desroche, *op. cit.*, p. 257.

39. Haim Darin-Drabkin, trans., *The Other Society* (New York: Harcourt, Brace, & World, Inc., 1962), p. 69. First published in Hebrew by the Hashomer Hatzair, Merhabia, Israel by Sirfiat Poalim, Ltd., 1961.

40. George Melnyk, *op. cit.*, p. 56.

41. Amia Lieblich, *Kibbutz Makom: Report from an Israeli Kibbutz* (London: André Deutsch, 1982), p. xx, cited in Melnyk, *op. cit.*, p. 60.

42. Melnyk, *op. cit.*, p. 57.

43. Darini-Drabkin, *op. cit.*, p. 87.

44. Harry Viteles, *History of the Co-operative Movement in Israel*, vol I (London: Vallentine and Mitchell, 1967), pp. 259-260; cited in Melnyk, *op. cit.*, p. 58.

45. Darin-Drabkin, *op. cit.*, p. 92.

46. Bruno Bettleheim, *The Children of the Dream* (London: Macmillan Co., Collier-Macmillan Ltd., 1969), p. 305.

47. Darin-Drabkin, *op. cit.*, pp. 101-120.

Chapter Seven

Communal Sharing Demands
An All-Female Society

Forerunners: Mary Ansell & Sarah Scott
Mary Bradley Lane, Mizora
Charlotte Perkins Gilman, Herland
Sally Miller Gearhart, The Wanderground
Suzette Haden Elgin, Native Tongue

The dream of equality has sometimes been expressed as a dream of social virtue; a desire to move society in the direction of more sharing, kindness, sociability, and loving. If the dreamer believes that the needed virtue is found mainly among females in the society,[1] the method of increasing social virtue would be the improving of the status of females so that society might be leavened more thoroughly with the virtue women carry. Such dreamers sought the reform of society, and both Mary Ansell and Sarah Scott fall into this category.

Others with similar feelings about women being carriers of social virtue, despairing of reform so long as society is dominated by males, felt that the goal can only be achieved by excluding males from the society. Three different stories exemplify this concept from a female perspective. The first two, Lane's and Gilman's, describe all female societies, thousands of years old. The third, Gearheart's, describes the superiority of a group of sharing "hill women" who were struggling against the old gross inequalities represented by urban people of both genders--a point not too far from that made in real life by Abimal Guzmán. A final, compromise solution, leaving depowered males in society but rather rigidly separating them from the virtuous women, is advocated by Suzette Haden Elgin. This can be called science fiction, but such futuristic stories belong to a history of communal sharing because, like More's *Utopia*, they were not written to entertain so much as to demonstrate the attractive possibility of communal sharing compared to the existent undesirable male world of property and hatreds that functions as its counterpoint.

The stories are written by women, and in each there is a strong emphasis on gender equality as part of the overall dream of community sharing. That this emphasis is unusual is evidenced by the very large number of communal dreams in which gender equality is not even given a passing thought. Sexual equality can easily be left behind in pursuing the dream of equality. Except for the positive example by the Shining Path in Peru, this ignoring of gender equality was quite familiar to anyone living through the rebellious 1960s or to those familiar with revolutionary events in the 19th century. It was also obvious to ladies in the civil rights movement where the liberation of males took precedence over the freeing of females. Even to the extent of leadership positions in the movement, this has been true. Black women, for example have a better chance of a leadership position in a white group.[2] This gender inequality has also been true in utopias where, except for Plato, women have been no better off in terms of equality than they were before.[3] Indeed even a discussion of poverty can ignore clear gender differences.[4] One of the topics at the 1995 Fourth World Conference on Women in Beijing was the fact that 70 percent of the world's poor are women, while females hold down only 14 percent of the managerial positions worldwide.[5]

Revolutionaries in the past who were dedicated to equality, even to gender equality, never went past the inequalities implicit in "woman's work." These stories, as well as others such as Marge Piercy's *Woman on the Edge of Time*, make clear that both "man's work" and "woman's work" need to be thoroughly examined by serious dreamers of social equality. Sex rôles left unchallenged all too often resulted in revolutionary ladies serving the coffee, cooking the meals, and warming the beds of the male revolutionaries who did all the planning and took all the credit.

While these stories are about communal sharing, they are also about women's rôles in the changed society. So it would not be at all surprising to find these books on the shelves of a feminist bookcenter because they all not only imply that communal sharing and feminist goals are intrinsically linked but suggest extreme feminist remedies; living without men at all or (in Elgin's case) living as though the men did not matter because otherwise equality was not possible.

The frustration was summarized by song lyrics cited in Elgin's *Native Tongue* entitled "Sorrowin' Song With the Words All Wrong,"[6] arguing that the only song a woman knows, the one she learns at birth, is a sorrowin' song with the words all wrong in the many tongues of earth; a language that does not lend itself to the things a woman wants to say. Although there is a great deal that women want to say, they have to try to say it in words that are all wrong.

The song lyrics suggest the pain and anger felt by women who often find it difficult to be heard and unlikely that they will effectively communicate in mixed gender company. Studies of communications between men and women have revealed astonishing inequities in the sense that males interrupt more and do so effectively by overpowering the conversation, and that women do a great deal more to keep the conversation going than do males. Males usually talk more and male language habits are treated as normal, while the female patterns are seen as abnormal. Yet it is in the female language patterns that one finds daily life structured in more cooperative and mutually empowering ways, enhancing relationships, and helping others to belong to themselves.[7] The study of language and language patterns, in other words, is part of the struggle for equality.

Communication in the normal world can actually garble rather than clarify thought. A similar problem can arise in philosophy or theology when one wishes to speak of something in the world of essence and discovers that the only language one has is a language of existence. The result is that people describe their God, for example, in the language of things and cannot avoid the reification that distorts the God concept. What is abstract and immaterial emerges as a material object.

Something of the same sort of belief is held by those who feel strongly that anticipations of the future conceived by men have had little appeal to women because, for the most part, their anticipations about equality are concerned with an economic equality that does not seem to be even minimally aware of the need for gender equality. A major exception to this was Plato, but others who tried to emulate the openness in *The Republic* to a general female participation in the society, such as Sir Thomas More, failed to come even close to gender equality.[8]

For hundreds of years women who dreamed of gender equality subordinated that dream to the one of economic equality because they were sold the rationalization that gender equality flowed out of economic equality, that you had to get the latter first. Many believed this. Linda Jenness, for example, argued in 1972 that the achievement of full liberation for women would require the elimination of the social and material basis for that oppression; it would require a fundamental change in the social structure of American society; i.e., a socialist revolution.[9] She even went further than this to state that there was no way that a revolutionary socialist organization could contradict the interests of women or the feminist goals because the whole purpose of the socialist organization was to promote and build *all* revolutionary developments. If people were revolutionaries, she thought, they would support feminism, because it's revolutionary.[10]

Not everyone agreed with this, however, particularly when it seemed evident that gender equality would be postponed until after "the revolution," and it was obvious that women's place in the struggle for that revolution was rarely equal. So it is not at all strange that some women went well beyond conventional dreams of equality and imagined a future that did not include men at all; a future in which women could communicate in their own language; a future where **they** could shape the society. In the beginning, however, the proposed solution was more moderate.

Forerunners:
Mary Ansell & Sarah Scott

Mary Ansell's book was published in 1697 amd pointed to the obvious advantage of education for women. Its full title was *A Serious Proposal to the Ladies for the Advancement of their True and Greatest Interest*. That Mary Ansell's intent was wider than simply improving the lot of women was clear from the dedication to Princess Anne of Denmark, heiress presumptive to the throne of England. Mary Ansell hoped that Princess Anne understood the goal of the book; "...the Bettering of the World, especially the most neglected part of it as to all Real Improvement, the Ladies."[11]

Mary Ansell wanted to improve the world by raising the level of the female half of the population. In order to accomplish this goal she skated dangerously close to the idea that marriage might not be the best thing for women in an age when marriage was almost the **only possible** goal of women. In the England of 1697 this idea may even have been nearly treasonable, so she didn't come right out and say it-- education for women might have been radical enough. She couched her proposal in ethical, moral, or religious language. Worry, she wrote, about being beautiful on the outside but an empty sepulcher on the inside: worry about neglecting one's soul. Think more, she argued, on the beauty of the mind and soul. She who has opportunities of heaven and of obtaining the love and admiration of God and the angels must not waste her time and endanger her charms by throwing them away on vain, insignificant men.[12] Instead, her readers should value that Beauty which endures for all Eternity, and not disparage the virtue which men ignore.

I would have you live up to the dignity of your nature, she wrote, expressing your thankfulness to God for the benefits you enjoy by a due improvement of them: As I know very many of you do, who value that piety often ignored by men. It grieved Mary Ansell that **other** females did not imitate such illustrious examples as these, and therefore she wanted to see the good examples increased in numbers and in visibility so that with virtue more in fashion, vice would be put out of countenance and sneak out of the world. It was clear, moreover, that because women have been unjustly denied opportunities of improvement on the outside, they were granted greater internal virtue and goodness. If the ladies would only manage that properly and remove external obstacles to their improvement, the noble ambition of improving the world could be realized.[13]

Her goal, therefore, was to show women how they might greatly improve their position and in so doing improve the overall condition of the world. Aside from the different spellings and dramatic language of her day, and the feeling that virtue and religion were somehow synonymous, she forcefully argued that if women had the incapacity to act prudently, it was not because of a natural deficiency but was an acquired characteristic due a faulty education. From infancy women were prevented from acquiring those advantages which they were later criticized for lacking, and encouraged in those vices which they were attacked for possessing. If our nature is spoiled, she wrote, instead of being improved, if from infancy we are nursed up in ignorance and vanity and taught to be proud, petulant, delicate, fantastic, humorous, and inconstant, it is no wonder that these characteristics emerge in all the future actions of our lives. And since ignorance is the cause of all sin, how can we women escape *this* who have been raised in *that*?[14]

Ignorance, then, was the cause of most female vices. Her remedy for the lack of a proper education for women was to erect a school that would have a double aspect: a retreat from the world as well as an educational institute that would fit women to do the greatest good in the world. This, she felt, would amend the present, and improve the future age by exchanging the shabby and sick for the sublime and the beautiful. Women would find a happiness, which when once possessed would convince that one could never do too much to obtain it. This education would make the women such holy and heavenly creatures as they one day hope to become in a more perfect manner. The happy retreat would introduce women to the paradise that their Mother Eve forfeited, where they will feast on pleasures that will never disappoint or disgust but always please.[15]

The Retreat or school would be a type of or a foretaste of heaven where the students would seek to magnify God, love one another, and communicate useful knowledge obtained by study and contemplation. This knowledge would provide sweet and durable delights that cast previous pitiful pleasures into the shade. But the Retreat would have more than knowledge and contemplation, it would also be the basis for many good works: offices of charity and beneficence to others that would benefit the world. The Retreat would stock the Kingdom with pious and prudent ladies whose good example, it was hoped, would so influence the rest of their sex that women would no longer be considered the useless and impertinent animals for which they are often mistaken because of the ill conduct of too many women.[16]

Mary Ansell saw this educational activity as a very serious business. There would be no impertinent visits, she wrote, no foolish amours, no idle amusements to distract one's thoughts and to waste one's precious time. This was all the more important for females to learn, she thought, because it was a dangerous thing to have all the opportunities for sinning in our power with the danger increased by all the bad precedents set by women around us. *Liberty*, she wrote in italics, *will corrupt an angel*.[17]

Virtue triumphant in an egalitarian society required a reduction in liberty, according to Mary Ansell, a reduction in choice. Mary Ansell would regimate her new society as much or more than would Sir Thomas More in his *Utopia*. It was evidently not imagined that people could grow sufficiently strong on the inside to resist available temptations; those temptations had to be kept out of the society for the protection of the people. Thus are social prisons imagined as emancipations.

This was not learning for the sake of education but for the sake of equality. What can be more provoking, she asked, than the idea of a designing male who thinks his own intellect is so strong that he can make women swallow anything, and lead them where he pleases. Such a person wants to reduce women to the vilest slavery and capture their understanding. Such a person should be justly condemned as insolent, and against that insolence she would place her educated woman not only as balance but as a force for good.[18] Women of such caliber could be an antidote to those expecting obedience merely on the basis of authority.[19]

Moreover these unmarried ladies would not suffer because they had no children to instruct. The whole world, she felt, was a single lady's family. Her opportunities were not lessened but increased by her being unconfined.[20]

Sarah Scott's book was published in London in 1767 with one of those long, chatty titles: *A Description of Millenium Hall and the Country Adjacent: Together with the Characters of the Inhabitants and such Historical Anecdotes and Reflections, as may excite in the reader Proper Sentiments of Humanity, and lead the Mind to the Love of Virtue.* It purported to be a long travel letter from a gentleman of consequence about a virtuous rural society of women who lived in a structure he called Millenium Hall--a fictitious name chosen so as to protect the inhabitants.

The story unfolds gradually as in a novel. The travellers' carriage broke down on a country road and while waiting for repairs the young man and lady went for a walk when they came upon Millenium Hall quite by chance. It was a large house in an idyllic setting of flowers, farm animals, and clean, healthy people. The walkers were invited into the house and saw many ladies engaged in intellectual pursuits. They were invited to spend the night while repairs were made to their vehicle.

The next morning the young man rose early and went out for fresh air and discovered a row of cottages, all very neat, with an old lady spinning at one of the doors. He strolled over to talk to her. The old lady said that she and others were very happy to have these cottages and that the ladies in the mansion were responsible. How, he asked? It seemed that when the good ladies came to the area they found the other villagers in a near starving condition. Few of us, she said, had rags to cover us, and few had enough to eat, except the two squires who were rich on the underpaid labor of others. She tried to be kind: perhaps the squires, living over a mile away, were ignorant of their poor condition. After all, she said, the ladies tell me I must not speak against them because we only see other people's faults clearly, while we are blind to our own.[21]

The resettled older ladies were taught to be kind and forgiving of their neighbors and eventually they did become so. They were inspected every day as to cleanliness and neatness because their houses would become homes for children brought to them. The ladies took every female child after the fifth one from poor people and after the child was weaned and could stand they sent it to the old ladies to care for and to teach as many knitting and spinning skills as possible before they were four or five years old, when they removed to one of the schools.

After breakfast, the two stranded travellers took another walk, this time into a beautiful wood and a temple dedicated to Solitude. Animals had no fear of humans, and the young man speculated that here was a place where the lion could lie down with the lamb. Another place looked like an enclosure and when they asked about it they learned that the ladies of Millenium Hall did not use the enclosure to hold wild animals who should be left alone, but instead used the enclosure to protect the inhabitants, women of unusual size, whether dwarfs or very tall people, who were constantly victimized on the outside.

The travelers wanted to know how this repository of social virtue began, and the stories about the individual inhabitants and how they came to live together in Millenium Hall were tales of exploited and badly used women whose relationships with males were invariably negative. After much travail they had decided to come together and pool their wealth so as to do the virtuous things they felt compelled to do, inspired perhaps by Mary Ansell's work or by a sense of what Sarah Scott described as the "true religion" that had been taught the young ladies.[22]

Millenial Hall, therefore, was a female island of kindness and benevolence in a sea of cruel indifference, with so much equality and a sufficiency of sharing that everyone in the area was comfortable. The rules for membership specified that, like on a kibbutz, a new member would deposit her wealth with the group. If she later left, she would get this back except for the interest the money had earned in the meantime. The purpose of this was to preserve an equal dependency on the group among the members. Bedrooms were private but eating was in common rooms and all amusements like musical instruments or books would be provided by the community. Very regular hours were to be kept, servants would be provided, and the ladies were expected to take turns presiding at the table. They would receive a small allowance for their plain clothing, but the costs of an illness would be borne by the group. Imprudent, petty, or turbulent behavior could be cause for dismissal if so voted by three-fourths of the group.[23]

Added a short time later were provisions for people to board there. The number of members at that moment was 30, with four additional ladies boarding, one of whom had 2 children, and five young girls who were also paying boarders. Sometimes widows came into the society for the year of their mourning.

Efforts were made right from the beginning to sow the seeds of a life of virtue, or service, getting people into occupations they enjoyed, and getting rid of all unnecessary ceremony. The whole society assembled early for morning prayers, for evening prayers at the end of the day, and, of course, they assembled at meal times; but all other ceremonies were abolished.

The women sometimes left the society. Death might change their circumstance or they might marry a gentlemen from the neighborhood. But the society had as many as it could handle and normally was forced to turn people away whom they would otherwise have admitted. So they formed a second home. Now they are about to establish a third, about three miles away.

The whole thing began with only two ladies who shared some years of sacrifice before they came into both freedom and money. The two ladies met a third in similar circumstances and decided to buy the house in the country so they could set up a place to all live together in such a way as to find both temporal as well as eternal happiness.[24]

They found a house that was sufficiently furnished that they could settle in rather quickly, and they rather soon took up the cause of the poor in the area. They instituted schools for the young and almshouses for the old, took in destitute daughters of persons in office and trained them for decent occupations. They used their large fortunes to provide houses for the newlyweds in their district along with some stock, cared for the sick and saw that adequate wages were received by the workers. This was how they lived for some twenty years.

When praised for their efforts at improving society, the women argued that they had not begun as reformers. We wished, a spokeswoman said, to regulate ourselves and endeavor to enforce the laws laid down to us, but beyond that small circle we did not try to go. All that is foreign to us and we have sufficient employment in improving ourselves. To mend the world requires abler hands.[25] Mary Ansell may have wanted to reform the world so as to do good, but Sarah Scott reversed this; the ladies did good works and let the reforms take care of themselves.

The travellers visited a school house that contained about fifty girls in neat uniforms, and all very clean. The girls were taught piety and the purest principles as well as practical skills of survival, training them according to their interests and abilities. A large garden was there to provide weeding as the principle recreation. They did service work for the main hall among their duties.

The boys' school had only about 25 pupils, and most of them small in size, because they were dismissed from school to labor as soon as they were able to perform any work, except when they were incapacitated by ill health. The double standard here was not noticed by the author and perhaps it would not have been noticed by her readers. This was an age that was influenced by Bernard Mandeville's publication in 1714 and 1723 of *The Fable of the Bees*. Mandeville, like some modern politicians, was against any form of welfare, against the poor laws established in Elizabeth I's time, and very much against education for the lower classes. He wrote as though he were speaking of boys alone, but in his thinking lower class females would not be educated at all, and boys would be severely limited. Going to school in comparison to working, he wrote, is idleness, and the longer boys continued in such an easy sort of life, the more unfit for work they'd be when the grew up. Neither strength nor inclination would be there. Men who were to remain and end their days in a laborious, tiresome, and painful station of life, he wrote, should be placed in it sooner rather than later so that they submit to it more patiently.[26] This attitude, echoes of which are still heard, may have been responsible for the author's neglect of the boys' education, or it may simply have been a double standard, unusual in placing women at the top of the standard.

The young man was so impressed that he praised them lavishly. So, as though to demonstrate that they had not gilded or romanticized the female as a class, the ladies of Millenial Hall hastened to inform the travellers that they were far from perfect. On the contrary, the spokeswoman said, we are sensible of great deficiencies in the performance of our duty. We are by no means perfect; we are just like anyone else in that regard.

The young man, however, missed the point, in his eagerness to theologize. Madam, he interrupted, do you imagine that what you do here is merely a **duty**? Absolutely, she responded, tying virtue to equality with bands of steel. We are told by God who cannot err, she said, that our time, our money, and our understandings, are entrusted with us as so many talents, for the use of which we must give a strict account. How we ought to use them he has likewise told us; as to our fortunes, in the most express terms, when he commands us to feed the hungry, to clothe the naked, to relieve the prisoner, and to take care of the sick. Those who have not an inheritance that enables them to do this are commanded to labor, in order to obtain means to relieve those who are incapable of gaining the necessaries of life. Can we then imagine that every one is not required to assist others to the utmost of his power, since we are commanded even to work for the means of doing so? God's mercy and bounty is universal, it flows unasked, and unmerited; we are bid to endeavor to imitate God as far as our nature will enable us to do it.

The only limit that we recognize, she said, is the lack of power to extend it further. Our faculties and time should be directed to the benefit of people, the encouragement of virtue and the suppression of vice. We seek opportunities to do good to the poor to whom we are stewards. And don't imagine that our lives are thus without pleasure. We have all that we need and more besides. Certainly we could spend more money on servants, travel, card parties, and clothes, but those activities do not give us nearly the pleasure that helping the poor and old does. Instead of these false pleasures, we endeavor to obey our Maker, to correct our defects in a constant sense of our own offenses, and to avoid the commission of them in the future.

The book ends with the plaintive hope of most authors that if what she described may tempt anyone to go and do likewise, she would count herself fortunate. "For my part, my thoughts are all engaged in a scheme to imitate them on a smaller scale."[27] A good idea that was, unfortunately, not adopted by sufficient people to make a difference, and so this moderate dream was replaced by the more radical one of entirely excluding the males from society as the *sine qua non* of social virtue. The first of these attempts was Mary E. Bradley Lane's *Mizora: A Prophecy* serialized in the Cinncinati *Commercial* from November 6, 1880 to February 5, 1881.

Mary Bradley Lane, **Mizora**

The author of this story concealed her authorship, perhaps even from her husband, by describing the story as a true account of a journey to the center of the earth found in the private papers of Princess Vera Zarovitch. The putative author was the Princess, a Russian adventurer-explorer who had been in Siberian exile, but who escaped to the North Pole and lived with Eskimos. One day in her boat she found herself in a whirlpool, pulled down into the Earth to the community of Mizora, a land of beautiful, blond women.[28]

The most astonishing thing about Mizora is the absence of men, but before the author gets to the explanation of that phenomenon, other differences are allowed to excite the imaginations of her readers. For example, education was not only free, but encouraged for everyone.

All expenses, including board, clothing and travel costs (presumably on the state owned railroads) were covered by the state. All of the wherewithal for serious scholarship and research were provided. So much did the Mizorans value education that educators were paid very handsome salaries. They believed that the higher the culture of a people, the more secure was their government and their happiness. In an interesting rephrasing of Adam Smith's invisible hand idea, the Mizorans felt that a prosperous people was always an educated people, "...and the freer the education, the wealthier they become."[29]

This was therefore, an appeal for a general, public education, but it was also an emphatic emphasis on the need to educate the female half of the population. She has the Princess say that in the world she had left education was a privilege only of the rich, and even in the most enlightened countries education did not reach everyone. Charitable institutions were limited and benefitted only a few. In Mizora, however, things were very different. Back in the old society philosophers were still travelling in grooves that had been worn down by past ages of ignorance and narrow-mindedness. Wealth and the organization of society and governments were privileges passed by heredity. On Mizora, however, "...nothing was hereditary but the prosperity and happiness of the whole people...."[30]

So it was a very different country, not just because there were no men, but because education was ranked so high. There were other differences as well. Food, for example, was almost entirely produced by chemical means. Agriculture, except for vegetables and fruit, had died out. There was no need for it. And because the annual food production no longer depended on uncertain elements, there was no poverty in Mizora, and no disease. People lived very long lives, looking as youthful at eighty as they did at thirty.

Princess Vera was intrigued by the art gallery at the National College; many portraits, but none of men. What was so strange was that no one seemed aware that they were missing an entire gender. What she felt besides curiosity over the lack of men was a high regard for the women in Mizora who all seemed ever gentle, tender, and kind. They were open-hearted and open-minded, and she found a great deal to admire. They had no envy or malice in them.

Courts and legal proceedings were unnecessary because law breaking was unknown. They hadn't had a thief in centuries. If a dispute arose about the law, they went to the library and looked up the law. If that didn't work, an impartial observer would decide the issue.

They all worked. Indolence to these women, she wrote, was as much a disgrace to them as a loss of virtue to the women of her country.[31] And they all did all sorts of labor so long as they were suited for it. No social favor or ignominy was attached to any kind of labor. There were no such distinctions. There were no paupers, no charities, no poverty. They felt strongly that they were all born equal, but similarly all should work.

They were careful of their beauty and yet used no makeup or any other kind of deception to enhance it. The impression was given that good food, good exercise, and good education brought about the beauty they cherished.

When the Princess asked where the men were, her guide was perplexed. Perhaps it is some extinct animal, she thought. So the Princess cut to the chase: where, she asked, is your other parent? This question too was met with surprise, because she only had the one--the mother. Finally she became even more explicit in her questions, while indicating that she didn't really miss men--she was just curious, but had to confess that she had never heard of a country where there were no men. In my country, she said, they are very important. The response from the guide was a placid "Possibly." Finally she came right out with it: Are you really a nation of women? Yes, she said, and have been for the last three thousand years. Will you tell me how this wonderful change came about, asked the Princess?[32]

The answer given was not a surprising one. In the beginning the country was peopled by two **races** -- male and female,[33] suggesting that the separation between the two genders was wide and perhaps unbridgeable. Children were born who were not desired, and attempts were made to prevent their live birth. Misery and despair haunted the nation. Plots, intrigues, murders, wars and stupid self-serving politicians compounded the misery; gradually placing Mizora in so great a jeopardy that the women who had begun to organize simply took over, refusing to share the power just as the men had done before them. They profited from the mistakes made by the government of men, and promulgated a constitution that excluded males from all affairs and privileges for one hundred years. The men tried to get power back, but a female scientist had discovered a means of reproducing female life with no male activity, and so the troublesome gender just died out. Women chose to have female babies by the new method, and by the end of that century there wasn't a single male left alive.[34]

Moreover the emphasis on Mothers and protecting the environment of the Mother foreshadowed the science of life ideas of Rosa Graul in

"Hilda's Home." Mary E. Bradley Lane had the guide state that on Mizora they devoted the most careful attention to the Mothers of our race. No retarding mental or moral influences were ever permitted to reach her. On the contrary, all the most agreeable contacts with nature, all that can cheer and ennoble in art or music was permitted to surround her. She aroused tenderness in all who met her. She was guarded from unwholesome agitation, and furnished with a nourishing and proper diet so that the child of a Mizora mother was always an improvement on herself. Among us, she said, children have no sorrows. We believe, she stated, that the present condition of our race proves that a being environed from its birth with none but elevating influences will grow up amiable and intelligent though inheriting unfavorable tendencies.[35]

Deep in the heart of the center of the earth, therefore, existed the land of Mizora, a land with no men, with eugenically designed beautiful blond women, and hardly any problems at all. Obviously if males are seen as the principal barrier to equality, a society that excludes males makes equality much easier. This was also the case in the next example.

Charlotte Perkins Gilman, *Herland*

This novel by Gilman, although published as such in 1979, was actually written in 1915 and serialized in the author's monthly journal called *The Forerunner*, which appeared from 1909 to 1916. Charlotte Perkins Gilman was the feminist author who sought to unite the socialist and feminist movements "...by demonstrating their essential and necessary interdependence.."[36]

The author was born in Hartford, Connecticut on July 3, 1860. Her father, Frederick Beecher Perkins, was an educated man who for a time was the head of the Boston Public Library. Unfortunately he was not a family man. He left his wife, Mary, shortly after Charlotte was born, and gave his family little financial or emotional support during her years at home. So both Charlotte and her brother developed in a cheerless, unhappy home, always on the edge of poverty.

When Charlotte herself married and had a child, Katherine, she became depressed, rejected the medical advice she was given, and fled to California leaving her husband and child behind. Later attempts to reconcile with her husband failed and she moved to California permanently with little Katherine. Charlotte ran a boarding house in California to support them both, but when her husband remarried, both parents agreed that Katherine should live with her father and the new wife, whom Katherine evidently really liked. In a sense Charlotte was copying the life of her father, and she was heavily criticized for "giving up" her child.

In 1892 she published *The Yellow Wallpaper*, a bitter story of a woman driven to insanity by a loving husband-doctor who imposed on his wife the same rest cure a neurologist had recommended for her before Charlotte had fled to California the first time. This began her writing career but she mainly supported herself by lecturing. *Women and Economics*, published in 1898, was so successful that it was translated into seven languages and gained her international recognition.

Herland is, as was More's *Utopia*, described from the memory of a traveler who said that he had left whole notebooks and lots of pictures behind--pictures of gorgeous gardens and of lovely women. The narrator was a man named Vandyck Jennings who had traveled with two other men, classmates and friends, who were equally interested in science. Their names were Terry O. Nicholson or Old Nick, and Jeff Margrave.

Terry's passion was exploration, but he was also a very handy man to have along on a trip because he was talented. He was good at mechanics and electricity and was the owner of boats and motor cars as well as being a good airman or pilot. In 1915 electricity seemed futuristic in its applicability, and air travel nearly science fiction. Even automobiles were scarce. Jeff, on the other hand, was a good botanist, poet, and medical doctor. Vandyck's specialties were sociology, geography, meteorology, and languages.

The three men were travelling up a major river (he won't say where because he wants to keep away missionaries, traders, and land-greedy expansionists) when they heard about a strange Woman Land in the high hills some distance away. All the legends agreed that only women and girl children lived there, no males at all. They might not have found it had not they been looking for something else and pushed just a little too far and found a place where obviously clothing had been dyed. A few scraps that they found indicated a developed civilization. Their guide said, however, not to travel further--that beyond this point it was Woman country and others who had gone to see it in the past had never come back.

The three decided to stay quiet about their possible discovery so they wouldn't have to share it with others. But all the way back, and while they were arranging to return, it was something they couldn't forget.

They were expecting to find some sort of primitive, matriarchal people who kept the males segregated and out of sight. That the society did without males entirely, they would never have guessed. Another thought they had was that it would be like a nunnery. No, that was too much organization and too peaceful, they thought. Women were always fighting each other and incapable of organization. There wouldn't be any inventions or progress because that's what men did. And so the speculation went on and on, trotting out most of the stereotypes men have of women and some women have of other women.

When they had gone as far as possible by boat, they took a biplane up to explore and the next day flew up to find people. What they found was a civilized country with parks, cities, and well kept roads, and no men. But, they said, this is a civilized country. "There must be men."[37]

The humor was intentional. The novel was a tool to poke fun at people's conceptions of women, and Mrs. Gilman had fun on almost every page. But the humor had a serious twist to it as well. The three male explorers saw only women from the air, some of them quite pretty. They therefore saw no danger. That's funny but it's serious as well. Blinded by their stereotypes they read into the females in Herland the gentle female characteristics they thought women possessed in their own society. So they landed the biplane some distance away from the village they had seen and prepared to walk back. Sure they would discover men on the way, they stocked up on cartridges for their weapons. There had to be men. They had seen babies!

The first women they saw were young ladies in a tree. They were dressed in tunics and kneebreeches and had short, shining hair. They were so much at home in the tree that they got away from the three men who climbed up to get them. Terry tried to trick them with a necklace he held out, and, although three climbed close, and one grabbed the necklace, they all got away. Vandyck, the narrator, was moved to remark: "Inhabitants evidently arboreal." "Civilized and still arboreal--peculiar people."[38]

So they walked to the village to which the three young ladies named Celis, Alima, and Ellador had run. The place had an odd look; plenty of palaces but no homes. Just little houses. There was no dirt, smoke, or noise. As they turned a corner they saw a band of women, evidently waiting, while looking behind they saw another group closing in. Quickly they were surrounded. By women who were unafraid. After a bit they were imprisoned.

The women wanted to teach the men their language and they wanted to learn the language of the three explorers. Still no men, and this bothered the three. "There is a different--atmosphere." "They don't seem to notice our being men," he went on. "They treat us--well--just as they do one another. It's as if our being men was a minor incident."[39]

The country was beautiful; parklike with many trees and flowers, and travel was in electric motorcars that went thirty miles per hour. When they learned enough of the language they discovered that there had not been men there for some 2,000 years. Nor for a long time had there been cattle or horses. There were no wild beasts and very few tame ones. The only animals that seemed familiar were cats, trained to kill mice but never birds.

Ethnically the people were white, and they had been in contact with the civilized world with ships, commerce, an army, and a king. At that early point they were bi-gender. Wars decimated them and they were driven from the coastland up into the hills. They were polygamous and slaveholding and during their early history they built their fortresses and other old buildings which were still in use. One time when their army was some distance away, a volcanic eruption shut off the pass. In the absence of most men the slaves rose, killing off the rest of the men, boys, and older women, intending to enslave the younger females, the virgins. But instead the virgins killed all the slaves. As a result all that was left in this mountainous kingdom were young virgin women and a few older women. After the calamity, only a few babies were born of women already pregnant. Two were boys but they soon died. "So they set to work, to bury the dead, to plow and sow, to care for one another."[40]

This went on for five or ten years. They worked together and grew stronger, wiser, and more attached to each other and then the miracle happened. One of the young women bore a child. Everyone thought a man must be involved, but none was found. So it was decided that the child was a gift from the gods and they placed the new mother in the Temple of Maaia, the Goddess of motherhood. To guard against fraud, they kept her under careful watch. Over the next few years she gave birth to five children--all female.[41]

Each of the new girls, when **she** was twenty-five years of age, began to bear children as well, and soon there was widespread hope in the community that they would not die out. As the older women passed from the scene so did memories of men, and as other women died all that were left were the 155 parthenogenetic women who founded a new race of sexually self-sufficient women. The original mother lived to be a hundred years of age and lived to see 125 great granddaughters born.

They inherited the devoted care of the original women, a functioning industry, careful records, and farms and gardens in full production. The first five daughters, and their twenty-five daughters as well grew up as a holy sisterhood, in the process eliminating certain masculine as well as feminine characteristics. The women had no men to fear and no need of protection. Mother-love was raised to its highest power. Nonetheless the explorers felt that the ladies lacked femininity, that is they lacked the graces that attract males, airs the men missed when not present.

The ideals of the new race of women were high: Beauty, Health, Strength, Intellect, and Goodness. Their religious feelings had been expressed with the usual gods and goddesses, but eventually the deity of their belief reflected their own lives and it became a Mother Goddess that turned into a sort of Maternal Pantheism--the sort of "mother everywhere and in everything" that a reader of *Wanderground* can sense so clearly or is so appreciated in American Indian religious beliefs.

The women devoted their lives to more than simple survival. They deliberately tried, as did Plato, to make the best kind of people through education. They had no wars, no kings, no priests, and no aristocracies. They were sisters who lived together and grew together not by competition but through mutual action.[42] They all worked without complaint. A person might argue that they didn't know any better, but the point was that this socialism or communism worked very well indeed. When the explorers tried to establish the value of competition, they failed entirely because the women needed no incentive to work. They wanted to help support their children.

The women did not know what the men meant by "poverty." Vandyck tried to explain the concept using the survival of the fittest story derived from the mistaken notion that nature is a brutal struggle in which the weak perish and only the strong survive. The real question, why a few have the most, and the most have so little was unasked and unanswered.

Of overwhelming significance was Motherhood. Not a vague idea such as human brotherhood or sisterhood, but a real working concept in full use. And the children were valued above everything else for they were the major center and focus of all their thinking. Every step of our advance, they said, was always considered for its effect on them, on the future of the race. In saying that they were MOTHERS, they felt they had said it all.[43]

And because they were all part of one organic whole their names did not separate them from each other. Individuation, of course, there was, but separation as with different last names there was not. They were all of one family. Why should everyone know which child belonged to which mother? Why indeed.

The country was about the size of the Netherlands with a population of about three million. The numbers were controlled by the women themselves. The children were carefully educated in critical and inventive skills and the people as a whole showed a high level of intelligence. Whereas before the three men had thought of the women as primitive, they were gradually coming to the realization that the women were superior in nearly every aspect of life.

For example, they had literally replanted an entire forest with different kinds of trees so that now every tree in that forest bore some kind of fruit. Soil was fertilized with treated human waste, with organic scraps and leavings, and plant waste from industry. When praised, the ladies were surprised that such a common sense idea as replenishing the soil that society depends on should merit praise.

The explorers had expected to find a society of women preoccupied with frills and furbelows but found they wore a practical and beautiful garment. They expected dull submissive monotony and found daring social inventiveness beyond their own and a mechanical and scientific development that was fully equal. They expected jealousy and found broad sisterly affection and fair-minded intelligence. They had expected hysteria and instead found calmness of temper with high standards of health and vigor. They expected possessiveness and found instead that everything was shared in common--there were not even private homes. The one large sisterhood, the "we" of the community covered every aspect of life. It was a natural socialism, that is, one that grew from within rather than imposed from without. It was also a practical socialism in that it evolved out of what worked rather than out of difficult to accept theories of economics and history.

The care of babies was considered education and only the most fit were entrusted with this task just as dentistry was a specialization and mothers did not drill in their children's teeth. So child care was also too specialized to leave in amateur hands, even loving amateur hands. The result? They hadn't had a criminal for 600 years.

The babies were reared in the warmer southern part of the country and only gradually introduced to the colder northern areas. Natural mothers stayed close to their children throughout the first year and then gradually began pulling away back to their own specialties. In all their time in Herland, the explorers never heard a baby cry except when one fell. The little children were **happy**.

But it was all too quiet for Terry. He wanted struggle, combat, something to oppose over which he could win. The contrast to him was as boring as a Sunday School picnic. He couldn't stand the untroubled peace, the unmeasured plenty, the steady health, the large good will and smooth management that ordered everything and left nothing undone.[44]

Terry was the devil's advocate, or the worst case scenario of the book. When the three explorers married their three girlfriends, the whole country was excited by the possibility of another way of having children. But the women did not imagine that they would have sex relations on a regular basis. This infuriated Terry especially. Thus it was Terry and Alina who had the most difficulty and finally brought about the end of the story. Terry insisted on his husbandly "rights" and hid himself in Alina's room. His belief was that every woman privately cherished the idea of being mastered, sexually. Alina didn't. She called for help, got it, and Terry was put on trial. The verdict was expulsion.

Thus Terry, Vandyck and his new wife, Ellador, left Herland to go back to what some call civilization. The story ends there, but the reader's imagination shrinks from the sense of Ellador's disappointment in the world outside of Herland. This unwritten suggestion of how inferior our world is compared with the simple and rational beauty of Herland is probably the strongest part of the book, underscoring feminism and social equality at the same time.

Sally Miller Gearhart, *The Wanderground*

In the opening pages of this book, published in 1979, one is swept up into a situation of danger perceived by a novice in the use of her mental equipment. She hears a noise like armor creaking, and then it stops. She waits, but it does not start again. Could it be a male from the City who has entered their Wanderground? This would be a bad thing, she knew from her lessons about the past when men owned all things, even the forests and hills. "'It's too simple,' she recited to herself, 'to condemn them all or to praise all of us. But for the sake of earth and all she holds, that simplicity must be our creed.'"[45]

The noise came from old fashioned armor worn by a hostile woman, named Margaret, rather than a man. She had been raped by two men outside the City and then, as a cruel joke, dressed in the old armor and set free. She was met by a woman named Seja who convinced the new woman that she had nothing to fear from this society of females who did without men.

The time of the tale is somewhere in the future. The powers of the mind are greater in several senses. One could talk with plants and animals, for example, and they talked back. One could stretch out one's mind and sense that which was some distance away. One could communicate with others, using only one's mind. But danger still existed. Men in the City had been told they lost their sexual potency outside the City walls. But some males, like those who had raped Margaret, were already aware that this wasn't true and might come into the countryside to dominate the women again.

Decades earlier, the hill women had escaped from the City and had each shared the painful recollections of her City experience, so that they would never forget why they had come together. One of the worst of those recollections was that of rape. Usually when remembered, memory shields would protect from too much pain. Seja was remembering Margaret's rape without shields and was thrown into a raging anger, which she tried to take out on her friend Alaka. Seja had to be held down by three women so that she would not harm Alaka. Her desire to kill the rapists was so strong that she acted it out against the wrong people, and had to be slowly brought back to serenity by her friends.

The sense of danger developing in the book is that men have discovered they can function outside the City and are moving across the wanderground. Evidence of this was the rape of Margaret, but also the bear trap that caught Cassandra, the watchdog, by the forepaws. Everything in the book to do with the women is loving and caring, while everything to do with men is pain and anger.

But all of this past or potential gender conflict is blended into a sweet story about the hill women who live in total harmony with plants and animals and with each other, living out their destiny until they return to mother or die. In some ways it is as though the hill women picked up where St. Francis had left off--lovingly tied to everyone and everything so that all of life becomes one organism, and the individual did not think of herself without thinking of collective relationships as well. A strong element of mysticism was involved as well, a level of spiritual awareness that Ann Lee might not have called a vision but less religious people certainly could. Gearhart wrote that the ecstasy experienced was not from the joy of riding the high wind but was from the awareness of a thousand operations functioning together with such precision within her body. She felt connected to everything, a blended-in part of an interwoven whole. "She felt herself to be an infinitely complex organism elaborating in its turn each complexity. 'To know the many in the one,' she remembered, 'is as rare as it is possible.'"[46]

The hill women formed a network in the City where some of them, like Ijeme, passed as males. Ijeme brought a young woman to her apartment so as to make her guise of a man look better; possible watchers would be less wary of a "man" who acted like themselves. The woman was out of history to a hill woman. Face thickly painted, hair stiff with lacquer, dress low-cut in front, tight, mid-thigh in length, and shoes that should have made it impossible to walk. The woman had been standing outside Ijeme's apartment building without an escort and Ijeme had sensed fear in the woman. This was a woman who dressed to please men.

She was frightened and did the only thing she thought the "man" wanted: she took off her clothing and wanted sex. When Ijeme resisted, the woman fought with Ijeme and in the struggle discovered that Ijeme was a woman as well. She ran to the window and screamed out Dike! Dike! as loudly as she could. Ijeme tried to stop her and the woman ran away, but her shoe caught in the fire escape and, screaming all the way down, she fell to her death.

Ijeme ran back to the hills and had to undergo a cleansing ceremony. She had committed the vilest of acts: however accidently, she had killed a woman.

The women in the City lived in a man's world where all the rules seemed designed to benefit the men. For example, a new dress code for women prohibited trousers or pants on a woman. She had to wear a skirt and hose in public at all times. She had to have a male escort at all times. Women who dissented, whether they were gay or straight, were hassled and if that didn't work, their brains were operated on to make them more biddable, or they were psyched into acting like whores or housewives, or doped up to make them tame.

These were the reasons women escaped from the City in whatever manner they could, why they snuck girl children out in laundry bags, why they endangered themselves. The hills were the only place to go to get away from the male-mad City. It was not just that the City was dominated by men, it was also madness--created in large part because men could not avoid doing something simply because it was possible. And so they almost destroyed the earth. Even long ago most women knew that they could have built what is called western civilization, but they rejected most of the ideas as unnecessary or destructive.[47]

It was also madness because the women living in the hills were called witches by some, and new witch trials began in a small town above Minneapolis, after some of the women who'd been captured talked about children being born of virgins without benefit of male sires. The reaction was swift and deadly. Long prison terms, children taken away and put in homes, physical threats to the people themselves and to any who tried to help or appeared sympathetic. State laws required every woman to be married, so as to prevent any talk of not needing males for reproduction. Any woman wearing pants was sent to a behavior modification clinic and came out wearing a dress and a vacant smile.

Shortly after all this the women who were the least able to conform began to move out of the City into the hills. If they were caught they were eventually killed. Sometimes they were captured by helicopters that dropped nets on the fleeing women. Sometimes hunting parties would be made up of beer guzzling good ol' boys who would spend a few days in the hills trying to capture a woman or two to rape and leave for dead. It was called a sport. Sometimes the women were tracked with dogs.

There is the possibility offered late in the book for some male involvement in a new, loving, and equal future, but there was also a strong doubt that males could ever do and sustain anything that nonviolent. It seemed that a great spiritual sort of communism was possible so long as the women were left alone. Although a slim possibility was held out as a slender hope, the world of future equity, serenity, and evolution lay in the hands of the women among us.

A final story, Suzette Haden Elgin's *Native Tongue* published in 1984, expresses the need for (as well as the success of) a sharing female society that found a means of separating itself from a bi-gender society wherein women were devalued and powerless.

Suzette Haden Elgin, *Native Tongue*

Suzette Haden Elgin contrasts a brief period in the late 20th century when women seemed to be moving into the main stream with a later enforced inferiority that resulted after it was scientifically proven that women were mentally inferior. Writing from the perspective of the century after females were degraded, Elgin wrote that future people saw that the idea of female equality was a romantic notion like the "noble savage;" a dangerous and cruel burden on the female population forced to act out an equality that was biologically impossible. For the protection of the female, males again took over leadership positions and kept women in subservient positions even though they were indispensable in many ways.[48]

One of the fields in which women excelled was in linguistics. The world of the future saw the earth face to face with many alien species who all spoke very different languages that the female linguists in particular could handle very well. Without apparently damaging the notion of male superiority, the women were the *sine qua non* of every negotiation between alien governments. Nonetheless females required the written permission of a man to buy a piece of fruit or to travel beyond the city's limits.[49] A woman had no rights. Her children, her body, her life were under a man's control. No female, by definition, had adult legal rights.

Native Tongue is the story of this society, how well or how badly women coped, and how they quietly worked their way to a place of gender equality **without** a revolution. The linguists had a form of economic equality that did not sound all that pleasant, perhaps, because the focus was not on that dream. They voluntarily lived lives of shared austerity and frugality, reminiscent of monasteries or communities of Anabaptists. The adult women were allowed to own only a modest wardrobe, minimal underwear, one item of jewelry, and no cosmetics at all.[50]

The linguists lived in communal group homes called households and there were thirteen of them for each of the tribes or clans of linguists. The rest of the world or universe lived in private houses, presumably with private property, the way people did in the twentieth century. This also made Elgin's future society resemble the imaginary world of Plato when philosopher queens and kings ruled over a producing majority. And as the philosopher rulers were the *sine qua non* of *The Republic*, so the linguists in Elgin's future were essential to the continuing pace of imperialism and economic expansion of the planet.

The linguists' homes were built into the earth to make them more defensible. One house was described as having only the fourth floor showing above ground. On returning home, Thomas, the head linguist, looked at it very carefully to see whether "the women" had made any changes to the outside or to the gardens. He wanted to nip potential changes in the bud so as to avoid the expense of tearing down whatever the women had constructed. Why tear them down? Because he had earlier given an order that no changes were allowed unless initiated by a male. So they had let the grass grow waist high before he complained and settled things. Now he had to look carefully when he came home to avoid unpleasant surprises.[51] A person had to be aware that when dealing with a woman one should not for an instant forget that one was dealing with an organism that was basically just a rather sophisticated child suffering from delusions of grandeur. A man could not treat a woman as though she were a man, as though she were equal.[52]

The women living at the Barren Houses, the residences for females without or beyond reproductive ability, had, over the years, conceived the idea of developing a woman's language that would allow them to communicate female thinking/feeling without male comprehension or interference. Work on this new woman's language began, very slowly, in the twentieth century when women could still be doctors, lawyers, and such and were not simply men's property as they were later. The new language had barely moved beyond conception when a brilliant young woman named Nazareth unknowingly began to build it, rather like a person might doodle or write poetry or draw pictures in a private diary. An older woman discovered what Nazareth was doing, and the star of the story was now visible. Creating, developing, and using this woman's language is what *Native Tongue* is all about.

Nazareth was married to a man she hated when she was fifteen, and she gave birth eight times to nine children (one set of twins). Her only experience of love was the time she fell in love with a male backup translator who was kind to her and gave her a few compliments. On the last day of negotiations, feeling she would never see him again, she ran up and told him that she loved him. He promptly told her father and her father told her husband. They chastised her for it and laughed long and hard at the thought of this miserable ugly woman who thought she could attract a man. There were no words to describe what they had done to her. She never felt love for a male again, not even for her sons. When she developed cancer at age 40, a meeting was held where several males determined that her diseased uterus should be removed and instead of regenerating her breasts they were to be removed as well. Her "womaning" was done, after all. The expectation was that after she was arbitrarily mutilated she would then be sent to a Barren House so that her husband could administer another insult by divorcing her and marrying someone else. A meeting was held in which her father and her husband contributed to the decision that gave eloquent testimony to the powerlessness of women, even over their own bodies. She had no choice in the matter. Now officially barren, with a husband who wanted to divorce her, Nazareth was moved to the Barren House, where the older ladies had been waiting for her for decades, waiting for when she could work more openly on the women's language with the other older women.

Barren House was no luxury place. It was like a barracks. For the feeble and ill the house provided twenty-three beds, all in the same big bedroom, lined up on either side. Not even a bit of partition to create an illusion of privacy. But it was the women's choice that it was this way, so that they could all share the sunshine and the view out of the windows and take pleasure in each other's company.

Coming out of that communality was the desire to have Laaden, the new language, up and running so that there would be a language just for women, so that one could "...say the things that women wanted to say and about which men always said: 'Why would anybody want to talk about *that*?'"

Nazareth was discharged from the hospital, and went directly to Barren House where the women showed her the progress that they had made on the woman's language. Nazareth insisted that the language be taught to infant girls even if it wasn't quite finished. More and more young girls would be able to speak it, and "...as more and more little girls acquire Laadan and begin to speak a language that expresses the perceptions of women rather than those of men, reality will begin to change."[53]

What if the men found out? Nazareth's answer was that it would be ten-twenty years before the men found out, plenty of time to devise women's responses to whatever hypothetical actions the men might take. In seven years every girl in Chornyak House knew Laadan and used it easily. The manual alphabet devised by Nazareth for signing to one another consisted in very tiny, hard to see, movements of fingers and hands that were in the lap of the speaker. Difficult to detect unless one was looking for it. The result was incredible: women didn't have to talk with men anymore and their dependence on males shrank to nearly zero. And the males did not know why. Adam, Nazareth's hated husband, speaking to Thomas, Nazareth's father, described the changes in a plaintive manner. Women, he said, do not nag or even whine or complain any more. They don't demand things and don't make idiotic objections to everything a man proposes. They don't argue. They don't even get sick! If there are still female illnesses, they are never mentioned.[54]

All the males except Thomas felt that the women had become saints.

Thomas suspected the existence of the women's language and moved to put a stop to it, but his nurse Michella, killed him before he could take any action. Michella had started off hating all the Linguists, but ended up loving the women linguists at Barren House, especially Nazareth. She killed Thomas to preserve their secret language, then killed herself as well.

Sometime later the men became vaguely aware of a new problem summarized by one of them as the disappearance of real women. Because women no longer needed to communicate with the men they stopped doing so.   To the men, therefore, the females in their households were alive, but little more. To the men the women were becoming intolerable, but there was nothing the men could do, no complaints they could actually make. They were helpless.[55] How could one "...accuse a woman, name her guilty, for ceasing to do every last thing he has demanded that she *not* do, all his life long.?"[56] Women were so courteous, so cooperative, and reasonable, and pleasant that they didn't seem real. Men were not really needed any longer because the frustration of not communicating was gone. Women needed each other but not the males, and their courteous indifference made it seem as though they weren't there at all! The men felt that it was no longer any good to go home to confess a shameful thing, or to take pride in an accomplishment, because the women were so dissatisfying-- it was as though they didn't need to talk to men anymore. They didn't.

The solution the men came up with was to build separate female households near the male households and the Barren Houses. This was great news for the ladies. Nazareth summed up the pleasure. We don't have to run away, she said, nor erect battlements and ramparts or move into caves with lasers at the ready. We just have to go about our business, but now with a lot less inconvenience than we've ever had before.[57]

As the book ended, the notion was expressed that the woman's language should now be shared with women outside of the Linguist groups and the reader was left with the idea of a quiet feminist revolution gradually spreading all over the world(s).

Endnotes
Chapter Seven

1. This notion is widely believed and is the main thrust of romantic fiction; the improving, civilizing influence of a woman on even the most dissolute male. This idea **may** be correct, but it needs empirical testing.

2. Steven A. Holmes, "In Fighting Racism, Is Sexism Ignored,?" *The New York Times*, September 11, 1994, p. 3E.

3. Elaine Hoffman Baruch, "Women in Men's Utopias," *Women in Search of Utopia: Mavericks and Mythmakers*, Ruby Rohrlich and Elaine Hoffman Baruch, eds. (New York: Schocken Books, 1984), p. 209.

4. Susan I. Thomas, *Gender and Poverty* (New York: Garland Publishing, Inc., 1994), pp. 13-26.

5. Barbara Crossette, "U.N. Documents Inequities for Women as World Forum Nears," *The New York Times*, August 18, 1995, p. 3.

6. Alleged to be the lyrics of a 20th century ballad set to an even older tune called "House of the Rising Sun," in Suzette Haden Elgin, *Native Tongue* (New York: Daw Books, Inc., 1984), pp. 264-265.

7. Barrie Thorne, Cheris Kramarae, and Nancy Henley, "Imagining a Different World of Talk," in Rohrlich and Baruch, *op. cit.*, pp. 180-186. Notes following the chapter suggest an extensive literature existing already in 1984 on the subject of female/male language differences.

8. See Elaine Hoffman Baruch, "Women in Men's Utopias," *op. cit.*, pp. 211-213.

9. Linda Jenness, ed., *Feminism and Socialism* (New York: Pathfinder Press, 1972), p. 6.

10. Ibid., pp. 13-14.

11.   Mary Ansell, *A Serious Proposal to the Ladies for the Advancement of their True and Greatest Interest* (London: Richard Wilkin at the King's Head in St. Paul's Church-Yard, 1697), dedication page. Princess Anne was the second daughter of James II who became queen after William and Mary had both died.

12. Ibid., p. 10.

13. Ibid., pp. 11-14.

14. Ibid., p. 19.

15. Ibid., p. 41.

16. Ibid., pp. 43-44.

17. Ibid., pp. 70-71.

18. Ibid., pp. 171-172.

19. Ibid., p. 205.

20. Ibid., p. 211.

21. Sarah Scott, *A Description of Millenium Hall and the Country Adjacent: Together with the Characters of the Inhabitants and such Historical Anecdotes and Reflections, as may excite in the reader Proper Sentiments of Humanity, and lead the Mind to the Love of Virtue*, Third Edition (London: Printed for J. Newberry at the Bible and Sun, St. Paul's Churchyard, 1767), pp. 15-16.

22. Ibid., p. 50.

23. Ibid., pp. 82-83.

24. Ibid., p. 139.

25. Ibid., p. 148.

26. Bernard Mandeville, *The Fable of the Bees*, Philip Harth, ed. (Harmondsworth: Penguin, 1970), pp. 294-295; Cited in Gertrude Himmelfarb, *The Idea of Poverty: England in the Early Industrial Age* (New York: Alfred A. Knopf, 1984), p. 30.

27. Sarah Scott, *op. cit.*, p. 262.

28. Mary E. Bradley Lane, *Mizora: A Prophecy*, in Ruby Rohrlich and Elaine H. Baruch, *op. cit.*, p. 117.

29. Ibid., p. 120.

30. Ibid., p. 121.

31. Ibid., p. 123.

32. Ibid., p. 126.

33. Ibid.

34. Ibid., p. 133.

35. Ibid., p. 136.

36. Ann J. Lane, "Introduction," in Charlotte Perkins Gilman, *Herland* (New York: Pantheon Books, 1979), p. vi.

37. Charlotte Perkins Gilman, *Herland* (New York: Pantheon Books, 1979), p. 11. Book written in 1915 and serialized in *The Forerunner*.

38. Ibid., p. 17.

39. Ibid., p. 30.

40. Ibid., p. 55.

41. Ibid., p. 56.

42. Piotr Alexeievich Kropotkin thought of this as mutual aid when he described the social anarchism of wild animals in Siberia in *Mutual Aid, A Factor of Evolution* (London: William Heinemann, Popular Edition, 1915).

43. Gilman, *op. cit.*, p. 66.

44. Ibid., p. 99.

45. Sally Miller Gearhart, *The Wanderground: Stories of the Hill Women* (Boston: Alyson Publications, Inc., 1979), p. 2.

46. Ibid., p. 107.

47. Ibid., p. 145.

48. Suzette Haden Elgin, *Native Tongue* (New York: Daw Books, Inc., 1984), pp. 72-73.

49. Ibid., p. 268.

50. Ibid., pp. 89-90.

51. Ibid., p. 102.

52. Ibid.

53. Ibid., p. 250.

54. Ibid., p. 275.

55. Ibid., p. 288.

56. Ibid., p. 289.

57. Ibid., pp. 295-296.

Chapter Eight

Communal Sharing Solves
The Riddle of History

Theoretical Foundations
Karl Marx and Friedrich Engels
Eduard Bernstein and Vladimir Ulyanov (Lenin)

Karl Marx was a nineteenth century philosophy student who aroused strong feelings in others; either he was seen as an overeducated underachiever or a gifted prophet who unlocked the riddle of history. His beginnings were deceptively mild, considering how strongly history reacts to his name.

He was born in 1818 in Trier, a modest Rhineland city on the Moselle River in west Germany. His family was Jewish and his father was a successful lawyer who worked for the city government. His upper middle class home in Trier is still regularly visited by tourists.

In the fall of 1835 when Karl was seventeen he left home for the University of Bonn. He disappointed his father while at Bonn because he seemed to get into trouble more than study, so his father insisted that the next year he would go to the University of Berlin, a relatively young but already prestigious school located in the capital of Prussia. In his high school senior thesis Karl had revealed grandiose ambitions about saving the world, and at both universities these ambitions were visible in his desire to become either Germany's best poet, or, later, Germany's finest historian of ideas. Along the way, Karl Marx became a student of Hegelian philosophy.

Theoretical Foundations

G.F.W. Hegel (1770-1831) was an idealist philosopher who believed that history was an unfolding of World Reason in time, an unfolding that occurred in human consciousness. This unfolding was propelled forward by what he called a dialectic process in which the simultaneous presence of conflicts brought about resolution which utilized the best qualities of the conflicting parts in a new focus of ideas. Resolution by resolution, then, history marched forward.

Socrates had used the dialectical process in conversational attempts to create the cognitive dissonance or conflict in the human mind necessary for truth to evolve. Socrates pushed his listeners toward the truth by creating conflict in their minds, a conflict demanding resolution. Plato had idealized this dialectic process and made it the means by which the student could attain knowledge of the invisible world of ideas. Hegel took this idea and raised it to the level of universal history, and the dialectic became the process of moving history forward through conflict resolution, resulting in an inevitable progress from lower to higher stages of history.

Hegel thought that the goal of the historical process was the overcoming of human alienation, understood as an unnatural separation between the human and the World Reason or the deity (recall Winstanley) in itself or in nature. This overcoming of alienation appeared to be a process as well. It represented a humanizing of the world, like turning wasteland into a city, in which human **labor** developed what was undeveloped. Parking lots instead of raw nature may seem mundane, but pyramids in ancient Egypt were not. At any rate when the historical process was complete and alienation was overcome, expected by Hegel to occur in the Germanic period of his lifetime, people's sense of All and of their belonging to that All would be complete. Hegel sounded as though his philosophy was affected by Buddhism. Hegel believed that history moved forward in stages in which progress could be marked by determining how many people knew that they were free. His sense of history, which was philosophy looking backward, saw an Oriental stage in which **one** knew freedom, then the Greco-Roman stage in which **some** knew that they were free, then finally a Germanic stage in which **all** would know that they were free.

Hegel's philosophy was complicated because it tried to include every living thing and every nuance of behavior over the centuries of human existence in a history of conflicting forces which eventually saw the triumph of good. Ludwig Feuerbach, an older student of Hegel somewhat ahead of Marx professionally, helped Marx by making a significant criticism of Hegel in 1843. Hegel, Feuerbach argued, had abstracted reason from real people, reified it, and then made a God out of it. Feuerbach argued that this error prevented people from understanding what Hegel really meant, and that to help Hegel he had to be read transformationally: substituting the word human every time Hegel used the word Spirit (Reason). This corrective action, however, **materialized** Hegel's idealistic philosophy so that Hegel appeared now to be describing an evolving history of real people rather than a World Reason unfolding in human minds.

Marx was born in a locality and at a time when the industrial revolution was gathering momentum, and it must have seemed to Marx and his contemporaries as it had to the French philosopher, St. Simon, that industrialization was the wave of the future. Karl Marx took this sense of the importance of the new industrialization and the Hegelian philosophy as revised by Feuerbach with him when he moved to Paris with his new wife, Jenny, in October 1843.

Paris was teeming with revolutionary ideas, but the ones which seized Marx's attentions were similar to those ideas people had been urging on him for at least two years: ideas of communism that came out of a French communist tradition and the activity of François Noël Babeuf (1760-1797).

Babeuf is considered by many to be the father of European communism, or perhaps, the nineteenth century versions of it, because it was he who argued that private property should not be shared but should be abolished entirely. An observer more than a participant in the French Revolution of 1789, Babeuf remained a radical even after the republic was established and the king executed. Living in Paris and working as a minor bureaucrat in the Subsistence Bureau of the Commune, he came to see how wealthy people in Paris exploited the food shortages in the city at the expense of the poor. In his newspaper, *The Tribune of the People*, Babeuf began to demand both political and economic equality. Imprisoned for these views by the government, his family suffered during his absence. His seven year old daughter died of hunger.[1] Former revolutionaries, he wrote, now a part of the hated government, had earlier argued correctly that political equality without economic equality was only a tantalizing illusion. The cruelest error of the revolutionary bodies, Babeuf felt, had been their failure to limit property and their abandonment of the people to the greedy speculations of the rich.[2] Showing once again the close connection between religious and secular striving, Babeuf wrote that Christ told us to love our neighbor and to do as we would be done by, but he had to admit that Christ's code of equality resulted in his execution.

Even though it was unlikely that the code of equality would be established, he failed to understand why his little girl of seven had to die when the allowance of bread was cut down to two ounces by the people in power. His other children grew so thin, he wrote, that he did not recognize them.[3] Babeuf believed that the purpose of government was the common welfare, but the fact of private property made it impossible for government to seek that common welfare. Private property, he wrote, sounding a great deal like Gerrard Winstanley, gave rise to all the vices of society. If the land did not belong to anyone, he wrote, if its fruits were for all, then its possession by a small number of men is a usurpation resulting from a few institutions that abuse and violate the fundamental law. Whenever an individual hoards the land and its fruits beyond what the hoarder needs, that land and fruit have been stolen from society.[4]

Before the terrible words *mine* and *thine* were invented, Babeuf wrote, before the existence of this cruel and brutal species called *masters*, and of that other species called *slaves*; before there were those so abominable as to *dare to have too much while others were dying of hunger*; what was the crime committed by such hungry people? Of what sin were they guilty? Not only is the chimera of the golden age long gone, he wrote, but so is the chimera of virtue.[5]

When he was released from prison Babeuf formed a new political club, the "Conspiracy of the Equals," pushing for an abolition of private property. He sounded almost like Rousseau in that he wanted to remove people from large cities and place them in villages. He argued in his *Manifesto of the Equals* that the urban and rural poor should seize the property of the rich by using the power of the state and make property communal. This meant revolution, because the state would have to be taken from those who were controlling it in the interests of the rich and powerful. Once the urban and rural poor had power and had abolished private property, consumption would be socialized by placing the fruit of everyone's labor in the common store, from which all could draw according to their needs, echoing Cabet's slogan that had by this time become very popular. Private property, which had created masters and slaves, must be replaced by communal property, which would teach people that **no one** could ever become richer or more powerful than another, and would assure to all as much sustenance as needed but no more.[6]

He called for equality with no equivocations. If a suggested production could not be divided up equally then it should not be produced at all. For example, yachts or autos that are more costly than homes might not be produced. He rejected milder forms of equality and tolerated no distinctions between people. How he would implement this in practice is difficult to imagine. But these were the ideas that motivated an attempted coup against the Directory in 1796, and a year later Babeuf was executed. A disciple, an Italian named Philippe Buonarrotti, preserved Babeuf's ideas and transmitted his ideas to the radicals of the early nineteenth century. In the process Buonarrotti, without a thought to the possible difficulties, turned Babeuf's agrarian communism into an industrial communism that better fit the changing circumstances of the early 1800s.[7]

Karl Marx and Friedrich Engels

At this time Marx read the manuscript of Friedrich Engels' *Conditions of the Working Class in England*, and the two men became friends. Karl's attention was diverted to the new forms of capitalism created by the industrial revolution across the English Channel in Britain and the plight of the working class living and working in conditions of virtual slavery.

This student of Hegel (adapted by Feuerbach) had a theory of history with no particular goal. He was introduced to Babeuf's revolutionary politics, as adapted by Buonarotti, when he moved to Paris in late 1843. This supplied revolution as a goal, but revolution on behalf of what or whom? At the same time Marx became aware through Engels of the wretched conditions of the British proletariat. All this came together in his mind. His historical theory now had a goal and an agent class, and Marx concluded that history was a record of class conflict that would culminate in a victory for the working class who would lead the world into a communist future. This was historical materialism and was patterned closely after Hegel's own historical analysis.

Marx argued that human history was a record of class conflict with class defined as relation to the means of production. There were, therefore, only two real classes: the owners and the non-owners of the means of production. Other "classes" to which Marx sometimes referred were the petite bourgeoisie or small industrialists or shop keepers who would meld into the proletariat during industrial crises, and the lumpen proletariat, the lowest in the socio-economic rankings, the people who had already lost the toss of the dice; the undeserving poor as opposed to the deserving poor. Whatever that may mean.

History moved forward in stages, as Hegel and others had argued. Each of Marx's stages was a different relation of production or mode of production, meaning a different way of organizing the components of production like the labor force, machinery if any, owners of property, and the nature of property. A stage would be characterized by its mode of production, and it would last until two simultaneous events occurred: the flexibility of the mode of production was exhausted, and a new mode of production had matured in the womb of the old. At this juncture the old mode of production or relations of property would give way to the new through a social revolution that would alter everything.[8]

Marx believed that history progressed in five stages: the **gens** period in the beginning reflecting primitive periods, an **ancient-slave** period correlating roughly with the Greco-Roman period, **feudalism**, **capitalism**, and finally **socialism-communism**. The names referred to the economic foundation of that stage of social history, which fundamentally characterized all of the superstructure or the rest of society. The gens period saw the rise of religion and private property, both the results of an existing alienation but both also great exacerbators of separateness. Religion caused people to worship their own best qualities as though they belonged to an Other, and property caused people to fragment their common heritage in the Earth's treasury.

Each mode of production (historical period) deepened alienation at the same time that it enjoyed technological progress. By the time humans had evolved to the capitalist period they were **deeply** alienated even though they were technologically superior to the previous historical periods. Although capitalism was contemporaneous with Marx, he analyzed it as if it were already past, hoping thereby to encourage people to relativize the period, to think of the capitalist period as temporary, just like the previous stages. A second reason for his analysis of a contemporary phenomenon was to show that at the heart of capitalism lay theft.

He accomplished the second goal by describing the production process as one in which the employer stole from the worker. Profit, Marx insisted in *Grundrisse*, was basically theft, because it was based on unpaid labor time.[9] Imagine, as Marx argued in *Capital*, that a worker was hired for twenty dollars a day. During the morning hours he/she produced goods worth twenty dollars. The worth of goods was determined by the amount of necessary, living labor time involved in their manufacture. Something taking four hours to make would be twice as valuable as that which took only two hours to manufacture. So if one argued that during the morning, goods worth twenty dollars were produced, then the worker could go home and all would be well. His or her pay would equal the contribution to the employer. But, alas, the worker was not free to go, but kept on for an additional number of hours, producing more goods for which the worker received no pay. Because the goods were priced as though the employer actually paid the worker all the time, the prices were higher than the costs of production would really warrant. This difference between costs and selling price, on average, was profit, and profit or what Marx called surplus value, was theft.

Capitalism, therefore, was a temporary mode of production like the ones that had preceded it, and its chief characteristic, profit, was actually theft. But this did not make capitalism a bad thing. Marx believed that there was a good side to this. Capitalism taught workers how to produce commodities socially, that is, together. Although this was important, social production was not capitalism's most valuable characteristic; that was to teach the workers how to produce in abundance.

Prior to capitalism people had manufactured commodities on more of an individual basis in the sense that factories were small and perhaps most production was done in individual homes. What capitalism did was to introduce factories that permitted, whatever the cost to the human workers, a great expansion in commodity production. Instead of being an anti-capitalist, Marx welcomed it even as he critiqued it. Capitalism was a necessary and valuable historical stage existing in time just before the final stage of socialism/communism because capitalism showed workers how to produce together the abundance that communism intended to share. Such productivity was not philanthropism on the part of the capitalist, it was an intrinsic part of the capitalist mode of production. In order for capitalism to exist there **had** to be surplus value or profits, even though such were the result of theft. In order for capitalism to exist, Marx argued in *Grundrisse*, labor must be turned into wealth, a wealth created by a productive process stimulated by the deplorable greed of the capitalist that nonetheless dramatically increased both worker productivity and the amount of goods available for consumption.[10]

Moreover, this increased production was achieved by a work force acting collectively in the factory and living communally outside the factory. The discipline of capitalism taught the workers how to produce together, and the realities of their socio-economic class meant that they lived together as well, concentrated in the slums around the factory. Goods produced were the result of their collective effort rather than that of any single individual, and, as Engels had demonstrated in his book, they lived together in abject poverty. Nonetheless, the workers produced by their unpaid surplus labor the capital destined to employ additional laborers in the future. The growth of capitalism was due to surplus value as well as to the productivity of the workers.

Marx was not praising capitalism. He was simply acknowledging the importance of it despite the fact that he also believed that in the factories that characterized the early nineteenth century capitalist system the workers had become overspecialized. The factory workers were turned into brainless machines, crippled monstrosities of their former selves, in a milieu where the machines were treated far better than the people.

In addition the workers were normally not paid enough to be able to purchase the products that they had created. The workers would thus be poor consumers, and this fact helped trigger the periodic economic crises which would cause more workers to be laid off, more employers to fail and join the working class, while the remaining capitalists became monopolists using more machinery and fewer workers. Over time, as a result of the smaller **human** work force, surplus value or profits would decline and industrial crises would occur at an even more rapid pace, until the whole system failed and the workers, whom capitalism had taught to work and live socialistically, would take over in what was called the proletarian revolution.

Capitalism was, therefore, eroding from within, helplessly creating the seeds of its own destruction. The degeneration could not be stopped, nor could the misery of the proletariat. This was a major reason why Marx did not favor trade unions all that much. The misery of the working class could not, he believed, be ameliorated without a revolution that put them in charge. That revolution would take place when the workers discovered that they **themselves** were the overwhelming majority of the population and that they **themselves** were the productive force which no longer needed capitalists as guide. The workers would see themselves as they really were: the real basis for the entire system. The workers would, in Hegel's words, develop a mind of their own. Precisely in labor where there seemed to be only some outsider's mind and ideas involved, the laboring servant would become aware, through a rediscovery of self by oneself, of having and being a mind of one's own.[11]

The revolution would fundamentally alter the mode of production just as revolution had done in the past. The capitalist period would abruptly end when the workers socialized the means of production, ending for all time the division of labor known as classes. No longer would there be owners and nonowners of the means of production, the rich and the poor. The means of production would be owned by everyone.

Revolutionaries in the volatile France of the 19th century had discovered that even a successful new revolution had a temporary period when sporadic violence in favor of the old system could still be a danger. It was not enough to have a revolution and then to put down arms to enjoy the future, because enemies remained who wanted to reverse the revolution back to where it had been before. As a result a concept developed called the dictatorship of the proletariat, which suggested that for a brief and temporary period after the revolution, until such time as the dust of the revolution had settled, the proletariat might well arm themselves with the power of the old state and use that power to repel any enemies of the revolution who revealed themselves. But as soon as this brief resistance of capitalists was over, the dictatorship of the proletariat was expected to disband and disappear, making way for the much more democratic community assemblies that would be the source of authority in the new age.

Because the proletarian revolution ended alienation for all time, Marx considered his system to be the solution to the riddle of history. This overcoming of alienation was essentially accomplished through the socialization of the means of production.   Once this massive socialization had occurred, Marx argued, there would no longer be a division of labor represented by a class structure, and private property would be abolished. With the abolition of private property came an end to the division between humans and nature. Communism that meant the end of separating private property was another word for naturalism. Marx wrote that communism is the positive overcoming of private property or human self-alienation, and thus is the actual appropriation of the human essence through and for the human. Communism is, he stated, the complete and conscious restoration of people to themselves within the total wealth of previous development. It is the restoration of the human as a *social*, that is a truly *human* being. This communism is completed naturalism and is humanism as well, and as completed humanism it is naturalism.   It is the genuine resolution of the antagonism between humans and nature and between one person and another.   Communism is the resolution of the conflicts between existence and essence, objectification and self-affirmation, freedom and necessity, individual and species. It is the solution to the riddle of history and knows itself as this solution.[12]

The revolution that would cause these wonderful things to happen was difficult to conceptualize clearly. It was a concept astonishingly difficult for them to operationalize. A person could easily determine when a train began to move, but how could a person know that the revolution was beginning? What would it look like? The French Revolution? Marx and Engels thought so, at least at first. Engels wrote that their conceptions of the nature and course of the 'social' revolution that was proclaimed in Paris in February 1848, or their ideas of the proletarian revolution were strongly colored by the memories of the prototypes of 1789 and 1830.[13]

The proletarian revolution in their minds became a climactic event like the French Revolution had been. But what did that say about the French Revolution? Did that mean that the French Revolution was the bourgeois revolution historical materialism described as the beginning of the capitalist period? If the answer is yes and one still expected to see the proletarian revolution in 1848 or 1851, that was not much time to allow for capitalism to develop the new socialist class and to exhaust itself. The issue was not clear, especially when it became evident that Karl Marx was so frustrated that he would accept any kind of revolution at all just to get things moving. Engels, writing in 1895, argued that he and Marx had failed to analyze correctly what was taking place back in 1848-1849.[14] Marx never became that reflective; he just became frustrated when revolutions did not come. He became convinced that a new economic crisis would bring on the revolution.[15] When that did not happen, he hoped that new events such as discovering gold in California or the invention of the steam locomotive would stimulate the crisis which would stimulate the revolution.

In 1895 Engels believed that he and Marx had been wrong in 1848-49 in thinking that the revolution was imminent because he could now see that economic conditions had not been ripe in 1848-49. But if the ripeness of economic conditions can only be judged after the fact, one could not know the revolution was at hand until afterwards when it might be too late to help.

Similarly, Marx and Engels seemed confused about when the revolution should occur. It might occur ahead of time, for example.[16] Or the proletarian revolution might occur as a result of a new peasant war.[17] Was a radical party needed to lead the working masses or would the proletariat somehow do it by themselves? They implied both. They were also unclear as to whether the revolution would be sudden and violent or gradual and peaceful.[18]

This confusion about revolution in men who anxiously sought it was part of the confused legacy left by Marx and Engels. The revolutionary Lenin and the revisionist Bernstein both inherited that muddy legacy and each sought to implement it in different ways: Lenin to justify seizing power in a basically feudal Russian society that had experienced only the beginnings of capitalism, and Bernstein who sought to implement it gradually over a long period of time in a Germany well along the capitalist path. Lenin's revolution would socialize the means of production by nationalizing it, making everything belong to the state. Bernstein, on the other hand, would achieve his goal without a dramatic socialization of the means of production. He would accomplish socialism by passing socialist laws in the legislature, which would gradually have a cumulative effect. The confusion in the legacy was an important reason why Marxism was applied in such different ways after his death in 1883.

Even so, in Marx's theory, the revolution was to usher in a period called socialism to be followed after some time by a second and final period called communism. The chief difference between these two periods revolved around the distribution of the social wealth. In socialism the operative slogan would be "From each according to their ability, to each according to their work." How much a person worked would determine the size of their reward. Work eight hours and receive eight hours worth of goods. This was equality, Marx argued, that covered over the inequalities of strength, age, and the number of a person's dependents. When socialism had been internalized, after perhaps a generation or two, society would inscribe the familiar slogan on its banner: "From each according to their ability, to each according to their needs." Need would be the basic criterion, and reward according to need would finally divorce one's work from the share of social wealth received. Work would still be expected, but no longer because it was the means to satisfy animal needs. Work in late socialism and in communism would be performed as a means to satisfy one's human nature, one's desire to create, to produce.

Authority in the new society, whether socialism or communism, would emerge from an association that was fairly identical with the community. In his answer to Proudhon, a French anarchist, Marx wrote in *The Poverty of Philosophy* that the working class in the course of its development would substitute for the old civil society an association that excludes classes and class antagonism, and there would be no more political power because political power was precisely the official expression of class antagonism in civil society.[19]

These associations would function in a really democratic manner, and be far more democratic than the democratic pretense under capitalism. What this meant specifically was not clear, but one thing it certainly did mean was that Marx's communism, except for a brief dictatorship of the proletariat, was intended to function in a system of democratic associations--not in authoritarian despotisms.

These associations would be led just as orchestras are led by conductors in order that music instead of noise results. So the associations were not anarchic either. Just what exactly they would be, besides the fairly vague concept of people **really** ruling, was left for the future to determine. Engels provided a small clue, however, when he spoke highly of two methods used by the Paris Commune of 1871: filling all posts by universal suffrage with easy recall provisions, and paying elected officials no more than the average workers' wages.[20]

Moreover, worldwide society would produce according to a single plan developed in these associations. The revolution and socialism might begin in one country but it would quickly spread throughout the world. The point of the plan was to be production for use, not for exchange, meaning that the planners could focus on what was needed rather than what would sell. And the people themselves, meeting in their associations, decided what needed to be produced. As these local plans blended (in some fashion not mentioned) they would constitute an economic plan for the whole world. Marx did not describe how this would occur. Even imagining such an unlikely complexity is difficult, particularly for an age without computers.

Although the plan was democratically prepared, when finished it functioned as the source of production discipline and coordination; as a source of authority. But the goal was the satisfaction of people's needs. Nowhere in Marx and Engel's writings does one gain the impression that the goal was the satisfaction of the plan rather than meeting the needs of the people. The plan was instrumental, not the end in itself.

The result of this planned economy, Marx felt, would be an unbroken, progressive development of industry and a practically limitless growth in production. Unfettering the productive capitalist system would result in abundance, and that is what would be shared in socialism and communism. By ending the private extraction of profit, and producing for use according to a rational plan, wealth would be created that would fundamentally change human life just as a river flowing over a former desert would bring new green life. Engels wrote that the new society would do away with extravagance and waste, end the devastation of the productive forces and products, and free the producing system to provide a fully sufficient existence for everyone.

Moreover, the work done in the new society was expected to be different. Not only would **all** adults work, but the work itself would be more like a hobby, something people felt like doing because they enjoyed doing it and because they did it well. In addition, the work would be varied to reduce boredom and fatigue. One might be a carpenter in the morning, a music critic in the afternoon, and an engineer in the evening; or like the examples on the kibbutz, perhaps a university teacher or author in the morning and a manual worker in the afternoon.

Women's work would be fundamentally transformed in the sense that occupations to relieve so-called "women's work" would exist that tapped particular interests and skills. If some workers, male or female, enjoyed cleaning houses, then that was one thing they would do. They might care for children in day care centers. Women would no longer be serving a life sentence tied to a particular home, but they would marry for love rather than security, and remain married only so long as love endured. The entire relationship between women and men and between women and society was expected to change dramatically.[21]

Agriculture and life in the country would also be changed. Land would no longer be privately owned but would be social property worked by cooperative associations of agricultural workers as part of their daily activities. Marx felt that communal work done on the farms would allow for greater production to be coordinated into the single economic plan. The result of these changes would be the reduction of differences between town and country. Large cities would be divided up into smaller, scattered communities, and rural areas would lose their sense of isolation by being closer to urban life. Because the same people would work in the towns as in the country, cultural differences would disappear. Scattered industry would receive purer water and cleaner air, and rural folk would benefit from nearby industrial jobs in the off season and from urban sewage used as fertilizer. Mixing town and country together would even out the population distribution and combine the best of both urban and rural worlds.[22]

Of course some people would have to lead the society in the sense of coordinating activities as would a conductor of an orchestra. These administrators would be elected by the associations, would be easily recalled, and would not be rewarded any more than the average worker would be. Additionally, the administrator would, like other people, have other occupations, do different things in addition to administering for part of the day. This varied activity would help prevent leaders from becoming too attached to leading. This plus the injunction that the new leaders would administer things rather than people sought to prevent the degeneration in virtue that Plato had also feared.

When operating successfully communism would also mean more leisure time for the worker. Rational, planned production, for use rather than trade, would reduce and then eliminate the excess production that had plagued capitalism. The time saved could be used to produce different things or to spend more time on intellectual pursuits. The massive introduction of machinery that had hurt capitalists by reducing surplus value had a different impact in communism: it would lower work requirements without lowering consumption levels or standards of living. The workers could gain more education in the arts and sciences and education would be available to all.[23] This spread of education both extensively and intensively would result in improvements in production as well as in people. Humans living and working in the new society would be renewing themselves and the world of wealth they had created. What was really worth preserving from history would be converted into the common property of the whole society where it would be developed further.[24]

A final benefit of communism was peace. The proletarian revolutions, first in one country and then around the world, demonstrated that people had left behind the narrow confines of bourgeois nationalism. The association would be worldwide. The main cause of conflict, the tension between classes, would have disappeared. Hostility between groups of people, expressive of former alienation, would wither away just as would the state and religion. Engels wrote glowingly about the American Iroquois as described by Lewis Morgan: everything ran smoothly without a hierarchy of power--no soldiers, gendarmes, police, nobles, kings, governors, prefects, judges, prisons, or trials. All disputes were settled by the whole body of those concerned.[25]

Although the primitive society which had so many noble features in its early communism was destined to perish, all of the subsequent human history of progress in mastering nature and improving production did not diminish the beauty of that early communist beginning. Communism in the future, Marx and Engels felt, would be far richer because it would be totally unalienated, humanistic, and worldwide. There would be an end to crime, an end to war, and a satisfaction of everyone's needs.

Distribution in the final stage of communism would be unequal, reflecting actual need. Distribution stores would be accessible and contain everything that a person might need. Perhaps this would be one very large store containing hardware as well as food or separate stores in a kind of mall. Marx did not give details on such matters. But the point was that everything a person might need was going to be available to them. They would not take more than they needed because the concept of individual selfishness at the expense of others would have been left behind as the socialized means of production influenced people to become more social and less individual. The commodities in the distribution center were put there by the people who had produced them. The rational plan, administered by the elected officials, would coordinate the shipments of a vast variety of goods to make sure, for example, that the milk stores had milk and the meat stores had meat. Perishables had to get to the right outlets in good time.

Marx made it very clear that, so far as he was concerned, the socialist/communist distribution of wealth **followed** or **flowed out** of the socialization of the means of production and not the other way around. Put another way, the communism Marx was describing was not caused by a redistribution of social wealth or by something like socialized medicine, however valuable those reforms might be. This was what a revisionist like Bernstein seemed to be saying: that people could legislate their way into communism, or, even worse, that classlessness did not really depend on a previous socialization of the means of production. Bernstein actually believed that democracy was the absence of class government. Democracy, he argued, was on principle the suppression of class government though it was not yet the actual suppression of classes.[26] Marx did not agree, of course, for whatever that was worth. However good the legislative goals of social democrats might be, the communism Marx was talking about was the **result** of the socialization of the means of production, and not the other way around.

And before a generalized distribution could even be considered, Marx insisted that *society* had to pay for some things that society as a whole needed. Depleted raw materials and older machinery needed replacing, a budget for production expansion earmarked additional funds, a reserve category for contingencies isolated other monies, as would funds for nonproductive but important areas such as schools and unemployment compensation. Only after funds were allocated for these sorts of expenses could a general distribution to **individuals** occur.[27]

Marx and Engels saw the communist future as the goal of human striving, what all of history had been in the process of becoming. The internal dynamic of history would culminate, they thought, in the beginnings of a really **human** history that in some ways was a return to the past and in others ways was a use of technological progress to create a future of great richness for everyone. Communism was the means by which alienation was overcome, and thus was the solution to the riddle of history. Marx believed that he had unlocked the secrets of history and was pointing the way to human emancipation for all time.

Eduard Bernstein and Vladimir Ulyanov (Lenin)

The longed for proletarian revolution did not occur during his or Engel's lifetime. However, Marx and Engel's ideas **were** implemented in the sense that they became the major focus of the Second International Working Men's Association from 1889 to about 1914. The International began as a revolutionary organization, and indeed it was such, but the revolutionary aspects of the organization were more rhetoric than real, and the people who made up the organization had vastly different ideas about the revolution and the society that was to follow it.

Members who gathered in meetings sang the same songs and rallied to the same slogans but understood them quite differently. The major cause of differences was the evolving democracies found in western countries compared to the despotisms in the east. If workers could be politically active, i.e., voting and running for office, and if unions were permitted, the members attending International meetings tended to favor compromise and incremental reform rather than revolution. They hoped that gradual, step by step approaches would ultimately lead to structural transformation in their own countries and then the world.

Delegates from despotic countries, however, where the clandestine political/union activity encouraged an ideological purity out of touch with real life, tended to seek sudden, total revolution as the only solution that made any sense. To them, overthrowing the entire system was the only way to make a single progressive step.[28]

These differences divided the Second International and rather quickly resulted in two distinct revolutionary directions: a soft, gradual approach associated with the name Eduard Bernstein, and a hard, violent approach associated with the name Lenin. Both altered the Marxian legacy by ignoring the parts that disagreed with their position, and proponents of each side felt they had the **only** legitimate interpretation of Marx and all others were apostasies.

Bernstein's revisionism weakened the revolutionary dimension of Marxism by drawing attention to the real accomplishments of party members who had won election to political office in the newly democratic but capitalistic Germany. By talking about gradual reform and a milder version of the dream Bernstein tried to adapt ideology to practice, something he thought Marx had not done sufficiently. Bernstein argued that Marx's great scientific spirit was, in the end, a slave to a doctrine. To express it figuratively, Bernstein wrote, Marx had raised a mighty building within the framework of a scaffolding he found existing, and in its erection he kept strictly to the laws of scientific architecture so long as they did not collide with the conditions which the construction of the scaffolding prescribed, but he neglected or evaded them when the scaffolding did not allow of their observance. Where the scaffolding put limits in the way of the building, instead of destroying the scaffolding, Marx changed the building itself at the cost of its right proportions and so made it all the more dependent on the scaffolding. My conviction, Bernstein wrote, is that wherever that dualism shows itself the scaffolding must fall if the building is to grow in its right proportions. In the latter case, and not in the former, does one find what is worthy to live in Marx.[29]

The ideology, in other words, ignored the real world when the real world conflicted with the ideology. If it could not be ignored it was interpreted in such a way as to not challenge the ideology. In this sense ideas of revolution came less from reality and more from some almost religious position. Alfred G. Meyer, writing about the ideology of the German Social Democrats (SPD) in the 1890s, said that the party's ideology became a set of slogans, or a set of war-cries. The ideology became a litany intoned again and again, and drummed into the listeners' heads at meetings and rallies. The same phrases were always used, fortified only by invective. It became language no longer for thinking, but for arousing. Moreover, regardless of its doctrines, the Marxist movement attracted large masses of workers because it gave them an exciting sense of self-liberation and self-education, a sense of belonging and participation, a sense of solidarity in defying their bosses, and a great feeling of comradery.[30]

To be sure, the SPD was not a church; but in many respects it behaved like a church, labelling those who questioned accepted dogmas as heretics or, in a more benign mood, suggesting that they had not sufficiently mastered Marxist theory, and in general relying on discipline and obedience for its continued existence as a militant movement.[31]

The revolution was treated as though it were the end of time, and party members like Louise Michel wrote about it in the Old Testament style of Isaiah or Daniel, discussing predictions happening in the fullness of time. Then, she wrote, the great uprising will come. The rising of the people will happen at its appointed moment, happening in the same way that continents develop. It will happen because the human race is ready for it. The uprising will come, and those whom I have loved will see it. O my beloved dead.[32] Louise Michel made it sound as though the revolution was in fact the resurrection. To her perhaps it was.

Bernstein wanted to realign ideology and reality, to replace the barricades with ballot boxes even if that meant doing away with the dictatorship of the proletariat as inconsistent with the desired democracy.[33] He argued that Marx's failure to provide details about the future socialist society made the revolution eschatological and caused utopian speculation rather than the reverse. It was far more important, he thought, to work for immediate goals like democracy. Moreover he did not agree that the class struggle was so visible nor was it inevitably moving to some future conclusion favorable to the workers. Capitalism, he felt, would be around for many years to come, and present day workers were becoming better off rather than more pauperized as Marx had predicted. He also argued that the transition period between capitalism and socialism would have to be longer because workers lacked the skills to take over. Capitalists would be needed to run things even after the revolution. Bernstein stressed nationalism over internationalism in that he felt that the workers should realize that they are citizens of particular countries.[34]

The revolutionary message of Marx was substantially softened under such attacks and the European Marxist movement in general drifted in the direction of what would later be called socialism rather than communism, meaning social democrats seeking social reform rather than violently seeking revolution.

Lenin, on the other hand, came from a Russia in the 1890s where there was no democracy, no active political parties, and no labor unions. Russia was a backward empire barely nudging into the industrial era, centuries behind the West both politically and economically. Its government was a feudal despotism straight out of the middle ages. The whim of the tsar or tsarina was law, and tenure was for life. Redress was either by coup or by revolution.

In such a society a revolutionary party was of course a secret affair and the internal politics of the party mirrored the despotism of the external world. The dictatorship outside was matched by the dictatorship imagined necessary on the inside of the party. Because the majority of the workers were still basically peasants ignorant of their glorious future, the party **led** them into revolution and beyond rather than coordinating their activities.

Rosa Luxemburg (1870-1919), a Polish revolutionary leader, resisted these tendencies and insisted on party democracy and mass involvement before leading into revolution. But Lenin (Vladimir Ilich Ulyanov, 1870-1924) and Feliks Dzerzhinskii (1877-1926) insisted on tight control over the workers; an impatience with democratic niceties characteristic of authoritarian personalities.

Lenin insisted, contra Bernstein, that the revolution must be violent and sudden, and must completely overthrow the social system. But how could Marxism, which focused on a workers' revolution at the end of capitalism, be applied to backward, feudal Russia? Here is where Lenin's theory of imperialism fit. Lenin argued that in the last stages of capitalism capital would be exported overseas to less developed countries. There cheap labor and raw materials would permit gross profits which could be brought back to the industrial country both to line the pockets of capitalists and to bribe workers to divert them from revolution. Moreover, even though the less developed country was still in feudalism, imperialism would create pockets of advanced capitalism and workers would be doubly revolutionary: against the capitalist, but also against the monarch or tsar. The backwardness of the country, oddly enough, made it more revolutionary rather than less. The revolution that Marxists sought would actually begin in a backward country like Russia, breaking the chain of profits on which imperialism depended. Capitalists in advanced countries would no longer be able to bribe their workers, the workers would grow angry, and the revolutions would then occur in the developed countries and become worldwide.

This thinking created a revolutionary role for the small proletariat in a feudal country like Russia, but to what end? The proletarian revolution that they sought was still too far away. In the language of historical materialism, feudal Russia still had not had the **bourgeois** revolution, the social upheaval that would create the contradictions that the proletarian revolution was intended to solve. To maintain a revolutionary role for the workers in a country like Russia, party leaders developed the idea that the workers should help the bourgeoisie to achieve **their** revolution so as to hasten the day of their own: the proletarian. Additionally, after the notion of minimum (bourgeois) revolution and maximum (proletarian) revolution was accepted and became almost old hat, they added the idea of permanent revolution--the proletariat in helping the bourgeoisie would retain whatever power and position they achieved in the bourgeois revolution so as to **shorten** the time until the next revolution. They did not realize that, although shortening the time allotted for capitalism would appeal to their frustrations, they would be shortening the capitalist period that Marx had felt so essential to build the wealth that socialism and communism were to share. Without a sufficiently long capitalism, the communism that succeeded it would share poverty.

In 1914 the outbreak of the First World War ended the Second International to all intents and purposes. In the late months of that war, however, two revolutions would occur. The revolution in Germany that established the Weimar Republic was supported by a German socialism that had, thanks to Bernstein, lost its revolutionary edge. In Russia after an initial, popular upheaval in March 1917, the revolution was guided eight months later into Marxist channels by Lenin and the Bolsheviks. For the first time in history, the dream of equality, the ideas of community of goods, of sharing, of brother/sisterhood, of the secular Kingdom of Heaven were going to be tried in practice for an entire state.

Endnotes
Chapter Eight

1. Edmund Wilson, *To the Finland Station: A Study in the Writing and Acting of History* (Garden City: Doubleday & Co., Inc., 1953), p. 70.

2. Ibid., p. 76.

3. Ibid.

4. Albert Fried And Ronald Sanders, eds., *Socialist Thought: A Documentary History* (Garden City: Doubleday & Co., Inc., 1964), p. 64. John Locke would agree with this position, but disagree with the implications of the idea.

5. Ibid., p. 70. Italics in the original.

6. Ibid., pp. 51-56.

7. James R. Ozinga, *Communism: The Story of the Idea and Its Implementation*, Second Edition (Englewood Cliffs, NJ: Prentice Hall, 1991), p. 12.

8. Karl Marx and Friedrich Engels, *Marx-Engels Selected Works (MESW)* in three volumes (Moscow: Progress Publishers, 1970),p. 504.

9. Karl Marx, *Grundrisse*, David McLellan, trans. and ed. (New York: Harper & Row, 1971), p. 151. Recall that Marx included raw materials and machinery in a prior calculation that had the factory owner paying surplus value to the suppliers. Such "frozen suplus value" was not, therefore, a part of the final calculation of profit.

10. Ibid., pp. 87-93.

11. George W. F. Hegel, *The Phenomenology of the Spirit* in Carl Friedrich, trans. and ed., *The Philosophy of Hegel* (New York: Random House, 1954), p. 409.

12. Karl Marx, "Economic and Philosophic Manuscripts of 1844," in Loyd D. Easton and Kurt H. Guddat, eds., *Writings of the Young Marx on Philosophy and Society* (Garden City, NY: Doubleday & Co., Inc., 1967), p. 304.

13. Friedrich Engels, "Preface to Marx's Class Struggles in France, 1848-1850," in *MESW, op. cit.*, vol 1, p. 189.

14. Ibid., p. 187.

15. Karl Marx, "Class Struggles in France, 1848-1850," *MESW, op. cit.*, vol 1, p. 289.

16. Engels, "Letter to J. Wedemeyer, April 12, 1853," *Marx-Engels Selected Correspondence* (Moscow: Foreign Languages Publishing House, n.d.), p. 94.

17. Marx, "Letter to Engels in Manchester, April 16, 1856," *MESW, op. cit.*, vol 1, p. 529.

18. Ibid., pp. 529 and 120, vol 2, p. 291, vol 3, p. 31; *Marx-Engels Selected Correspondence*, p. 94; and *Marx-Engels Selected Works in Two Volumes* (London: Martin Lawrence, Ltd., 1942), p. 614.

19. Karl Marx, *The Poverty of Philosophy* (Moscow: Foreign Languages Publishing House, n.d.), p. 167.

20. Friedrich Engels, "Introduction to the Civil War in France," *MESW, op. cit.*, vol 2, p. 188.

21. Friedrich Engels, "Origin of the Family, Private Property and the State," in ibid., vol 3, pp. 248-255.

22. Friedrich Engels, *Herr Eugene Dühring's Revolution in Science (Anti-Dühring)* (New York: International Publishers, 1939), pp. 323-324; and *The Housing Question* (New York: International Publishers, n.d.), pp. 36, 95-96.

23. Karl Marx, *Grundrisse, op. cit.*, pp. 74-76, 142.

24. Ibid., pp. 148-149, and Friedrich Engels, *The Housing Question,* *op. cit.*, pp. 29-30.

25. Friedrich Engels, "Origins of the Family, Private Property and the State," *MESW, op. cit.*, vol 3, p. 266.

26. Eduard Bernstein, *Evolutionary Socialism*, Edith C. Harvey, trans. (New York: B. W. Huebsch, 1912), pp. 142-144.

27. Karl Marx, "Critique of the Gotha Programme," in *MESW, op. cit.*, vol 3, pp. 16-17.

28. James R. Ozinga, *op. cit.*, pp. 73-74.

29. Eduard Bernstein, *op. cit.*, pp. 210-211.

30. Alfred G. Meyer, *The Feminism and Socialism of Lily Braun* (Bloomington, IN: Indiana University Press, 1985), p. 42.

31. Ibid., p. 85.

32. Bullit Lowry and Elizabeth Ellington Günther, *The Red Virgin-- Memoirs of Louise Michel* (University, AL: University of Alabama Press, 1981), p. 196.

33. Eduard Bernstein, *op. cit.*, p. 146.

34. Ibid., pp. 148ff.

Chapter Nine

Practical Communism as a Failed State Ideology

Russia
China
Cold War Communism: Cambodia and Cuba

The implementation of communism in both Russia and China resulted in the imposition of a harsh authoritarian rule even though the purpose of the revolution was to bring about equality, abundance, and a society of brothers and sisters. Russia and China were backward societies in that both were still basically feudal, poor, and hungry when the ideology of communism was applied. In both societies, instead of describing the organizational form of equality and caring, communism became the method of overcoming poverty and backwardness. When discussed at all communism was a distant goal, as the brother/sisterhood concept would be among a group of Christians. The communism in both societies became the method of **building** the capitalism necessary for future wealth, and that building became the operative ideology while communism itself became a distant dream of affluence manipulated on behalf of the leader, whether that was Stalin in Russia or Mao Zedong in China.

Russia

The attempts to implement the dream in Russia took place in the four year span between 1917 when the Bolsheviks seized power and 1921 when the Communist Party of the Soviet Union at its Tenth Party Congress caved in to authoritarian rule and voted to prohibit all disagreement with top party leaders. Eventually the ideology shifted from communism to physical survival, and attempts to legislate Russia into the golden age gave way to attempts to build the wealth that Russia lacked. After 1928 the ideology was inseparable from the five year plans that annually ratcheted output targets ever higher in an effort to catch up with and surpass Western production levels. Communism came to mean passing the United States in affluence, both in the 1930s and later under Khrushchev in the early 1960s.[1]

In a way this sorry eventuality was predictable if one considers the discussions among the revolutionary theorists in the late nineteenth century. They sought to apply an ideology to feudal Russia which was meant to be applied to the last stages of capitalism. Such a discussion did not mean that **they** were wrong to do this; Marx was wrong in anticipating that his proletarian revolution would occur in advanced capitalist countries. It still hasn't occurred there despite the passage of well over a century. The problem that arose was not that Marxism was a holy canon that should never be reinterpreted, but rather that the Russian revolutionary discussion had unforeseen consequences. The Russians concluded that because they lived in a society still feudal, the next revolution for them according to historical materialism was the bourgeois one. But Russia had very few bourgeoisie because of the nature and brevity of the Russian industrialization.

What industrialization had occurred in Russia in the latter half of the nineteenth century developed under the control of the tsarist government and was implemented for the purpose of strengthening the state. Such selective capitalism did not do Russia much good because in the terrible war in the Crimea (1854-1856) she lost to Britain and her allies France, Turkey, and Sardinia. In the war with tiny Japan (1904-1905), the Russians lost badly, and the resulting discouragement helped begin the 1905 disturbances that historians call a revolution. In World War I (1914-1918) Russia did not do well against Germany either, but then neither did France and Britain. Moreover, the selective capitalization in Russia organized from the top down meant the kind of state control of investment capital that precluded an evolution of private entrepreneurs or capitalists as had occurred in Britain.

The Russian revolutionaries realized that these facts meant that there was an extremely low number of capitalists with which to accomplish a capitalist (bourgeois) revolution to begin the process that would eventually lead to the proletarian triumph. According to theory they weren't even in the game until all that happened. So, as noted in Chapter Eight, the idea arose that the already existing industrial workers would assist the weak bourgeoisie to achieve the bourgeois revolution.

Assisting in this revolution would open the door to the capitalist mode of production, still some distance, of course, from the proletarian revolution they also sought. To avoid the discouraging prospects of such a lengthy wait before the **real** revolution occurred, revolutionary theorists decided that they could **shorten** the capitalist time period by retaining whatever power or position they had attained during the bourgeois revolution, implementing what they called a permanent revolution. It did not occur to them that in shortening capitalism they were inhibiting the growth of the wealth they hoped to share.

And, moving from theory to practice, what the Russian rebels did not anticipate was that this desire to shorten the length of capitalism would result in an absurdly short eight months long capitalist period running from March to November 1917. Lenin, writing just after the Bolsheviks seized power in 1917, stated that the bourgeois revolution in Russia had begun with the 1905 Russian "revolution" and had culminated in the revolution in March 1917, while the November 1917 affair allowed the Bolsheviks to "...march fearlessly toward socialism."[2] This shortening of the capitalist period fundamentally distorted their efforts to implement the dream. But that is getting ahead of the story.

Russia, as an ally of Britain and France, entered the war in 1914 against Germany. There was a good deal of fanfare in the beginning; troops marching to the colors, parades of weapons and troops before the tsar and tsarina, troops and weapons blessed by the leader of the Russian Orthodox Church, and the usual bombastic claims of early victory against a demoralized enemy. However, they marched off to war singularly unprepared to fight a modern war. Many Russian troops were unarmed, and some were armed with weapons that weren't modern in the previous war against Japan and were barely modern in the Crimea against the British. Cavalry charges were made against machine gun emplacements, for example. Had Germany not been fighting a two front war, Russia would have been overwhelmed. As it was, the war settled down into a dull and dangerous trench war that drained Russia of manpower and depleted scarce reserves. By 1917 cities were hard pressed to find food and fuel in the winter, while the rural areas were increasingly the scenes of peasant riots against the economic and cultural ties that held them in perpetual bondage on the landlords' estates.

In March 1917 strikes and demonstrations broke out in Petrograd, then the capital of Russia. What the people wanted was food to eat and fuel to keep warm. The demonstrations and strikes, **not** led by any party or group, grew from very small beginnings into a sizable force. Cossacks refused to dispel the crowds because they were merely demonstrating for food. The Russian Army stationed in Petrograd refused to fire on fellow Russians. Only the small and basically ineffectual police force tried to hold back the demonstrations, but the police eventually found themselves barricaded in their police stations.

Tsar Nicholas II, tried to get back to Petrograd from Mogilév where he had been trying to lead the stalled Russian war effort, but he could not get back. His train was stopped by railroad workers who refused to allow it through, and he abdicated in favor of his brother who refused the honor unless elected by the people. In this confusion an election was impossible so the Romanov dynasty came to an inglorious end.

The absence of political order caused a fairly liberal provisional government to emerge from the weak parliament called the Duma, the tsar's timid response to the revolution in 1905. At about the same time a rival government called the Soviet of Workers and Soldiers' Deputies organized itself. The Soviet, as it was called, was more democratic, more in touch with common people, and more leftist than the provisional government, but the provisional government had a legitimacy that the Soviet did not have. This balance gradually began shifting in the direction of the Soviet because the provisional government made three errors that eventually cost it its life. These errors, of course, become very visible in hindsight. It is far easier to spot errors after the fact than during the process itself, whether that is a football game or governmental activity.

The first error was costly: the provisional government continued the war against Germany despite the fact that it was draining Russia and was principally responsible for the people's revolution in March. Continuing the war was not a good idea; it was not successful militarily and it cost the provisional government a great deal of support.

Secondly, the provisional government appointed a committee to study the land question rather than simply giving the peasants the land the government did not control anyway. Instead of recognizing the strong momentum in the countryside running against landlords and siding with the revolutionary flow, the provisional government listened to the many landlords who supported them and gave people the impression that they desired to return to the old system people thought they had left behind. In many cases peasant seizures of landlords' estates made the question of land ownership academic anyway. Giving the land to the peasants would have created for the provisional government the appearance of being both liberal and in control; not solving this volatile issue through inaction simply made more enemies. It was a serious mistake.

Thirdly, their legitimacy was temporary. Even their name underscored their temporariness. Instead of calling for nearly **immediate** elections to a constituent assembly to write a new constitution for a new government, the provisional government postponed these elections over and over again; and in the process, during the radicalizing environment in the summer and fall of 1917, they stretched their own legitimacy to the breaking point.

The Soviet of Workers and Soldier's Deputies, on the other hand, basically composed of delegates from the military and the factories, provided an increasingly attractive alternative between March and November 1917 as the provisional government erred its way into oblivion. In the beginning the Soviet was only loosely socialist, with a minority of Leninists (Bolsheviks) in attendance, and lacked any clear direction. This changed after Lenin was allowed to return to Russia in April 1917. A sealed train, authorized by the Germans, took him and his party from their exile in Zurich across wartime Germany to Finland where he could change trains to travel to Petrograd.

When he arrived at the Finland Station in Petrograd, he astounded his mostly Bolshevik audience by calling for **Soviet** power and appearing to know exactly what to do. The Bolsheviks did not control the Soviet at this point, but, Lenin argued, this could change. As, of course, it did. His other slogans were clear and meant sincerely; Peace, Bread to the Worker, Land to the Tiller, and Worker Control of Industry. Sort of a Leninist version of Winstanley's Work Together, Eat Bread Together.

As the summer months came and went, the situation in Petrograd and Moscow grew worse rather than better, and the more radical ideas pushed by the Bolsheviks seemed more and more reasonable to a population ever more anxious for solutions. The tsarist army was disintegrating even though the war was continuing. Lenin realized that the time to act was upon them. His theories about imperialism and the final end of capitalism seemed to be materializing before his eyes. He wrote that doubt was out of the question, that they were on the threshold of a world proletarian revolution, and that of all of the proletarians in the world only the Russians had the freedom to act.[3] Other Bolshevik leaders were reluctant, and he had to threaten to resign before they would agree to act. After a good deal of discussion and an exposé of their seizure plans in a rival newspaper, the Bolsheviks finally moved against the government. They seized communications, stormed the Winter Palace, overpowered the weak defenses, arrested the officers of the provisional government, and established a Soviet government led by Bolsheviks.

For the first time in history, Marxists were in charge of a state. This state was not at the end of productive capitalism but at its beginning.

It was, however, at the end of a debilitating and draining war. There was **no** wealth to share, there wasn't even food. By 1921 cannibalism would reappear in the Russian countryside, a ghastly mockery of the humanist aspirations of the revolution just a few years before.

In spite of all this there were very strong efforts by Lenin, immediately after arriving in Russia from Zurich, to distinguish **his** party from those who had made up the majority of the Second International. He urged his followers to change the name of their party from Bolshevik to Communist, arguing that the social democratic parties had "betrayed" the revolution. The word communist, instead of being synonymous with the word socialist in the Marxist lexicon, began referring instead to Lenin's Bolsheviks. They were the communists. After the formation of the Third International in 1919, membership of which was open only to "communists" or Marxists who agreed with Lenin's seizure of power in Russia (many did not), it became apparent to the world that the word that formerly designated the higher stage of socialism now designated the Bolshevik party in charge of a very backward country.

Oddly enough, however, despite the renaming of the party and the use of the word "communism" to separate Leninist Marxists from other Marxists around the world, communism did not really change meaning in Russia. Instead of treating the word as basically devoid of any real meaning, people, including Lenin, talked as though the word still referred to a higher stage of socialism coming in the future. Lenin did not argue that this higher stage had been achieved in Russia. Far from it. He was well aware that Russia was a long, long way from communism of equality, brother/sisterhood and a sharing of affluence, particularly if one considered the man in the street whose idea of communism frequently seemed to be the removal of all social restraints on behavior. Men raped women under the illusion that women now belonged to everyone, still property but now property belonging to any that desired it. Peoples' homes were broken into under the illusion that no one had a right to have something not possessed by others; like wine and whiskey. Lenin anticipated this by stating darkly in July 1917 that although the great socialists had anticipated the coming of communism, they did not assume either the low productivity in Russia or the "unthinking man on the street capable of spoiling, without reflection, the stores of social wealth and of demanding the impossible."[4]

Although Lenin knew this before the November seizure of power, he felt that these Russian limitations could be ignored because he was supremely confident that revolutions in other countries would quickly come to the aid of the Russian revolutionaries. The idea of an **international** revolution was an object of belief not to be questioned at this point. According to the theory of imperialism, Russia had been the weak link in the international chain of imperialistic profiteering. That link was now broken, he argued, and it was only a matter of time before the revolutionary fervor in the advanced industrial countries rose to the point of explosion. They would then show the Russians what to do.

So even though he seemed to identify the word "communist" with his own party and ideology, he was well aware that it had not yet come in Russia and that it would be a long time coming. He wrote in January 1918, just two months after gaining power, that he had no illusions about their just having entered the period of *transition* to socialism, about not yet having reached socialism. But, he continued, if you say that our state is a socialistic Republic of Soviets, you will be right--as right as those who call many Western bourgeois republics democratic republics although everybody knows that not even a very democratic republic is completely democratic. No, we are far from having completed the transition from capitalism to socialism, he wrote. To do so we need the international proletariat. We have no illusions on that score and the road leading from capitalism to socialism is fraught with difficulties.[5]

The idea of equality expressed as **communism** was at this point still attached to a dream of the future. In the early days after the Bolshevik seizure of power in Russia the dream lived on. In the same volume that deplored the possibility of a Russian communism because of low productivity and unthinking people on the streets, Lenin argued that the communism coming in the Russian future would be a part of a new and different world. The entire society, he thought, would be like one office and one factory with equal work and pay for everyone. What would eventually govern this society was a sort of factory discipline so internalized as to be unnoticed. This discipline would result in people's observation of simple, fundamental rules of social life. When this had occurred, the initial stage of socialism could be left behind. The way would be clear for the introduction of communism, the second and higher level, and the coercive powers of a state would no longer be needed.[6]

Even earlier, in 1913, Lenin's idea of communism was clearer and more optimistic. The distinction between town and country and between manual and mental work would disappear. Social wealth would be easily produced because capitalism would not be holding back productivity. New technology, symbolized by electricity, would make everyone's task easier and shorter, and open up an international fresh start in which oppression, poverty, privilege, and disunity would disappear. Agriculture and industry would unify around collective labor. Children's education would combine productive labor with instruction and gymnastics, resulting in improved social producers and more fully developed human beings. There would be neither rich nor poor because everyone would draw from the common store, and the shelves in those stores would be laden with goods because people working for themselves worked much harder than they did for others. For Lenin as it was for Marx, communism meant the **emancipation** of humanity.[7]

This was Lenin's dream of what the future would hold, and this view of the future would also be that of the Bolshevik party as a whole, since these ideas had been already published in party papers in 1913. In 1917-1918, however, the Bolsheviks faced the question of not just **what** the future society would look like, but also **how** to get there.

At first one could argue that they should wait until expected revolutions occurred in the developed countries, because then the developed countries would take the lead and show the Bolsheviks what to do. But as time passed, and the only "revolutions" after the war were a mild one in Germany (Weimar Republic) and a coup in Hungary that briefly seemed promising (Bela Kun), it became clear that revolutions elsewhere were not going to happen as Lenin's theory of imperialism had predicted. The Bolsheviks were on their own, ruling the only country in the world professing to have had a socialist revolution. The Russian leaders began to look around them with some pride. Despite the beginnings of terrible civil wars in 1918, awful chaos in the country, and interventions against them by some fourteen nations, they demonstrated that they could remain in power. Simply continuing to stay in power, at first longer than the ten weeks of the Paris Commune of 1871, then longer than a year, then two years...assumed great significance. The torch of human emancipation they carried was carried by *the Bolsheviks* alone, and this notion lent a pleasant communist gloss to what would otherwise appear to be simply staying in power; a use of ideology bureaucrats have perfected all over the world. Even when the disastrous treaty of Brest-Litovsk in March

1918 that ended the war with Germany seemed the worst thing ever to happen to Russia, they could **still** argue that the treaty allowed them to stay in power. Listeners would nod their heads in agreement. Staying in power had become a significant thing in itself and whatever means had to be used to continue in power were justified on the basis of the dream. Naturally the baby is in danger of being thrown out with the bath water but the dangers of narrow authoritarianism were blunted by the ends supposedly sought.

And those goals **were** still being sought in the early years. Despite the bloody civil war, military seizure of territory, foreign interventions, lack of food and fuel, rampant inflation, and a shrinking Russian empire, the ideological goal was at this point still not forgotten. Many of the Bolsheviks became impatient for **some** movement toward communism. This created a momentum of **legislating** the nation into that desired future, particularly during 1918 and 1919. Some of the new laws did not last long, but the intent was there. This was not Revisionism, because they felt that they had gone past the proletarian revolution.

Laws were passed and decrees issued that recognized the end of the war with Germany, established worker control of factories, abolished property in land and nationalized all wealth including that held in banks, permitted no hired labor, elected a Council of People's Commissars to run things, affirmed the rights of all ethnic groups, abolished all classes and class distinctions, civil grades, and ranks and insignias in the army, replaced the former legal system with revolutionary tribunals, separated the Russian Orthodox church from the state, appointed a Patriarch for the church that had not had one since Peter the Great, liberalized marriage and divorce, abolished inheritance, and nationalized all mineral rights, industry, commerce, and foreign trade. The socialization of the means of production clearly meant the **nationalization** of the means of production to Lenin and the Bolsheviks. They may have been pressed by the very real needs of the moment, or they simply may not have understood any other way of accomplishing that goal; but their otherwise decent efforts failed to realize that nationalizing the means of production placed all economic initiative in the hands of the state--the entity that was supposed to wither and disappear.

In March 1919 the Communist party (Bolshevik) adopted the Second Party Program. This Program called for the emancipation of women, an end to ethnic privilege, full democracy, the right of former tsarist colonies to separate from Moscow, and for vast improvements in housing and schooling. Industry and agriculture should be improved so that the work day was only six hours. Later in the Third Party Program adopted in 1961, the Program designed to move the Soviet Union to the beginnings of full communism, it was obvious that although the rhetoric of communism had not been forgotten, the means of reaching it were entirely economic.

The affluence for everyone to share, however, which Marx had assumed would flow automatically out of the socialization of the means of production, **had to be built** in Russia. Right from the beginning the dream was sidetracked in order to build the basis of the dream, and *building the wealth rather than sharing the wealth became the goal.* In the language of Chalmers Johnson, the goal-culture was subsumed into the transfer-culture, as the ideology became the dogma of production.[8]

This tendency was reinforced by continuing intimations of illiberal authoritarianism and the justification of that authoritarianism on the basis of the need to stay in power and the need to build wealth rapidly. Examples are not difficult to find. Two days after seizing power all opposition newspapers were closed down. About seven weeks after November 7th, *Cheka* was established to maintain order. *Cheka*, the Russian initials for the All Russian Commission for Suppression of Counter-revolution, Sabotage, and Speculation, was the forerunner of the KGB. This paramilitary organization dispensed what was called "proletarian justice," summarily executing offenders when it seemed necessary. The Cadet party was declared counter-revolutionary as early as December 1917.

In January 1918 the elected Constituent Assembly was prevented from meeting, the Red Army was organized under Trotskii, complete with ranks and insignia, and the death penalty for desertion was brought back. Former Tsarist officers were hired to flesh out the Red Army, and former capitalists were hired at high wages to bring productivity back to the factories. And the final example of the way things were going was the *coup de grâce* to hopes for communism: the prohibition on factionalism at the Tenth Party Congress. Keep the same leaders in power and produce, produce, produce! The objectives might be understandable, but this was **not** why they had become revolutionaries. Their method of reaching their goal had become their goal.

After 1921 it might be argued that some attempts were made, perhaps not wisely or well, to create a communist society. The collectivization of agriculture, for example, created agricultural communes that might be imagined as similar to examples of communism in earlier chapters.

Stalin began the collectivization of agriculture with great suddenness in 1928. The reason was not ideological, that is, he did not push the Soviet Union in this direction because he wanted the countryside to be more communistic. The reasons had more to do with control of the countryside and the need to extract an agricultural surplus from the rural areas despite rural opposition.

The countryside had undergone tremendous changes since the Bolsheviks took over in 1917. The large estates, from which a surplus could be regularly expected, had been eliminated by peasant unrest. The result was a strong movement away from large estates to approximately 25.5 million individual peasant farms. Most of these were small farms of less than thirty acres and they tended to be under-equipped and inefficiently run.[9] A surplus of grain was less evident here, and with so many peasant farmers involved it proved difficult to even locate a possible surplus. During the mid 1920s, moreover, farmers began to learn the old lessons of withholding grain from the market so as to force up the price. The cities needed to be fed, but Stalin also needed an agricultural surplus to export so that he could pay for industrial imports.

In December 1927 Stalin ordered that force be used to extract grain from peasant hoarders, and early the next year he ordered the forced collectivization of the rural areas of the Soviet Union. Of the approximately 25 million peasant farms, about 24 percent were run by poor peasants who in general possessed neither livestock or machinery. The largest group, about 72 percent, was made up of middle peasants who had modest livings and wanted no radical changes. Only about 4 percent were the rich peasants or *kulaki*; industrious and prosperous farmers who wanted no part of collectivization.[10]

The only peasants who welcomed the collectivization were those who had something to gain from the move to collective farms. All those, whether middle or rich peasants, who had livestock and equipment of their own, saw collectivization as a loss of individual property to the collective. These latter folk tended to resist collectivization, and all resisters were labelled *kulaki*.

The collectivization of agriculture in the Soviet Union, therefore, quickly became a class war against the middle and rich peasants who resisted. The ideology was used not only to mask the systematic murder of millions of people in the name of the dream of a better future, but was also used to mask the greed of the poor peasants who were promised the cattle and machinery of the middle and rich peasants who were killed or moved away in boxcars, like unvalued cattle, with a one-way ticket to a gulag in Siberia.

The result of these policies was a terrible chaos in the countryside; the systematic uprooting of the most productive and efficient farmers; coupled with a forcible extraction of grain by the state that often left none to be sown as seed in the following year. Famine, caused by Stalin's short-sighted stubbornness, cost millions of lives particularly in Ukraine. Cannibalism ironically returned to the black earth area that was so rich in agricultural potential. The drive to collectivize slowed a bit in 1930 but never really stopped, and by 1938 some 93.5 percent of all farms were collectivized.[11]

The collectivization campaign was brutal and it benefitted no one: neither the state, nor the farms, nor the peasants. Because they didn't want to lose their animals or machinery to the collective, peasants frequently slaughtered and ate their animals and destroyed their tools before coming to the collective. Ironically some died from overeating while millions died from famine. But the net result was that the collective received neither the livestock nor the machinery. What was shared was poverty. Although the government introduced the death penalty for destroying livestock or machinery, the collectives started from very poor levels and were, for several decades, systematically underfinanced by a state eager to purchase industrialization no matter what the cost to agriculture or to people who needed food to survive. As a result the collective agriculture in the Soviet Union was a poor relation to the industrial sector throughout most of Soviet history.

The collective farm, *kollektivnoie khoziaistovo*, was theoretically an agricultural cooperative operated by its members. Still in theory, the collective was composed of volunteers and run democratically. Members acting through their associations on the farm elected their officers, determined who should join or be excluded from the collective, selected production goals, and determined the level of remuneration to pay themselves. Theoretically. Speaking practically none of the above was true. They were normally not volunteers, they were often forced to collectivize at gunpoint. The party selected officials to lead the collective, printed their names on a ballot and let the members elect them in a travesty of a political process. State officials, often hundreds of miles away in different climate zones, told the collective farm officials when to plant and when to harvest, how much the state required this year and how much to pay the members. The machinery of the collective was not owned by the members but by the state and kept at machine tractor stations (MTS) under party control until 1958 when the MTS were disbanded.[12]

The only continuously successful part of collective farms was the private plot. Usually no more than 2 acres per peasant, the private plot by law was limited to 1 cow, 2 calves, 1 sow, 10 sheep or goats, unlimited fowl and rabbits, and not more than 20 beehives.[13] Because the peasant could sell the produce from the private plot on the open market, these plots received the most intensive attention from farmers who paid far less attention to the collective farm needs. This was a major irritant to the ideologue who thought people should work harder on the collective acres, but the private plots produced such a large quantity of eggs, vegetables and meat that moves against them were counterproductive. The country depended on private plots.

The loss of capital in the rural areas, combined with the annual underinvestment in agriculture by the state, made it impossible for the collectives to succeed in any real sense, even if the forced nature of their beginning could have been forgotten. The ending of the machine tractor stations sent many thousands of skilled mechanics and laborers into the collectives and this had a positive but limited effect on production. Except for a brief period in the mid-1950s when new lands in Kazakhstan were brought into cultivation, Soviet agriculture dismally failed to keep pace with the growth in the Soviet population.

As an example of forced communization imperfectly implemented, the Soviet collectivization of agriculture should be ranked, along with other elements of the Stalin era, the furthest possible distance from the humanitarian, sharing goals that should define communism.

The Russian revolutionaries three years after they had seized power had but a slim chance to resist nearly a millennium of authoritarianism so as to implement a meaningful communist society. That they did not succeed is not surprising. What is astounding is that they did not seem to recognize what they failed to accomplish. What they succeeded in building was not communism, but a nineteenth century economic system one might call authoritarian capitalism.

Daniel Chirot's description of the five stages or ages of Western industrial development makes this assessment easier to understand. Chirot wrote that the ages, with their approximate dates, were:

(1) The cotton-textile age led by Great Britain from about the 1780s into the 1830s.

(2) The rail and iron age, dominated again by Britain, running from

the 1840s into the early 1870s.

(3) The steel and organic chemistry age, one that also saw the development of new industries based on the production and the use of electrical machinery, which ran from the 1870s to World War I. The American and German economies dominated.

(4) The age of automobiles and petrochemicals running from the 1910s to the 1970s. The United States became the overwhelmingly hegemonic economy.

(5) The age of electronics, information, and biotechnology. This last age began in the 1970s and should continue well into the first half of the next century. The dominating economy is not yet clear, although certainly the Japanese and West Europeans seem capable of replacing the Americans.[14]

Those who planned the construction of wealth in the Soviet Union were people like Lenin and Stalin and their cohorts who fixated on the third age as modern capitalism. When they looked to see what capitalism was, that was what they saw. They didn't look again. So, held back by the devastations of two world wars they succeeded finally in constructing a stage three economy they imagined might challenge a United States economy already at the end of stage four and about to enter stage five. What is truly amazing is that Western economists believed the challenge as thoroughly as did Soviet leaders. It is no wonder then that the technology implied by "Star Wars" frightened Soviet leaders and helped to cause the dissolution of the USSR; it highlighted the tremendous gulf between the two economies.

Not only had the Soviets not built communism, they had not even built a modern capitalism. (That's more than a little sad.)

China

The difficulty in analyzing China is that China imported so much of the Bolshevik experience. Probably one of the most significant impacts of the Bolshevik seizure of power in 1917 was the signal given to Chinese liberals that anti-capitalist Marxism could be used to justify a modernizing revolution in a backward country. One did not have to wait until capitalism had developed and waned; the process could be hastened by Marxist revolutionaries eager to move history forward.

In the Marxist society begun by Li Dazhao in 1917, revolutionary Marxism was discussed with reference to China. This topic picked up considerable excitement after the November seizure of power by the Bolsheviks. One of the people involved in this small society was Mao

Zedong.

Why were intellectuals seeking an anti-West revolutionary ideology that might apply to China? They were anti-West because of the extremely humiliating imperialism suffered by China in the 19th century. Western countries, Britain in particular, treated China as a profitable way stop on the Britain - India trade route. Chinese tea became very popular in Britain and ships would carry this cargo from China to Britain, but from India to China there were few cargos picked up in India that could be sold in China or traded for the tea. In the absence of such cargoes the tea trade from China to Britain developed into a silver drain as cash had to be paid for the tea. The solution was opium, picked up in India, and sold in China where its addictive nature would guarantee a continuing market and make the importing of tea much more profitable.

The Chinese government prohibited the sale of opium, but British ships smuggled the product in with the help of well-paid Chinese. As a result war broke out between China and Britain and for twenty-one years (1839-1860), China fought unsuccessfully against Britain in what were loosely called the Opium Wars. The humiliating loss by China not only permitted the sale of opium, but cost the Chinese control over several port areas, including Hong Kong and Shanghai. Queen Victoria declared Hong Kong to be a British Crown Colony in April 1843.[15] Other Western nations forced concessions as well.

The right to send missionaries to China was nearly as difficult to obtain as the right to sell opium. Perhaps because the opium and the missionary often came on the same boat, the Chinese position might be understandable. The Christian religion appealed to some Chinese, but to many others it was a foreign intrusion that China was powerless to prevent. When Chinese were kidnapped and forcibly removed to South, Central, and North America for use as cheap labor, the Chinese often blamed *all* foreign devils. In this context a Roman Catholic convent could believably be accused of kidnapping or killing Chinese children. This anti-Christian violence stimulated Western military retaliation which the Chinese central government could not repel. The more the Chinese rebelled, therefore, the worse their position became.

Even so revolts occurred, and some were communist. The Taiping rebels, for example, were active from 1850 to 1864. They were led by a man who believed he was a special emissary of the Christian God. Hong Xiuquan declared himself the Heavenly King in charge of the Heavenly Kingdom of Great Peace with its capital in Nanjing. The

Taiping rebels wanted a social revolution that would drive out the Manchu rulers of China, end private ownership of land, improve the status of women, end the opium traffic, and set up a communal society.[16]

Taiping rebels were suppressed by Western military invasions, which further weakened China, particularly in the northeast where Russia established Nikolaievsk, and Vladivostok. British and French forces temporarily occupied Beijing where they spent several days looting and burning the summer palace outside the city.

Floods, famines, plagues, internal disorders, and loss of former satellites Vietnam, Taiwan, Okinawa, and Korea continued China's downward spiral. A disastrous war was lost to Japan, and both Germany and Italy made new demands. The United States forced itself into the predator ranks with its Open Door policy. All this humiliation fed into the Boxer Rebellion in 1899; an anti-foreign and anti-Christian movement that weakened China even more. A confrontation on the Amur River gave Russia the pretext for invading Manchuria.

China faced a heavy burden of humiliation and a crisis of modernization that forced intellectuals to look for revolutionary solutions, preferably solutions that avoided capitalism and were anti-West. The emperor abdicated in 1912, but the year before revolutionaries under Sun Yat Sen had already established the Guomindang (Nationalist) government in the area around Nanjing. After World War I when the Versailles Treaty awarded former German holdings in China to Japan rather than back to China, the humiliation worsened. On May 4, 1919 students, intellectuals, merchants, and workers demonstrated against the West and against weak Chinese governments. Conditions in China radicalized and it was in this context that Marxism emerged as a possible solution to China's problems.

The Bolshevik seizure of power had demonstrated that Marxism could be applied to a backward society even before capitalism had developed very far. It seemed anti-West because the West was so hostile to the Bolshevik takeover. Moreover, Marxism did not insist on capitalism but transcended it--an idea that appealed to the notion of Chinese superiority. In the beginning Bolshevik Russia did not seem imperialistic toward China and this was a plus. Many other aspects of Marxism could be interpreted as basically Chinese thoughts; the dialectic of Hegel and Marx could be conceived, for example, as the yin and the yang of Taoism. In 1921 when the Third International (Comintern) called a meeting, a delegation from China attended, representing a new Chinese Communist party (CCP).

The new party took orders from the Comintern, which meant orders from Moscow. Initially these orders were to attach themselves to the Guomindang reform movement under Chiang Kai Shek. This backfired in 1927 when Chiang moved against the CCP and nearly destroyed it. Mao Zedong and others fled to the south where they established peasant armies to fight against Chiang, but their position became untenable in 1934, and they were forced to flee the area. This began the Long March, a long dangerous trek from the south of China to the northwest, a journey that decimated the party and left Mao Zedong in charge in Yenan. He was no longer taking orders from the Comintern, which stupidly wanted Mao and the Red Army to take cities so that they would have a proletariat! When the Red Army had attempted this, disaster normally followed, so Mao stopped listening to Comintern orders and developed his party and his army from peasant rather than proletarian forces.

With the Long March over, and the Red Army encamped at Yenan, Mao Zedong had his first intimations of what communist life might be like. There was hardship at Yenan, but there was also brother and sisterhood. Hardship was shared and made less burdensome. Everyone seemed to be pulling in the same direction--not for themselves, but for the good of the whole. Although Mao would sometimes sound like a Soviet Marxist, the Yenan experience encapsulated his idea of the communist future. After 1949 when the Red Army successfully drove Guomindang forces across the sea to Taiwan, Mao Zedong would continue to seek that Yenan experience for the whole Chinese population.

During the early period after 1949 when Mao's influence was stronger, material incentives were played down in favor of ideological or spiritual incentives. He did not insist that everyone live in poverty, but he did feel that spiritual factors were more important than material wealth. Because there was so much pressure to make material factors more important, Mao probably overdid the spiritual side. Neither he nor Deng Xiaoping who succeeded Mao properly understood the balance between spiritual and material factors and both pushed one to the near exclusion of the other.

During the Great Leap Forward (GLF) in 1958-1960, for example, it appeared as though the Chinese were getting onto the production bandwagon begun by the Soviets, seeking communism by outproducing Great Britain. But there was a kicker in the Great Leap Forward. The rural communes were supposed to bypass socialism and move directly into communism. This rural communism would spread throughout the entire decentralized society. In the later years after the failure of the GLF, during the Mao-sponsored Cultural Revolution from 1966 to 1976, party bureaucrats were repeatedly told to go to the peasants for answers, for inspiration, for a sense of how to conduct party and national life. The Yenan experience was still to be picked up from the peasantry, from common, uneducated people. Centuries before it would have been mechanic preachers but still the emphasis on the common: when Adam delved and Eve span, who was then the gentleman? After Mao's death in 1976, there was no one with influence left to push China in this revolutionary direction. The country appeared happy to drift into a pursuit of material wealth while still under the control of the aging CPC.

Mao Zedong was by no means perfect, nor was he necessarily correct about the course he proposed for China. He may not have been a good Marxist, whatever that might mean. He romanticized the peasantry as Marx romanticized the proletariat. Someone might argue that Mao's leftwing ideological approach would have been a major disaster for China, arguing professorially that there is a time for revolution and a time to put things back together. Mao often gave the impression that he wanted to pull apart (and keep apart) what others had put together. Such critical people use a different perspective than is being used here. Here the perspective is that of successfully implementing communism. That perspective suggests that China's inability to follow Mao was the disaster, not Mao Zedong himself. One might argue that to follow the Gang of Four, as they were called in 1976, was tantamount to leading China away from success toward chaos and confusion. There is no denying that this was probably true. The definition of success would vary, however, between a communist and a member of the CPC. The communist would argue that success meant the spread of the spirit of Yenan over the entire billion population of China and until that was accomplished nothing was a success no matter what was produced or gained. The party member might have other ideas, of course, arguing that the spirit of Yenan was not appropriate for an industrialized country like China with a hydrogen bomb and a major voice in world affairs in 1976. Who was right?

Communism was implemented neither in Russia nor in China. In Russia it had only the briefest of chances before losing out to authoritarianism. In China the possibility of communism was at least as remote as for Russia, but as long as Mao sought to recreate the Yenan experience in Chinese life, there was some room for hope. When Mao died in 1976, however, the dream died with him.

Cold War Communism
Cambodia and Cuba

Communism was the governing ideology in many other countries in the world besides Russia and China, particularly in the three decades from 1950 to 1980. In every case revolutionary leaders thought they were choosing a Marxist kind of communism, but not because they had had a proletarian revolution at the end of a successful capitalism. On the contrary, in every case the experience of Russia or China was replicated. The countries concerned were agricultural rather than industrial, poor in a pre-capitalist sense, illiterate, politically authoritarian, and looking for an economic miracle.

Moreover, communism or Marxism-Leninism was selected as a revolutionary ideology for the so-called national liberation movements in places like Ethiopia, Angola, Nicaragua, and Cuba **after** the leftist revolutionaries had seized power. In Cambodia, on the other hand, the Khmer Rouge were communists prior to their successful seizure of power in 1975. But in all five cases Cold War hostility shaped the desire for communism. The revolutionaries were pushed by that hostility into making a decision between East and West, between some sort of Western-oriented democracy that seemed like the old corrupt regime or a Marxist-Leninist regime that seemed more in tune with their goals.

In some ways the decision was easy. When they took power, these revolutionaries were already leaning left, away from the corrupt "democracies" that had characterized the previous regimes against which they had fought. In addition, the previous regimes had been clients of or parts of Western imperialism and so the leaning away from that was understandable.

When the rebels took power in these poor countries they quickly learned that there were only three ways to go. First, they could try to stay unaligned with either superpower and make it entirely on their own. This was unattractively slow and didn't appeal at all, except to the Khmer because of their ideological commitment to a Chinese style agricultural communism for Cambodia (Kampuchea). Second, the new leaders could reestablish ties with the West. Ties with Western powers, however, had earlier been part of the problem against which they had fought. The second choice would have seemed a betrayal of their principles. Third, these new governments could opt for alliance with the Soviet Union. This would spite the West as well as providing needed economic and military assistance from a non-Western source. Cuba, for example, picked the third choice and linked up with the USSR while Cambodia tried the first choice with a little assistance from China for the few years that they held power. As a result they were encouraged to imitate the structures then present in either the Soviet Union or China: central committees, communist parties, and, of course, five year plans and collectivized agricultures under state control.

In both countries there was a great need to reconstruct the society and build some sort of prosperity, and the prospect of a sustainable, state-controlled construction of wealth was difficult to resist. Also, revolutionaries knew that they would qualify for generous assistance from the Soviet Union (or China in Cambodia's case) because during the Cold War both Soviet Russia and China (as well as the United States) paid well for international friends. This strange fact was often manipulated by smaller nations to generate financial assistance at rather high levels. Albania was a case in point; shifting allegiances from Yugoslavia's Tito to Russia's Stalin to China's Mao Zedong, and then back to a kind of nonalignment.

In the 19th century, during the "Great Game," Russia and Britain fought for influence in central Asia. In the late 1950s, 1960s and 1970s, the struggle for pawns consumed the United States and the Soviet Union, and the communism adopted in smaller countries should be called "Cold War Communism," implying that communism would not have been adopted in these areas had it not been for the continuing stupidity known as the Cold War. The Cold War was a period of overt hostility between the Soviet Union and/or China and the United States that often involved using proxy forces in "little wars" as part of an international struggle to gain friends and influence. Soviet leaders unwisely acted as though any international growth in U.S. influence would stifle the Soviet Union, and leaders in Washington D.C. unwisely felt that any new communism in the world meant increasing the size of some terrible world cancer. The Cold War was a silly dance which made it appear that if one partner took a step forward the other had to step back. Both Soviet Russia and China (as well as the United States) were guilty of incredible blindness about the regimes they supported. They created their own headaches, some of which are highlighted by this chapter.

Just one example of this Cold War blindness might suffice. Cold War communism associated with the third world liberation movements arose in part as a reaction to a U. S. foreign policy that made little sense at the time and even less in retrospect. U.S. economic and military support for corrupt right wing dictatorships, such as the government in El Salvador, was the policy that caused a good deal of Cold War communism. The United States was a responsible cause for the emergence of this sort of communism in many areas of the world. Documents that were released in 1993 revealed that American leaders **knew** about death squad activities by El Salvador officials. Support for the Salvadorian government went on anyway.   The actions of the sadistic death squads included arbitrary arrests, barbarous torture and the murder of innocent men, women, children and even babies on the slightest whim of the official in charge.   Despite the knowledge of the names and positions of specific officials involved in such actions, the United States funded the Salvadorian government's opposition to leftist guerrillas to the tune of $1 billion in the 1980s.[17] That's like fearing the devil instead of loving God.

The communism in East Europe from 1948 to 1989 can be called "Enforced Communism" to suggest that the only reason communist governments ruled this area was the intimidating presence of Soviet military power. Cold War communism did not develop because of an outside military power, but because of an attractive, external ideology that was anti-West. The chosen ideology opposed the philosophy of the regime one was fighting.   So if liberation warriors were fighting Western-oriented, capitalist governments their ideology gravitated toward the East and advocated state communism.   In the case of revolutionaries in East Europe in 1989, for example, the situation was reversed; their ideologies were democratic in orientation and leaned to capitalism, at least until after the communist power was overthrown in 1989.

At any rate the nature of the previous regime usually dictated revolutionary ideology. People generally were rebels first, and then because they had to explain their rebellion, they sought an ideology as different from the ruling one as possible to justify their anti-regime position. During the Cold War the different ideological positions were precast so that a new rebel would quickly understand that if one were against the oppression funded by the United States one opted for a liberation movement based on some kind of socialism or communism. However, the actual choice of Marxism-Leninism normally came after the revolutionary leader was in power, like Fidel Castro in 1961, two years after winning control of Cuba.

When the Cold War still dominated the thinking of superpower leaders, both of the insecure superpowers needed fairly constant reassurances of the continuing loyalties of their pawns, demonstrations they were not being lost to the other side. If those assurances were not strong enough, the superpower often treated the pawn as though it had already gone to the other side, like a suspicious and not very bright parent with teenage children. For example, Imre Nagy, the leader of Hungary in 1956, had an idea that Hungary could be neutral in the East-West struggle and that Hungary did not have to belong to the Warsaw Pact formed the year before. For another example Alexander Dubcek, the leader of Czechoslovakia in 1968, helped bring about a reform movement called the new Action Program of the Czechoslovak Communist party that hoped to create a "socialism with a human face." Both of these examples were taken by Soviet leaders as movements toward the West. Similarly, to take two examples from the other side, political events in 1954 Guatemala moved a bit toward the left, and in 1983 the wavering pro-American position of leaders on the tiny Caribbean island called Grenada plus the presence of Cuban workers enlarging an airstrip on Grenada seemed to US leaders as movements toward the East.   In all four cases, Hungary, Czechoslovakia, Guatemala, and Grenada, the superpower that imagined the pawns to be shifting invaded the smaller territory to ensure that such movement did not occur. States in the Soviet sphere were free to choose governments favored by Moscow.   Such states were called slaves by the West. States in the Western sphere were free to choose governments approved by Washington D.C.. Such governments were called friends by the West, and if the hypocrisy were noticed, it was never mentioned.

Sometimes these suspicions that ideological change was desired were correct. Often the internal struggle in a country trying to throw off its colonial past was funded by one or the other superpower with an eye toward winning a new pawn to its side. In order to qualify for this funding, the internal group usually had to appear more rather than less like the funder: a group funded by the United States would try not to appear too authoritarian and inhumane and as democratic as possible, while a group funded by the Soviet Union would make speeches dealing with proletarian goals despite the lack of a proletariat, and found it was easier to use symbols of Marxism-Leninism than to lose the funding. The difficulty was, however, that the more one side looked like the funding superpower the more the other superpower sought to destabilize it.   The result generally was a prolonging of the conflict which prevented any implementation of the desired democracy or communism. This stupidity went on for decades.

The two examples chosen to illustrate cold war communism stand out from the general description above by virtue of the fact that the nature of the new emerging governments was a surprise both to Washington D.C. and to Moscow. The first is Cambodia, while the second is Cuba.

Cambodia, a poor and tiny nation situated south of Laos and west of Vietnam in southeast Asia, has had a rich, long history, dating from at least the 5th century when their capital, Kambodja, was located near Ho Chi Minh City (Saigon). In the 9th century the Khmer extended their rule northward into Burma, and the capital in the 12th century was Anghor where the temple of Angkor Wat represented the highest development of Khmer art.

In the 19th century Cambodia became a part of the French Indochinese empire which did not fully survive World War II. In 1947 Cambodia received partial independence by becoming a constitutional monarchy under Prince Norodom Sihanouk. In 1949 Cambodian independence was recognized. During the years when France was struggling to suppress the Viet Minh (Vietnamese rebels led by Ho Chi Minh), Cambodia raised some military support against the Viet Minh. Later when the United States took over the Vietnamese struggle, and Cambodia sought to maintain neutrality, neither side would permit it. By 1970 that neutrality was irretrievably shattered, and a period of great suffering began for the people of Cambodia.

Southern Vietnamese communist forces were supplied from North Vietnam along the long trail that partly ran through Cambodia. The U.S. decided to interrupt this supply line by invading Cambodia in 1970, and followed up with prolonged bombing allegedly to prevent any new use of the area by the Vietnamese. The bombing was so extensive, however, that the already poor country was reduced to extremely primitive conditions, and the former rice exporter became a very hungry nation unable to feed itself as the dropped chemical defoliants, fiery napalm, and explosives killed the vegetation.[18] At least a million people were killed, and three million became refugees who fled to the cities, especially the capital, Phnom Penh. This created a new problem--feeding, housing, and clothing vast numbers of dislocated people torn from the rural areas.

As if this were not bad enough, a right-wing coup toppled the government of Prince Sihanouk and replaced it with a right wing leader with a palindromic name, Lon Nol, who had to be propped up with American assistance from 1970 to 1975. Not only was the U.S. bombing the countryside, it was also responsible for the Cambodian government and assumed responsibility for the refugees uprooted by the bombing, providing food, medical supplies, and equipment until 1975. Bombing with one hand while feeding with the other was an irony only a dedicated Cold Warrior could understand.

Opposition both to Lon Nol and the American presence was led by a group who called themselves the Red Khmer, or in French, the Khmer Rouge. This was a group of inexperienced intellectuals who become communists while studying in French universities and who came back to their country to struggle for a Cambodian communism against those who oppressed and invaded the country. Both Vietnamese and U.S. activities caused this to appear as patriotism because the intensive bombing pushed the hated Vietnamese deeper into Cambodia where they seized territory from local Cambodians. It seemed patriotic in the beginning to move against the Vietnamese, and the Red Khmer seized those areas and, in the process, became a larger territorial force.

At the same time the Red Khmer became the dominant force in the political coalition set up by Prince Sihanouk, then in Chinese exile, and began leading the fight against Lon Nol. Some Soviet and Chinese help was given but American arms left by retreating Lon Nol troops proved easy to find. The Red Khmer quickly became the dominant force in the Cambodian society, and when Lon Nol fled the country in 1975, he left behind a political vacuum, devastation, and suffering that was the result of the one-sided war.

The Americans left as well in 1975, taking their essential food and medical supplies with them. Widespread starvation was expected, but the U.S. left anyway.[19] What was left behind was a swollen urban population unable to care for itself and a devastated countryside either destroyed by bombing or by fighting.

The Red Khmer solved this problem by abruptly evacuating the cities. People were moved at gun point, and this was not a time to be sick or too old to move easily, because everyone was forced to evacuate and march into the countryside on their own power. Transportation and food supplies was either inadequate or nonexistent. The sheer numbers of internal refugees overwhelmed the new Red Khmer leaders. Many thousands of people died as a result of poor planning and the absence of any food or transportation. Some died because of the inhuman treatment by sadistic or tired guards who had seen too much misery. Executions sometimes appeared planned, as when former Lon Nol supporters were involved, and sometimes unplanned as the result of impulse. The movement of refugees was a time of terror, hunger, and great weariness. Would this many people or more have died anyway in the cities where no one could help them? Perhaps or perhaps not, but the manner of the evacuations made it appear as though the *people* were the enemy rather than the source of revolutionary strength and purpose.

The Red Khmer wanted to get people back to the land quickly so that food could be grown. The arbitrary manner of accomplishing this end testified to their ideological rejection of all dependent cities and industries and influenced the Shining Path development on the other side of the world. Both the genocidal evacuation and the arbitrary agricultural resettlement were costly efforts to achieve rural self-sufficiency. But crops had not yet been planted, irrigation schemes to provide a three crop year were still at the planning stage, and many of the evacuated people were ill equipped to farm the land. Agricultural cooperatives based on an older village-unit system were the basis of a rapid collectivization begun in the early months of 1976 and harshly pushed because the leaders, who had neither administered nor farmed before, felt that collectivization was better than the cooperatives. So peasant homes and temples were wiped out as property was confiscated. Very simple housing was constructed. Families worked separately in work teams and only slept together. Schooling for the young was minimal. Long workdays were common. So was hunger. In 1977 the cities were partially repopulated but the industries permitted were much smaller than those that had been there before. The Khmer Rouge seemed to be replicating Mao Zedong but correcting what were seen as his mistakes.

In the initial period there seemed to be no mention of Marxism-Leninism. The communists involved in the Red Khmer were known as *Angkar* (Organization) or *Angkar Loeu* (Organization on High) or even *Angkar Padevat* (Red Organization). There was secrecy, little visible politics, and a clear identification with the lower classes of society, which made the Red Khmer appear to be deeply revolutionary, and profoundly egalitarian. In September 1977 the secrecy ended when it was announced that the Cambodian revolution was led by Pol Pot (b. 1928) who headed the Communist party.

By 1978 the harshness of the situation was beginning to ease, but refugee reports suggested that random cruelty, killings, and beatings were continuing. Whether this communist experiment would have developed into something beneficial to the people of Cambodia, despite its cruel beginnings, became an academic point in December 1978 when Cambodia was overrun by a Vietnamese invasion. For the next eleven years some 150,000 Vietnamese troops were required to keep order and to maintain the Viet sponsored government. In 1989 the Vietnamese forces were withdrawn, and Cambodia embarked on a very shaky search for peace and stability. After years of negotiations Cambodia returned to a constitutional monarchy with the same leader that it had in the beginning, Prince Sihanouk. The Red Khmer, and its leader Pol Pot, became a small but still active part of the new political picture. The events suggested that the ideological fervor of the 1975-78 period may have been as much anti-West as pro-communist.

Cuba, another example of Cold War communism, is a large island about ninety miles south of Key West and inhabited by about ten million people. The island belonged to Spain until the Spanish-American War of the 1890s and after that the United States acted as though it belonged to the U.S. Regular interference with Cuban politics, the establishment of profitable trade relationships with owners of large agricultural estates, and the use of Havana as a playground by the criminal and rich from the U.S. made Cuba a colony of the United States in everything but name.

In the nineteenth century communist ideas had come to Cuba as they had to other parts of Latin America. The ideas had come through books, immigrants, and tourists; creating an intellectual leftism that stimulated an emerging anti-imperialist nationalism. Individuals who considered themselves communist were normally just a bit more radical than other liberal groups that arose and often the radicalness had more to do with anarchism than it did with Marxism.

This state of affairs began to change in 1925 when the Cuban Communist party was formed. The individuals forming this party sided with Lenin in the international struggle over whether violent revolution or peaceful reform was the way to achieve socialism and communism. The new party became a part of the Communist International (Comintern) or Third International that Lenin had begun in 1919. The Cuban Communist party was a small group that frequently divided on ideological issues, like a small church might, and it rather ineffectively sought to work with the small and uneducated labor forces in the country.

The Comintern did not pay much attention to the Cuban Communist party, nor to other parties in Latin America. This area of the world was somewhat written off by the Soviet Union because of its geographical distance from Moscow and because these areas of Latin America were considered to be in the backyard of the United States. So the communist parties of Latin America were usually ignored by the Russians in favor of trade agreements with Latin American capitalist governments. The communist parties, the Cuban one included, were instructed to work for reform in their countries, but not to upset things by trying to lead a revolution against their governments. As a result the Latin American parties were unlikely sources of revolutionary agitation.

The United States acted as though this were not true, however, and persistently funded anti-communist political leaders who repressed alleged communists (and democrats) in the name of liberty. In Cuba this tendency was carried to new heights by the American support of Fulgencio Batista who canceled elections he was unsure of winning in 1952. Batista seized power and moved against all political parties, including the communist party even though they represented no threat to his power.

Batista's problem was not going to come from the Cuban Communist party. His problem was going to come from a young lawyer named Fidel Castro Ruz who was the son of a planter who had immigrated from Spain. He was a young, bourgeois Roman Catholic. He came from a well-off Cuban economic group who were denied access to real power by the oligarchy of wealth and privilege organized around the sugar interests. When Batista seized power in 1952, Castro's opposition became a focal point for liberals who opposed Batista and his supporters because they intensely disliked his reactionary policies and because they wanted a chance at power. The hero of the liberals, including Castro, was not Karl Marx but José Martí (1853-1895), a romantic idealist who symbolized Cuban independence from Spain but who also had impressive leftist credentials.

José Martí was born in Havana and was, like Castro, the son of Spanish immigrants. At the age of seventeen he was already a staunch advocate of Cuban independence from Spain. He was arrested and banished to Spain, and while there he received degrees in law, philosophy, and letters. He travelled to France, Mexico, and Guatemala before coming back to Cuba in time to be rebanished in 1879. He then took up residence in the slums of New York City and supported himself as an art critic for the *New York Sun* while privately working for Cuban independence through his writings.[20]

His ideology seemed to be a romantic idealism that sought to improve lower class conditions. This moderation changed after the Haymarket Square riot on May 4, 1886. A bomb thrown by demonstrating workers had killed a policeman, and the action galvanized either opposition or support for working class movements. Martí sided with the workers, and his own ideology of romantic idealism deepened to represent working class concerns. He knew of Karl Marx, even wrote an obituary tribute to him in 1883, but his identification with Marx was more through Marx's humanism and his support of the working class than through any great attachment to Marx's image of communism in the future. Martí blended his knowledge of Marxism with his desire to see Cuba free and his hostility to the United States where he was then living, as he put it, "in the bowels of the monster."[21]

Independence from Spain came in 1898. Dominance by the United States followed, usually exercised through oppressive Cuban governments so tied to the United States that to be against one was to be against the other. It was easy to assume that much of Cuba's problem came from U.S. interference and domination.

Castro's opposition to Batista in Cuba was in this context of a liberal, anti-American ideology that followed the ideas of Martí far more than Marx. On July 26, 1953 a small force led by Castro unsuccessfully stormed the army barracks at Moncada. Although this mission was a failure, their next attempt did not fail. Their name came from the failed first mission: the *26 Julio* movement, but their second mission established a base in the mountains of Oriente Province for the approximately three hundred guerrillas.

In 1955 a manifesto or statement of purpose was published for the group calling for a restoration of political democracy, social justice, a return to the 1940 constitution that Batista's seizure of power had usurped, and the breakup of large agricultural plantations so that land could be redistributed to peasants. The demands of these liberals in the mountains of Cuba were actually more radical than the expectations of the Cuban communist party, partly because the liberals were willing to fight to achieve their goals. Party members were anti-Batista, and most of them wished Castro well, but none participated in the uprising. Moscow discouraged such activity in Cuba.

So when Castro and the *26 Julio* movement were victorious over Batista's forces in 1959, the Cuban Communist party was not involved, nor was Fidel himself a communist. The new Cuban regime sought economic assistance from the United States as well as from other nations, including the Soviet Union. In the beginning the new regime was like any other, rather confused and tangled up in its own rhetoric. Hardly anyone paid attention to this non-event in such a small country as Cuba. Castro himself said, twenty five years later, that no mention was made then of a Marxist-Leninist Party, or of socialism or internationalism; capitalism was not even mentioned by name. Indeed, Castro said, very few would have understood its true meaning at the time.[22]   And yet in December 1961, two years after victory, Fidel Castro announced that he was a Marxist-Leninist and tied Cuba ideologically to the Soviet Union many thousands of miles away and thumbed his nose at the very near United States. The reasons for this apparent switch from liberal to communist were not difficult to find: earlier that year Cuba was invaded by Cuban refugees that had been funded and trained by the American CIA. This was the abortive Bay of Pigs invasion planned in the Eisenhower administration and implemented in the early part of Kennedy's presidency. A less obvious reason was Castro's perception that Cuba needed more than liberal solutions could provide; it needed a revolution; it needed to shake itself out of its poor country status by the application of a Cuban command economy that operated according to central direction; it needed massive programs in literacy and health care improvements that centralized government direction fit better than the slower democratic procedures.

Although Castro could be faulted for not returning to the 1940 constitution as he had promised, very little else in the 1955 Manifesto was threatened by the switch to Marxism-Leninism. Indeed, relying on private enterprise to accomplish his social goals implied a reliance on the United States that he felt had earlier proven detrimental to Cuban development. By declaring himself a communist Castro found the ideological justification for the nationalization of U.S. owned enterprises without compensation to the former owners. This, he felt, was repaying the Cuban people for past imperialistic oppression.

After his abrupt change Castro balanced himself between a purged Cuban Communist party and a smaller 26th of July movement. The party expelled people who didn't agree with Castro. The 26th of July movement lost many liberal members who felt unable to follow him into Marxism-Leninism. The party now became **his** party and the Latin American *caudillo* type of government organization was in place. Cuba became a communist country in the sense that it was led by a communist party.

All this activity convinced the United States government to establish an embargo against Cuba and to prevent American citizens from travelling there. This punished Castro and Cuba for receiving economic aid from the Soviet Union, aid at very high levels until 1989: at least $3 billion per year which works out to an astonishing $100 per second.[23] One of the major ways this aid was given was through the

Soviet purchase of Cuban sugar at inflated prices and the sale to Cuba of Russian and East European manufactured goods at reduced prices.

Considering all this assistance from Moscow, Fidel Castro was astonishingly independent in foreign policy. One would think that with this level of economic assistance Fidel Castro would be a very dutiful subject. But for many years the reverse seemed to be true in foreign policy. The Cubans deliberately and openly sought to promote violent revolution in Latin America, despite the clearly contrary wishes of the Soviet leadership.

In the 1960s particularly, the Cuban leaders tried very hard to export their own version of the revolution that was somewhat like the Chinese; armed conflict against government forces until victorious. Cuba wasn't any more successful in exporting their revolution, however, than Russia had been decades before in Europe or the Chinese in Indonesia. Instead of exporting revolution Cuba seemed able to export only people, as so many thousands of Cubans emigrated to the United States that southern Florida was permanently changed. The foreign policy adventurism came to a gradual end, however, after the 1967 failure of a Cuban sponsored insurrection in Bolivia that cost the life of Che Guevara, a Cuban revolutionary who had gone to Bolivia to lead the struggle.

Castro appeared to become humbler, concentrated on Cuban internal problems, and became a cooperative partner of Soviet international ambitions. Instead of being the maverick of the socialist world seeking **his** kind of revolution in other countries, Castro and the Cuban military began to assist already existing revolutions in other countries like Angola and Ethiopia. During the 1970s and 1980s thousands of Cuban military were used overseas. In December 1989 *The New York Times* reported a Castro announcement about Cuban casualties in Africa since 1974. According to his statement some 400,000 soldiers and technical advisers were sent to Africa, and 2,289 were killed there, with over 2,000 of them killed in Angola.[24] This was a heavy price for the 10 million people of Cuba to bear.

The technical advisers sent to Africa and later to Grenada and Nicaragua were civilian professional people like doctors and teachers and engineers. The United States tended to play down the possibility that these advisers were really civilian, while the Cuban authorities often made it seem that most overseas Cuban personnel were non-military. Of course it was difficult to distinguish since a teacher can pick up a gun as well as a soldier.

Many of the accomplishments of the Cuban regime during the heyday of its existence have been tarnished by the ending of the Cold War and Castro's refusal to bend with the winds of change. At one time it was easy to state that in Cuba literacy was very high, medical care was about the best in Latin America, child labor had been abolished, and land was redistributed to peasant farmers. Life was never affluent in Cuba, but occasional rationing was bearable. Freedom was circumscribed by what Castro deemed permissible, but many millions of people either did not mind this or didn't care sufficiently to do something about it. Those that did draw attention to themselves found long terms in prison as their reward.

When things began to change in the former Soviet Union in the late 1980s, Castro banned the sale of **Soviet** publications in Cuba that he felt had gone too far away from the party line. As early as 1989 he called the weekly *Moscow News* and the monthly *Sputnik* promoters of bourgeois democracy and the American way of life. Readers of those two publications, he felt, could be led astray into believing that socialism had failed, that it was not historically inevitable. Castro dramatically rejected the Gorbachev type of reforms out of hand. He said that if destiny assigned Cuba the role of one day being among the last defenders of socialism in a world in which the Yankees have replaced Hitler as world dominators, then the Cubans will know how to defend this bulwark to the last drop of blood.[25] Perhaps Castro was gambling that Gorbachev would fail and new conservatives would emerge as Soviet leaders. That, of course, did not happen. What did occur was that the Soviet Union fell apart and by the end of 1991 had ceased to exist. As the Cold War disappeared and Russia's President Yeltsin seemed one of America's new friends, Castro's conservative attitude toward reform and change increasingly isolated both him and Cuba from the mainstream of world events.

For all of Castro's noted accomplishments, he seemed stuck for much of the early 1990s, mired in ideological platitudes of increasing irrelevance. Instead of a leftist hero of sorts, Fidel Castro became more an object of pity caught shivering in the breeze of a history that had passed him by. Some evidence of change began to be visible in late 1994 and 1995 as the government allowed the appointment of a Cardinal for the Cuban church, made gentle moves away from full employment toward a more capitalist economy, and even permitted the endorsement of an organization dedicated to a peaceful transition to democracy headed by an old Castro opponent, Eloy Gutiérrez Menoyo. Reports suggest that the party is declining in influence compared to the army, a situation reminiscent of Poland just before the great changes in 1989-1990.[26]

In summary, therefore, attempts to implement Marx's answer to the riddle of history, attempts to bring about theoretical communism, have failed. The modern ideology, just as experiments in the past, could not be sustained for long, and then generally only by the use of authoritarian force. Clearly this raises questions about the future of communal sharing ideas, and that is the subject for the next chapter.

Endnotes
Chapter Nine

1. James R. Ozinga, *The Relevance of Marx and Lenin to the Soviet Transition to Communism*, PhD. Dissertation, Michigan State University, 1968, on microfilm from the University of Michigan collection at Ann Arbor, Michigan.

2. Lenin, *Collected Works (CW)* (Moscow: Foreign Languages Publishing House, 1964), vol 26, p. 170.

3. Ibid., p. 77.

4. Lenin, *State and Revolution* (New York: Vanguard Press, 1929), p. 201.

5. Lenin, *CW, op. cit.*, vol 26, pp. 464-465.

6. Lenin, *State and Revolution, op. cit.*, pp. 155, 189, 193-4, 205-206.

7. Lenin, *CW, op. cit.*, vol 19, pp. 62, 92.

8. Chalmers Johnson, "Comparing Communist Nations," in Chalmers Johnson, ed., *Change in Communist Systems* (Stanford, CA: Stanford University Press, 1970), pp. 7-9.

9. Basil Dmytryshyn, *A History of Russia* (Engelwood Cliffs: Prentice Hall, Inc., 1977), p. 534.

10. Ibid.

11. Ibid., p. 535. This figure does not clarify the necessary distinction between collective farms and state farms. State farms (*sovkhozi*) predated the collective farms (*kolkhozi*) and were expanded in the era of collectivization, but their number was always small compared to the collective farms. In 1940, for example, there were 243,500 collective farms and 4,159 state farms. See Michael T. Florinsky, ed., *McGraw-Hill Encyclopedia of Russia and the Soviet Union* (New York:

McGraw-Hill, 1961), pp. 280 and 533. According to a different count made around 1933 before collectivization was complete, approximately 68 percent of all cultivated land was farmed by collective farms and only 10 percent by state farms, leaving some 22 percent still in private hands. See Nicholas V. Riasanovsky, *A History of Russia* (New York: Oxford University Press, 1993), p. 498. These figures changed after 1933, however, both because collectivization was pushed harder after 1933 and because the virgin lands expansion (1953-55) was essentially a state farm operation. See Florinsky, *op. cit.*, p. 532.

12. Michael Florinsky, ed., *McGraw-Hill Encyclopedia of Russia and the Soviet Union* (New York: McGraw Hill Book Co., 1961), p. 280.

13. Basil Dmytryshyn, *op. cit.*, p. 537.

14. Daniel Chirot, ed., *The Crisis of Leninism and the Decline of the Left: The Revolutions of 1989* (Seattle: University of Washington Press, 1991), p. 6.

15. Colin Macherras, *Modern China: A Chronology from 1842 to the Present* (San Francisco: W. W. Freeman & Co., 1982), pp. 24, 25.

16. O. Edmund Clubb, *Twentieth-Century China*, Second Edition (New York: Columbia University Press, 1972),p. 13. For a wider description of women's status in prerevolutionary China see Kay Ann Johnson, *Women, the Family, and Peasant Revolution in China* (Chicago: University of Chicago Press, 1982), pp. 7-26.

17. Clifford Krauss, "U.S. Aware of Killings, Worked with Salvador's Rightists, Papers Suggest," *The New York Times*, November 9, 1993, p. 4. Allegations about Central Intelligence Agency involvement in killings in Guatemala in 1990 and 1992 surfaced in a 700 page report in July 1995. See Tim Weiner, "C.I.A. Says Agents Deceived Superiors on Guatemala Role," *The New York Times*, July 26, 1995, p. 1; and "C.I.A. Agent's Link to Deaths in Guatemala Still Uncertain," ibid., July 27, 1995, p. 4.

18. Gavan McCormack, "The Cambodian Revolution 1975-1978: The Problem of Knowing the Truth," *Journal of Contemporary Asia*, vol 10, 1980, p. 77.

19. Ibid.

20.   Ramon Eduardo Ruiz, *Cuba: The Making of a Revolution* (Amherst, MA: University of Massachusetts Press, 1968), p. 62.

21. Ibid., pp. 68-71, 73.

22.   Fidel Castro, "Cuba Cannot Export Revolution, Nor Can the United States Prevent It," Speech, Santiago de Cuba, January 1,1984 (La Habana, Editora Politica, 1984), p. 6.

23. Arlene Idol Broadhurst, "Foreign Policy and Internationalism: The Case of Cuba," in Lawrence Whetten, *The Present State of Communist Internationalism* (Lexington, MA: D. C. Heath, 1983), pp. 160-162.

24.   Larry Rohter, "Castro Says He'll Resist Changes Like Those Sweeping Bloc," *The New York Times*, December 9, 1989, p. 7.

25. Ibid.

26. See Larry Rohter, "Cuba's New Cardinal Leads a Bolder Church," *The New York Times*, December 29, 1994, p. 1; "Cuba in Ideological Retreat, To Lay Off Many Thousands," ibid., May 13, 1995, p. 1; "Cubans Find the Army Rising as the Party Sinks," ibid., June 8, 1995, p. 1; and Mireya Navarro, "Castro Confers With Exiled Foe," ibid., June 28, 1995, p. 1. For the reference to Poland see Jerzy J. Wiatr, *The Soldier and the Nation: The Role of the Military in Polish Politics, 1918-1985* (Boulder, CO: Westview Press, 1988).

Chapter Ten

Sharing in a Postcommunist World
A Future Paradigm

The Continuing Need
The Problem of Size
The Problem of Duration
Equality of Opportunity

Despite all the distortions and misapplications, the successes and failures, of both sharing ideas and communism throughout history, the dream of equality continues to the present as though the ideas are a physical part of us, reborn with each new generation. In truth, however, the recurring dream is part of our future as well as our past because the gross inequalities that trigger the dream continue to exist. The desire for communal sharing is more than a mild nostalgia for community;[1] it is a continuing effort to redress the major problem of history: the large continuing gap between the rich and the poor.

TABLE 1[2]
INCOME LEVELS

City	Poorest	Richest	Difference	Ratio
New York	$5,237	110,199	104,962	21.04
Los Angeles	6,821	123,098	116,277	18.05
Chicago	4,743	86,632	81,889	18.27
Houston	5,591	97,536	91,945	17.44
Philadelphia	4,745	74,664	69,919	15.74
San Diego	8,611	103,921	95,310	12.07
Detroit	3,109	63,625	60, 516	20.47
Dallas	6,478	107,475	101,267	16.59
Phoenix	7,357	87,279	79,922	11.86
San Antonio	5,041	73,739	68,698	14.63

The Continuing Need

That problem has not gone away. It is clear that what communal experiments reacted to in the past is still very much with us. If new eruptions of communal fervor have learned nothing from the past, if passé models of communism are again attempted, we will be like robots mindlessly going through prescribed steps of a dance leading nowhere. Both sides of the problem need to be addressed. The first is the large income gaps that still occur even in a rich nation like the United States. Those gaps are worse elsewhere.

In Table 1 the median annual dollar income of the poorest and the richest fifths of the population is compared for each of ten major cities of the United States. The size of the difference is one measure of the gap, the ratio of the incomes is another. When the gap remains this wide the dream of equality has fertile soil in which to grow.

And, as Table 2 reveals, the gap is worse outside of the United States, particularly in the over 80 percent of the world that is "drowning in poverty and misery."[3] The expectation that poor countries are simply behind and will catch up with the rich ones lies behind the euphemism "emerging markets," which suggests that in time all countries can be wealthy. Even if this were true, the gap between the rich world and the poor world would still remain even if the total wealth of a country dramatically increased. This gap will continue to pressure violent attempts to implement the dream of equality.

TABLE 2[4]
INCOME DISTRIBUTION: LATIN AMERICAN AVERAGES
Per Capita Income in 1960 dollars

Class Division	1960	1970	1970 Difference	Ratio
20 % poorest	53.00	55.00	2,575	47.82
30 % next highest	118.00	167.00	2,463	15.75
20 % next highest	243.00	306.00	2,324	8.59
20 % next highest	424.00	616.00	2,014	4.27
10 % highest	1.643.00	1,945.00	689	1.35
(5 % highest)	2,305.00	2,630.00	0	1

Just a glance at the two tables reveals the stark contrast within a country or region and between the wealthy world and the poor world, and the data even suggest that the poor in the United States are better off than the wealthy in some poor countries. That may be true, but when the children of the United States were compared with the children of seventeen other industrialized countries in a recent Luxembourg Income Study, the largest income gap between rich and poor children was in the United States ($65,536). Seventeen other wealthy countries had smaller gaps[5] The future looks as bleak as the past.

Another expectation is that the lower end of the scale will slowly improve or at least that people at the lower end will gradually work themselves out of poverty if, it is argued, liberals don't get involved spending government money which destroys initiative and perpetuates the problem. But that argument and expectation do not wash either. Real wages for the least-skilled in the United States since 1979 have been **declining**, making it very difficult to work one's way out of poverty. Those with more education and skills saw their wages increase over the same period, *creating a widening gap in incomes*. Table 3 makes this explicit.

TABLE 3
COMPARISON OF 1992 U.S. WAGES WITH 1979 WAGES[6]

| CATEGORY | MALES | | FEMALES | |
	1992	CHANGE	1992	CHANGE
High school dropout	$21,620	-23.3%	$14,944	-7.4%
High school graduate	28,993	-17.0	20,372	+0.9
Some college	34,794	-7.3	24,695	+7.6
College graduate	50,331	+5.2	34,429	+19.1

This trend in the U.S. looks even bleaker when one considers that in the future the trend toward wider income gaps should increase as the need for unskilled labor diminishes in the new information age, and the old fashioned, underfunded educational system continues to graduate barely literate young people with few if any computer skills and no practice in thinking. Anyone who anticipates that the next few decades are going to be smooth sailing is looking at the data wearing ideological blinders. More people will be unemployed and unemployable because the educational system's crowded classrooms haven't changed and the job market has. All the factory jobs that were formerly done by unskilled labor will now be done by computers and automated machinery, and the poorer the school the less well prepared are the students.[7] How long will it be before a new Luddite revolution occurs and people attack computers with sledge hammers to vent their frustration in the name of equality? How large a military does the rich world need to keep the poor world away? The present gaps in income need ameliorating if they are not to continue as triggers of violent, frustrating attempts to achieve equality.

But the efforts to change society must change as well, and that is a major point of this book. Violent efforts to achieve equality will be a part of the future, and those efforts will probably be similar to those in the past. Without some heavy rethinking resistance to the dream will also continue as it has in the past, even though forcibly suppressing more equality is foolish. In general it is economically counterproductive. New thinking needs to be done. Some economists, for example, are now suggesting that greater income equality in a nation actually contributes to faster economic growth rather than the opposite.[8] These ideas are new, but they are by no means the only new thinking that needs to be done. The entire unrewarding historical dance of action and reaction and action with regard to communism needs to be rethought. Not only does the cause or trigger of the dream of equality need to be blunted by reducing income gaps, but the dream itself needs to be thoroughly re-examined so as to avoid routinely repeating the mistakes of the past.

The need to reduce income disparity is obvious. The need to change the dream is not. Consider, however, the twenty-one real-life examples of communal sharing and communism that have been described. Even to one sympathetic to the egalitarian dream there are two related problems that leap out of the data, which make changing the dream imperative: the very small size of the groups and their brief duration. When these two problems are faced head on, the solution is clear: the absolute part of the dream needs to be compromised.

The Problem of Size

Size is a problem because it has apparently been a factor in the success or failure of communist experiments. For the implementation of equality small groups have predominated, whereas for liberty large groups have been more the case. Neither equality nor liberty in the past have worked well on their own--they both need the balance of the other. But, interestingly enough, they have not worked all that well in the wrong sized groups either. The size of the group in which either is implemented seems to be a critical factor in whether or not either is achieved.

Liberty, for example, doesn't work all that well in a small group because the freedom to be different, to choose differently, is stifled by the need for everyone to perform the multiple tasks that the social system requires. For example, if a family of ten people were marooned on an island, the freedom to specialize and do one's own thing would not really be there. Each member of the group would have to do many different things in order for the small society to function. No one could specialize in that one thing that gave them the most pleasure. Jules Verne's *The Mysterious Island* is an example of this, where the society on the island consisted in the beginning of only five men.[9] Plato also understood this, and the opening pages of *The Republic* testify to the importance of group size. Aristotle insisted that one MUST live in something large enough like a polis (city state) in order to find happiness because the village or community was just too small for the sort of specialization required for happiness. So liberty in a small group has weak applicability. But liberty works just fine in large or even very large groups.

Equality or the community of goods, on the other hand, seems just the opposite. It has worked well in the past only when it was implemented in small groups. Only when the size was fairly small did the ideal occasionally approach a full implementation in practice with a duration measured in decades. If the size of the communal experiment were too large, liberty suffered; and not only liberty but progress as that is normally understood. These had to suffer because the degree of authoritarianism necessary in such a large society to maintain the communal sharing caused liberty to be pushed aside and progress became the captive of the command economy. Egalitarianism in the large, therefore, retards development and demands authoritarianism.[10]

So the size of the group is important to consider, but size is, within limits, flexible. The Perfectionists of Oneida New York were rather successful, and their size was about two hundred people. A kibbutz, on the other hand, is a successful implementation of communism that ranges in size from about one hundred to two thousand per kibbutz.[11] The overall number of kibbutzniks is much larger, of course, because there are many different kibbutzim in Israel. The smaller size of the Perfectionist group meant they could all live in one **very** large house and imagine themselves to be a large family.[12]

Tables 4A and 4B consider the approximate size of eighteen real life examples of communal sharing separated into two groups. Category A is enforced egalitarianism because the power of the state is behind the equality. Category B describes voluntary egalitarianism even though the kibbutzim could be considered part of the Israeli state.

TABLE 4A
SIZE OF COMMUNAL SHARING EXPERIMENTS

China	1,100,000,000
Soviet Union	278,000,000
Cuba	10,000,000
Angola	9,000,000
Cambodia	7,000,000
Haiti	6,000,000
Nicaragua	4,000,000

Obviously experiments that have the power of the state behind them were much larger than those that did not, meaning that in these enforced circumstances the population of the state communal societies would include a great number of people who did not share the ideological goals. Their cooperation was the result of the enforced egalitarianism. An assumption could be made, on the other hand, that almost all of the people in category B, especially at first, believed in the ideology at the base of their society. Their cooperation could be thought of as voluntary. The category B entries are therefore more reliable indicators of size potential than the state examples (category A). The two groupings are not entirely satisfactory, however. Haiti in the enforced group and the kibbutzim in the voluntary group suggest that the groups are not as neat as one might hope. This is always a problem when dealing with the real world.

The smaller size reduces the necessity of authoritarianism, especially after the death of the charismatic leader. If one is thinking of a future implementation of communal sharing and equality, a small group certainly seems preferable. Of course, this suggests grave difficulties if one is imagining the entire world as involved in the experiment. The data suggest that when the theoretical group moves beyond societies that approximate 6,425[13] members, among whom a sort of extended family network can be maintained, one moves into authoritarian territory. Although it is theoretically possible to have a world made up of small societies arranged in some sort of federal relationship, the mind boggles at the difficulties of attaining such a world. Even dividing up the United States, which has an approximate population of 250 million would require the setting up of some 39,000 societies if the group membership could not exceed 6,425. If fifty states are difficult to hold together, imagine the problems with a number 780 times as large! In theory something like this is possible, but in practice it is impossible unless it would slowly grow from below over many generations.

TABLE 4B
SIZE OF COMMUNAL SHARING EXPERIMENTS

Kibbutzim	350,000
Anabaptists	35,000
German Peasants	21,000
Shakers	6,300
Shining Path	5,000
Early Christians	3,000
Zapatistas	2,000
Icarians at Nauvoo	1,500
Pythagoreans	800
Perfectionists	260
Diggers	150
Settlement Houses	100

It may be possible to determine optimum size by experiment, and so allow practice to discover what worked best, perhaps even allowing a heroic figure to intervene when a group became too large or too small. Such possibilities, however, exist more in myth than in the hard light of reality. One is compelled to derive data not from such imagined experiments but from real life adventures which take on a life of their own once they are begun. But that does not mean that the problem of size has not been discussed. It has. Plato thought that there was an optimum size for communities in general and wrote of this in *The Republic*. Jean Jacques Rousseau (1712-1778) suggested that the country of France was too large for his communes and suggested splitting the country up into communities having populations like that of the Genevan city-state that he so admired. Mulford Sibley thought that Rousseau meant a number like 20,000 per community, over three times the data-suggested size of 6,425, but there is no indication whether Rousseau meant just adults, just males, or whatever.[14] At the population level estimated for 1750 in France of 24 million, Rousseau's figure would mean at least 1,200 communities. At present levels of France's population, over twice the size, it would mean at least 2,717 separate communes. The point Rousseau was making was that his ideal equal and democratic society needed to be fairly small. He wrote in Book II of his *Social Contract* that as nature has set limits to the stature of a properly formed human, outside of which it produces only giants and dwarfs; so likewise, with regard to the best constitution of a state, there are limits to its possible extent so that it may be neither too great to enable it to be well governed, nor too small to enable it to maintain itself single-handed. There is in every body politic, he wrote, a *maximum* of force which it cannot exceed, and which is often diminished as the state is aggrandized. The more extended is the social bond, the more it is weakened; and, in general, a small state is proportionally stronger than a large one.[15]

These limits were somewhat flexible, Rousseau hastened to add. It was impossible, he wrote, to express numerically a fixed ratio between the extent of land and the number of people that were reciprocally sufficient because of the differences in fertility of the soil, climate, fecundity of the female population, etc., all matters which made quite a difference.[16] At the end of the twentieth century it was obvious that information flow technology had an impact on size as well. But in general small was better because people knew each other, knew their rulers, and did not require the multiplying levels of bureaucracy in between the executive and the people.

In a larger society, levels of complexity make it difficult to imagine the implementation of very much equality. The modern information revolution may provide an exception to this because technology has made it difficult *not* to share everything with all the technically competent sisters and brothers operating in cyberspace. Even property rights are abolished or at least ignored when copyrighted material cannot be protected because of the freedom of access. In this instance technology reduces property rights as an unintended function of increased complexity, **but** the access is limited to technically competent sisters and brothers with computer access, raising the question of whether the new cyperspace elite is a modern day equivalent for the 144,000 untainted males in the book of Revelations. Past attempts at equality in real life have only worked in situations of considerable simplicity. Conceptual experiments, such as Marge Piercy's *Woman On the Edge of Time*, suggest a simplicity achieved by very complex technology, for example, but even so, this simplicity was for a world of groups of about 600 people, a tenth of the group size mentioned earlier. There seems no way around this problem. Attempts to implement any serious form of equality in a large and complex society either always fail during the preliminary stages (hence the need for the "dictatorship of the proletariat") or require such authoritarianism that the decrease in liberty makes the equality experiment unattractive.

The Problem of Duration

The second problem to consider is that communal sharing experiments have not lasted long. They do not seem to have the nearly automatic life or renewal capacity of liberty oriented systems that move from generation to generation with no apparent effort. Equality systems seem artificial, requiring extensive efforts, whether internal or external or both, to continue from year to year even when they are sustained by strong religious/ideological ideas. Think of all the short-lived communes formed by university students in the 1960s.

Recall the case studies of the previous chapters and again distinguish real life experiments from conceptual possibilities. The list is shorter than one might think after considering so many examples, but so was the normal life span of real experiments. In Table 5 below, this duration problem is addressed by ranking real life communal sharing experiments from longest to shortest in duration. The actual time can vary slightly from that given in the Table, but such variation should make little difference. The twenty-one entrees in Table 5 average nearly 37 years.

If one takes the dictionary definition of the word "generation" as the time span from the birth of the parents to the birth of the children, or approximately twenty years, then this average figure represents almost two generations. Other examples of communal sharing exist and could

TABLE 5
ESTIMATED DURATION OF COMMUNAL SHARING EXPERIMENTS

Anabaptists in Middle Europe	114 years (1534-1648)
Shakers around Mt. Lebanon, New York	110 years (1780-1890)
Kibbutzim in both Palestine and Israel	87 years (1909-1996+)
Russia and the Soviet Union	74 years (1917-1991)
Settlement Houses: Jane Addams	50 years (1890-1940)
Lillian Wald	50 years (1890-1940)
Mary Simkhovitch	50 years (1890-1940)
China	47 years (1949-1996+)
Cuba	35 years (1961-1996+)
Perfectionists in Oneida, New York	35 years (1845-1880)
Early Christian Sharing	30 years (40-70)
Angola	21 years (1975-1996+)
The Shining Path in Peru	16 years (1980-1996+)
Nicaragua	11 years (1979-1990)
Icarians at Nauvoo, Illinois	6 years (1850-1856)
The Diggers	3 years (1649-1652)
Cambodia	3 years (1975-1978)
Haiti	3 years (1990-91/1994-1996+)
Zapatistas of Chiapas	2 years (1994-1996+)
German Peasants	1 year (1524-1525)
Pythagoreans	1 year? (Sixth Century BC)

be added to the Table, but their similar duration would not significantly change the average. Two generations, ironically, seemed to be the time period Friedrich Engels estimated was necessary for socialism, but he anticipated full communism following those generations, not the end of the movement.[17] Thirty-seven years is a very short time considering the depths of the dream of equality.

Another way of looking at the problem is to consider **when** the communal experiments occurred. The dream of equality is constant,

TABLE 6
CHRONOLOGY OF COMMUNAL EXPERIMENTS

Pythagoreans	Sixth Century BC
Early Christian Sharing	40-70AD
German Peasants	1524-1525
Anabaptists in Middle Europe	1534-1648
Diggers	1649-1652
Shakers	1780-1890
Perfectionists	1845-1880
Icarians	1850-1856
Settlement Houses	1890-1940
Kibbutzim	1909-1996+
Russia	1917-1991
China	1949-1996+
Cuba	1961-1996+
Angola	1975-1996+
Cambodia	1975-1991
Nicaragua	1979-1990
Shining Path	1980-1996+
Haiti	1990-91/1994-96+
Zapatistas	1994-1996+

but implementations have not been. Table 6 chronologically rearranges the examples from Table 5.

Over 600 years separate the first and second examples but over 1500 years divide the second from the third. After that examples occur regularly. The first gap may be due to a lack of information. The second gap can be due to the emergence of two new religions (Christianity and Islam) as well as the existence of the so-called Dark Ages (476-1000AD). It is more likely, however, that the second gap resulted from the religious conceptualization of an earthly paradise; as in a real Eden Garden in Persia where reentry was prevented by original sin or by a guardian angel at the gate of the Garden. Even though earthly, the paradise was as difficult to attain as the spiritual one in heaven. Eventually, though, this religious lock on the vision of equality was broken. The causes were probably a combination of the Aristotelian, non-Christian learning coming from Moslem scholars in northern Africa, the Renaissance, the Crusades, and the Protestant Reformation. Changes in the way people thought raised the issue of equal liberty.

Communal sharing experiments lasting an average of 37 years suggest that the systems stressing equality are blips in the normal pattern and are not automatically sustainable, or self-sustainable. When the pressure to continue was removed in one way or another, the new generation seldom saw the need to continue the experiment. They were surrounded by an alternative that appeared more attractive, generally a liberty maximizing alternative with a good deal of inequality. This suggests that pushing equality to the point where separation into a smaller society occurs is pushing equality too hard. This suggests as well that the equality-stressing society is artificial and not self-sustaining partly because it is a small simplicity in a much larger complexity, but also because it has to reduce liberty. The equality system is not the norm but the exception. The need to push equality against the resisting flow of liberty is what demands an authoritarian or dictatorial system. Then both because of the embattled circumstances and the allure of authoritarianism, the implementation of communal sharing is from the top down, without regard for whether there was really anything to share or whether people were even willing to share. It's like commanding someone to love. That would be stupid, but so is forcing ideological obedience. Ideological leaders **knew** what others needed without asking them and that is a dangerous experiment to live through as millions of people have already discovered. Equality under these circumstances required too much coercion, and liberty, of course, flew out of the window. It was sorely missed. Liberty is one of those things that is never so valued as when it is lost.

The result is that all too often there have been serious implementation difficulties; so many that examples can be used as an excuse to block dreams of equality. This opposition is no solution because the dreams keep coming back in one guise or another. They are not, as Mercutio imagined, the children of an idle brain, born of vain fantasy.[18] They arise out of legitimate memories and are triggered by very real income gaps. It is time that history is used to avoid the mistakes made by earlier people which have created a continuing need for equality dreams to flourish despite the tarnished quality of past attempts. Otherwise the future will merely provide continuing evidence of the dream's dogged persistence.

Equality of Opportunity

There may be a way out of the perpetual problem if absolutes are left behind. The moment this is done, of course, there is the danger that nothing can be accomplished. Without the absolutist anchor one feels adrift. For example, if one wants, like Cabet, to argue that some forms of private property are permissible in the sharing society, where does one draw the line? Too little equality and one has a sort of socialized capitalism, something conservatives in the United States argue we already have. Too much equality and the need for authoritarianism becomes very real.

Although it is not easy, if absolutes can be left behind one is in the position James Harrington (1611-1667) was in; trying to slip a different kind of utopia between More's regimented communist island ideas with too little liberty and Britain's veneration of private property for the few with far too little equality for the many. James Harrington's *Oceana* was a precedent for this kind of moderation. He tried to **repair** society rather than to restructure it completely. His ideal society was more republican than communist, and his attitude toward property and property sharing indicated a sense of the importance of an equality goal that was a good distance from the absolute.

Harrington was part of the chaotic seventeenth century in Britain and a victim of the political see-saw that occurred. He had been an official of Charles I's court, and when the King was executed by parliamentary forces, Harrington retired to his estates at the age of 37, like others, pondering the future nature of the British political system. Thomas Hobbes published his analysis of what Britain needed in his book, *The Leviathan* in 1651. Hobbes argued for the restoration of a strong monarchy because he imagined that people lived in a dangerous anarchy prior to civil society. A strong sovereign was therefore needed to keep order and make civilization possible. Hobbes would have been more popular if he had argued that the sovereign's power came from God. But because Hobbes was an atheist he argued on different grounds and found himself isolated from other seventeenth century royalists who justified the king's power by reference to a royal genealogy that went back to Adam and God. So Hobbes' ideas did not serve, but other intellectuals felt that their ideas might have a better reception.

The Commonwealth of Oceana was published both in answer to Hobbes and to express Harrington's ideas about the relation between property distribution and social stability. The novel was dedicated to the anti-royalist Oliver Cromwell, the victor in the civil war, and was sufficiently successful that a group of influential people calling themselves "Harringtonians" petitioned Parliament in 1659 to consider establishing a commonwealth patterned after his utopia.

In 1661 Harrington wrote his *System of Politics* continuing the discussion of his ideas, but, despite his earlier popularity, the timing was ill-considered for any discussion of a commonwealth that did not need a king. The political system had shifted again and in 1660 the new king, Charles II, had been restored to the throne. Charles II did not care for Harrington's ideas. Harrington was arrested and imprisoned in 1661 and was harshly treated for several months before being released in ill health both physically and mentally. So although his ideas were moderate, he still got in deep trouble because his moderation was judged by an absolutist with power.

Harrington was concerned about property distribution. His original contribution in *Oceana* was that the key to an analysis of any society was the distribution of property within that state. He wanted neither a narrow concentration of property in the hands of the few nor a too-wide decentralization of property in the hands of the many. Concentration in *neither* was desirable, but **balance** between them was. The nature of that balance determined whether the society was involved in civil war or was stable. Hobbes had argued that if one wanted stability one must choose a strong monarch whose force of arms would create the stability. Harrington argued that the choice between a strong king or a strong parliament was not the important one; the big question with reference to stability was the balance of property ownership, just as today the big question refers to how to reduce the size of the income gap. He wrote in *Oceana* that dominion was property, both real and personal property; lands, money, or goods. So, he argued, the nature of any empire can be determined by considering the proportion or balance of dominion or property in land. The proportion or balance of dominion or property in land determined the **nature** of the empire.[19]

Both Plato and Aristotle had argued that governments could be distinguished by the number of people involved, i.e., one, few, many, and by whether the rulers ruled in their own interest or in the interest of the society as a whole. Harrington's contribution was to describe a different understanding of what creates the nature of a political system: the distribution of property, both in lands and in goods. He argued that the real elements of power were riches, wealth, and property.[20] It was a more economic understanding of the political system. Concerned only with liberty, political systems can be described as republics or monarchies and not ever refer to the very important issue of property balance. Harrington pointed the way to change this method of political analysis over three centuries ago. In the language of the seventeenth century, he wrote that if one man were the sole landlord of a territory he had an absolute monarchy. If, however, a nobility plus a clergy were landlords, one has a mixed monarchy. But if the whole people were landlords, then one had a commonwealth.

The commonwealth was not based on the abolition of private property but rather on a sufficient redistribution of property so that many more possessed it. For example, he argued that everyone being a landlord could mean everyone owning property, or it could mean that the property was so **widely** distributed that no one person or number of people could overbalance it.[21]

The balance of property ownership was correlated to the need of force in the society to achieve order, which was related to the balance between the political and economic system. The point made, contra Hobbes, was that force was an unreliable base of a society, that the more one depended on force the more unreliable was the form of government and the more unstable the political and economic system. Force was most necessary when the balance between property distribution and political power was skewed, as for example, the people having the most property, but with the political power in the hands of a single person, the king. The people in this example would not be dependent on the king for food, and would not need to serve the king so that the king would need to use his army to keep order. The royal army, in turn, would require vast supplies of goods and money, which would have to be wrested from the independent population through taxation. Not a stable structure, and civil war would probably ensue.[22]

In a republic when the number of property holders was increased, Harrington felt, there was a corresponding increase in the number of good soldiers, gentlemen, commoners or whatever.[23]

Public morality was also improved by increasing the number of property holders. Harrington's theory of balance argued that the source of all political power ought to be the ownership of property. That kind of balance made for stability. "Not having things makes men obedient; having things makes them independent."[24] This is why established interests do not want change, even moderate change such as is being discussed here. Established elites want people obedient, not independent, and that means maintaining large income gaps.

Harrington's compromise position, not taken literally but as an indicator of direction, suggests a way to handle the problem of the recurring dream of equality appearing like an artificial confrontation with liberty. In making this compromise, advocates of equality would be taking a lesson from those who successfully advocated liberty long ago. The liberty that people had to settle for was far less than perfect liberty, far less than absolute freedom. People who live together in villages, towns, and cities cannot avoid circumscribing each other's individual liberty in order for society to function. People's freedom to act as they wish so long as they do not hurt others sounds quite individualistic in theory but in practice the social constraints on individual freedoms are no small matter. Restrictions on liberty are necessary because of the social setting for the individual and the need to stop fouling our nests and those of our children.

A belief in individualism, after all, is **socially** grounded. Victor Ferkiss said it some years ago. Notions of discrete individualism discontinuous with society are lies designed to prevent social action. Ferkiss correctly argued that if we realized the extent to which our "individualism" is already shaped by society we would use that consciousness to make the shaping process more fully reciprocal, less one-sided. In so doing we would not only mold society, but through that remolding reshape ourselves.[25]

If egalitarians could see these interrelationships and accept the necessity of compromise, accept a future society that has more equality than presently possessed but a long way from absolute sisterhood/brotherhood, they might be on their way to achieving something real and lasting. The restrictions in the hoped for equality would match the existing restrictions on liberty already accepted.

This would not mean the end of the dream because the dream has always been about a good deal more than equality. It has also been about virtue, about innocence, about honor, and about a closeness with the God of your choice. Relative equality expressed in a **real equality of opportunity** would allow the remaining elements of the dream to bud and even flower if our words didn't get in the way. Dorothy Bryant's excellent book, *The Kin of the Ata are Waiting For You*, suggested a solution to the problem of words. The lesson taught by the Ata was that words obscure the dream, and this can be true of the dream of equality as well. Attempts to describe it profoundly rather than to implement it simply spend too much time splitting hairs about what kind of equality is sought or what to call the new system or whether it fits into some preconceived notion of rational justice, when the possession of the dream compatible with liberty is all that is really important.

And because the concern is the dream rather than words describing the dream, perhaps the dream can stimulate a non-absolute, softer vision of equal liberty that could be implemented without a revolution in a more loving society. It can take people as they are and suggest incremental steps that move them toward greater equality, but **not** total equality; a bit away from individualism and a bit more toward community, a bit away from Me or I and a bit more toward Us.

As with Harrington's *Oceana*, absolute equality (or liberty) would neither be expected nor desired. Harrington stood for a **balance of property holding** that would place private property in many more hands than in his own day, but private property would not be destroyed. In the past we have too often argued the need to *eradicate* the income gap as though the goal was to have no gap at all. Seeking the absolute creates so much opposition that the goal is entirely prevented. A new and different approach may succeed where this has failed. Wise people have always maintained that **the pathway should be the goal, not the goal itself**. Applying that Zen kind of thinking to this problem suggests that what leads to equality might be far more significant a goal than equality itself. The goal of the dreamer should be the *seeking* of equality. Because of the overriding danger of damaging liberty, equality, like happiness, is not something that should be sought directly. It can, however, be productively sought indirectly, by seeking that which leads to greater equality; by giving up on the absolute vision and searching instead for a formula that grants **more** equality while holding liberty as constant as possible.

Could Harrington's compromise be updated to function as a more realistic vehicle for the dream of equality than any other visible in the past? It is worth thinking about because such a new compromise could remove the two big problems of size and duration and create something like equal liberty. Private property would still exist. Public ownership would be avoided as much as possible. The result might nonetheless be a free and equal society of caring, sharing people. Just as with the balance between selfishness and altruism mentioned in Chapter One, so also the adjustment necessary to achieve an optimum balance between liberty and equality may well be within the possible. Instead of an equality of position and people, it may be as simple as a *real equality of opportunity*. Simple to imagine, difficult to implement, but *it is possible*. One beginning would be to seek a student/teacher ratio of 21 to 1 in our schools. It has been demonstrated that a higher ratio disadvantages students, while a lower ratio disadvantages taxpayers.[26]

Another beginning would be the continuation of some form of affirmative action until equality of opportunity becomes real, even though affirmative action is unpopular among conservatives. Affirmative action, in John E. Roemer's language, is special compensation for those who were denied access to privilege in the past. Equality of opportunity, in this view, requires that people be compensated for handicaps induced by factors over which they have no control. This is a use of affirmative action to achieve equality of opportunity and in no way is ever intended to create equality of welfare. People do have free will, Roemer argued, echoing Victor Ferkiss, they can make choices, but what the effective student/teacher ratio and affirmative action can help create are the conditions where that choice is a **real** one.[27]

Neither of these two ideas are perfect solutions. The better student/teacher ratio maximizes the percentage of students who graduate, but the best may be 80 percent, by no means everyone. Affirmative action can compensate and even reverse in some senses previous discrimination, but it is difficult to dislodge the phrase from its unpopular liberal ambience or the idea that affirmative action causes reverse discrimination. Pursuing affirmative action may therefore seem counterproductive for one seeking equal liberty, but what that view does not understand is that the reason for this is the old emotive language used, not the concept of affirmative action itself. A recent study reported by the U.S. Labor Department, for example, has argued that affirmative action has **not** resulted in many legal cases where reverse-discrimination has been charged. The survey indicated that less than 3 percent of the more than 3,000 discrimination opinions from 1990-1994 were reverse-discrimination opinions. Moreover, in this small number of cases very few were found to be reverse discrimination (6 out of almost 100).[28] It would seem that affirmative action is not harming liberty at all, but as to whether it is helping, the answer is mixed.

There is no question that affirmative action programs have resulted in greater equality of desired positions, but the negative spin of affirmative action can occur when those who are promoted on this basis are presumed not competent; merely promoted or retained because of skin pigmentation or belonging to a favored ethnic minority. This is an old story, and it is not caused by affirmative action. Despite this negative connotation, a continuation of affirmative action seems important to ensure that minorities continue to be promoted to positions where their competence can be demonstrated, instead of being assumed to be non-competent because of race or skin color. When affirmative action is properly carried out it should only mean that when all qualifications are equal, minority applicants should be given prefer-ence.[29] That's not reverse discrimination so much as it is a device to reverse the discrimination. Even liberals at times get confused. Words get in the way, frequently, and especially is this possible when research into the effectiveness of the program is hard to find.

Achieving greater equality of opportunity without affirmative action is difficult, but perhaps it could be done if we were serious about equal education for everyone and could figure out how to balance hiring so that every group has a fair chance. There is no reason why this cannot be done. All it takes is the willingness.

Keep in mind that the solution is a compromise, and that perhaps the methods need to be moderate as well. Over a century ago one of the left Hegelians, Ludwig Feuerbach, wrote that he wanted people to find the determining factor of their lives in a loving that he saw as a body and soul actively living for others, for humanity, for universal ends. These words can get in the way of the solution because they demand a sacrifice that seems too heavy, but even more to the point they get in the way when it is forgotten, as Feuerbach himself pointed out, that these universal ends can only find actuality in concrete human form. If I want equality I want equal people, *people with equal liberty*,[30] and I am then for whatever is necessary to enable people to possess an equal shot at life. In the language of liberation theology I must *do the truth*, engage in what can be called orthopraxis; activity designed to correct maladjustments or deformities, which is "...far more important and far more consistent with the gospel than simply assenting to the truth (orthodoxy)."[31] Let the people alone, as Adam Smith argued in another context, let them alone to differentiate all they wish after that golden moment of choice is past; but let us create for ourselves and our children the moment of equal choice.

Income gaps need to become smaller. Would a moderate negative income tax provide the answer? A test program might be attempted, so that the numbers we share as we argue could be based in some sort of reality. This program would provide income from the government to all those whose income fell below an agreed upon level. The money to accomplish this redistribution would come from an additional tax on the rich, so that the income gap was being cut from both ends. The rich mustn't be so taxed that the incentive to excel is removed, nor the poor so supported that the incentive to try is destroyed. The middle passage that avoids these dangers needs to be found.

It would be very easy to find arguments for one side or another, easier even to find politicians who would support several sides, but the real issue is not addressed by that activity. The point is to do **more** than simply talk about equality, the point is to achieve the minimum level consistent with liberty--equality of opportunity. If that can be made real, human history in the 21st century may become quite an improvement.

Real equality of opportunity could gradually change society so sufficiently that only minor adjustments would afterward be necessary. All people could have hope and rise or fail according to their own efforts. All they would be guaranteed would be equality of opportunity. Society might not appear very different for a long time, but the more moderate goal of equality of opportunity could be bettering people's lives and improving society while we think of what else we might do.

If this could be accomplished maybe we would be in a different ball game and show that a social learning curve does exist. Why have so many people in the past fled from communist systems, even at great risk to their lives? Liberty is the main answer: they didn't have it and they wanted it. Why has the dream of equality continued to bubble up all these centuries? Equality is the main answer: people didn't have it, and they wanted it. **Both** liberty and equality are important in a balance that maintains both. Such a balance is a realistic equality of opportunity.

Examples from the Soviet Union or China or Cuba illustrate that equality without liberty resembled the equality provided in a prison. Equality existed, but the enforcement of that equality, necessitated by the autocratic system, required guards who quickly become the first among equals, as in George Orwell's *Animal Farm*. Members of communist parties in countries ruled by those parties usually became members to get ahead, to get the better job, not because they had sympathy with communist ideas. Similarly, prison guards do not usually become guards because they are idealists wishing to rehabilitate prisoners. Equality without freedom is no answer.

Liberty without equality is no answer either. It is not even the better of the two positions. If the seesaw is not balanced both positions are out of line. Systems allegedly capitalist and democratic, organized like liberal republics in countries like the United States, Canada, or Great Britain regularly provide a high degree of liberty, but the equality is either very weak or almost absent. Justice might be blind but judges, lawyers, and juries are not. Fair treatment happens to pink-skinned samples of affluence far more frequently than it does to poor people of color. Insisting on equality of opportunity is shushed away by those who possess power because even that minimum of equality would allegedly interfere with their liberty to become more powerful. There is no denying that liberty is a **precious** commodity even to the poor, but its value is lessened considerably if all one has with the liberty is poverty, anger, and the absence of hope. People may be free to eat all they want but if the table is bare they have hunger along with their liberty.

History is full of examples. Liberty societies sometimes act as though foreign dictators and bullies who ignore human rights and who steal bread from their own hungry people should be rewarded with guns, tanks, and money sometimes legally, sometimes illegally. Liberty, unbalanced by equality, is no panacea.

Equality systems have frequently been unattractive as well. Sometimes the communism went very, very wrong and lost its goal while retaining the name. Cambodian peasants in 1975 come to mind, old and sick and tired and marching out of Phom Penh at the point of a gun. Or Anabaptists in Münster in early 1535 when King Jan was living high, while his subjects ate grass and rats in the name of equality. Or one of the millions of individual horror stories from the gulag era in Soviet Russia. Countries stressing equality have funded and trained assassination squads to rid them of alleged enemies and in the process bombed and maimed little children in the name of humanity. Their priorities were topsy turvy. Clearly, the ideology of sharing is something with which one has to be careful; unbalanced with liberty it is no panacea.

Liberty when supervised by an intelligent citizenry with a broadened property base and grounded in a *real* equality of opportunity could work well if we didn't get hung up in words. The freedom made possible by liberty is not an end in itself but a means to an end; it is the ability to achieve a desired future state both individually in the society and socially for the society as a whole. But any liberty is meaningless that provides only the appearance of choice with no means of implementing individual decisions.[32] Real liberty needs the power of implementation of realistic choice, and for that one needs something that could be called equal liberty, or a liberty balanced by an equality of opportunity: an equal liberty that might also be called an ecological humanism.

Under such circumstances, the authoritarian, liberty-denying communal sharing will not be a future paradigm so much as it will be a remembered cure for an illness humans used to have: the inhumane gaps between the haves and the have-nots. In the past sick people were bled by barbers before the development of modern medicine. Some people may even have been helped by these strange methods. But not many. It is time the medicine for sick societies was also modernized. Instead of bleeding them through conflicts and hatreds, **we can heal them**. The Tree of Life is for the healing of nations. We should start using it.

Then those that follow us, our children and our grandchildren, would not only understand what made the dream exciting for so many centuries, but they would also wonder what took us so long to implement it properly, to get rid of the strange twentieth century compulsion to fight communism by maintaining the social illness that caused it in the first place.

Perhaps it will take a decade or a century or maybe another millennium before humans learn that the slogans of the French Revolution: Liberty, Fraternity, and Equality *can coexist* in the same society at the same time. It takes effort, intelligence, and love to seek the balance. Dreams, after all, empower, showing us that we can "...move beyond words and history, beyond the possible to the imagined, and into a life both ancient and new...."[33] In this instance success is moving beyond stable equilibrium characterized by harmony, discipline, regularity, predictability, and adaptation. The old way only identifies roads already travelled. Moving beyond this means not knowing the future, following instincts that recognize the positive role of instability and the unknowability of the long-term future. "This is not only a state of matter, but first of all a state of spirit. And therefore we must change our mentality, our way of living, our way of doing things, our paradigm."[34]

Maybe, like in the days of our kindergarten, we can learn to share our toys and play fair. And if we did learn this lesson we would find that the *pathway* to the "Kingdom" is an extremely satisfying goal by itself. We have obscured this for twenty-four centuries. When will the kingdom come, asked his disciples. It will not come by waiting for it, Jesus seems to have answered, because it is already here, spread out upon the earth and people just do not see it.[35]

If these words are true, the pathway has been here all along, **on earth**, as it was in the Garden of our beginning.

Endnotes
Chapter Ten

1.   Richard Sakwa, *Russian Politics and Society* (New York: Routledge, 1933), p. 403.

2. Andrew A Beveridge, "Cities: The Difference in Income," *The New York Times*, December 26, 1994, p. 20.

3. Aleksandr I. Solzhenitsyn, "To Tame Savage Capitalism," *The New York Times*, November 28, 1993, p. 11.

4.   Adapted from James Wilke, ed., *Statistical Abstract of Latin America*, vol 30, part I (Los Angeles, CA: UCLA Latin American Center Publications, 1993), p. 441.   The section marked 1970 Differences and Ratio were added to the Table.   Caution is needed when comparing even the lowest fifth of Table 2 with Table 1 because Table 1 is urban income only while Table 2 averages urban and rural incomes.   Additionally, Table 1 compares top and bottom fifths of the population while Table 2 compares the lower 20 percent with the upper 5 percent.

5. Keith Bradsher, "Low Ranking for Poor American Children: U.S. Youth Among Worst Off in Study of 18 Industrialized Nations," *The New York Times*, August 14, 1995, p. 7.

6. Table adapted from Bureau of Labor Statistics data reported in Peter T. Kilborn, "Up From Welfare: It's Harder and Harder," *The New York Times*, April 16, 1995, p. 1E.

7. See for example, Lena Williams, "Computer Gap Worries Blacks," *The New York Times*, May 25, 1995, p. 1B.

8. See, for example, Sylvia Nasar, "Economics of Equality: A New View," *The New York Times*, January 8, 1994, p. 17.   She was reporting on a major shift in economists' thinking visible at the American Economics Association conference in Boston and reflecting word done by Nancy Birdsall of the Inter-American Development Bank

and Richard Sabot of Williams College.

9. Jules Verne, *The Mysterious Island* (New York: Charles Scribner's Sons, 1927), p. 6.

10. The enforced agricultural egalitarianism in the Russian 19th and 20th centuries whether pushed by tsar, landlord, or commissar was a clear example of the retarding consequences of too much equality in a large society.

11. Bruno Bettleheim, *The Children of the Dream* (London: Macmillan Co., Collier-Macmillan Ltd., 1969), p. 331.

12. Rosabeth Moss Kanter, *Commitment and Community: Communes and Utopias in Sociological Perspective* (Cambridge: Harvard University Press, 1972), p. 9; cited in George Melnyk, *The Search for Community: From Utopia to a Cooperative Society* (Montreal: Black Rose Books, 1985), p. 85.

13. The number was derived by averaging Table 3B using 2,000 for the kibbutz group since the discussion refers to individual groups.

14. Mulford Sibley, *Political Ideas and Ideologies* (New York: Harper and Row, 1970), p. 406.

15. Jean Jacques Rousseau, *The Social Contract or Principles of Political Right*, translated, edited, with commentary by Charles M. Sherover (New York: New American Library, 1974), II, 9, p. 75.

16. Ibid., II, 10, pp. 79-80.

17. Friedrich Engels, "Introduction to the Civil War in France," *Marx-Engels Selected Works (MESW)*, vol 2, p. 189.

18. William Shakespeare, *The Tragedy of Romeo and Juliet*, Act I, scene iv, lines 99-100 in William Wright, ed., *The Complete Works of William Shakespeare* (Garden City: Doubleday & Co., Inc., 1936), p. 322.

19. James Harrington,. *The Political Writings*, Charles Blitzer, ed. (New York: Liberal Arts Press, Inc., 1955), p. 44.

20. Michael Downs, *James Harrington* (Boston: Twayne Publishers, 1977), p. 18.

21. James Harrington, *op. cit.*, pp. 44-45.

22. Michael Downs, *op. cit.*, p. 20.

23. Ibid., p. 26.

24. Ibid., p. 33.

25. Victor Ferkiss, *The Future of Technological Civilization* (New York: Braziller, 1974), pp. 151-152.

26. This ratio is empirically derived from a study of twenty eight school districts in Michigan over a time frame of fifteen years. See Robbin Hough, "Fundamental Theorem of System Structure; an Application to the Study of Community School Organizations," *Journal of Systems Research*, vol 10:4, 1993, pp. 57-72.

27. John E. Roemer, *A Future for Socialism* (Cambridge: Harvard University Press), pp. 11-12.

28. "Reverse Discrimination Complaints Rare, a Labor Study Reports," *The New York Times*, March 31, 1995, p. 10.

29. Farai Chideya, "Equality? I'm Still Waiting," *The New York Times*, March 11, 1995, p. 17.

30. Melvin Cherno, "Introduction to Ludwig Feuerbach," in Ludwig Feuerbach, *The Essence of Faith According to Luther*, Melvin Cherno, trans. (New York: Harper & Row, 1967), pp. 18-19.

31. Arthur McGovern, *Marxism: An American Christian Perspective* (Maryknoll: Orbis Books, 1990), p. 178.

32. Victor Ferkiss, *op. cit.*, p. 159.

33. Gloria Steinem, Speech for Take Our Daughters to Work Day, 1994, cited in Gloria Steinem, *Moving Beyond Words* (New York: Simon & Schuster, 1994), p. 15.

34.   Karin Jurse, "Challenges of Systems Approach to Leadership," paper prepared at the School of Business and Economics, University of Maribor, Slovenia presented at the Ninth International Conference on General Systems Theory, Amsterdam, April 1995, pp. 3,8.

35.   *Gospel of Thomas* 113, a serial collection of Jesus' sayings dating from about 50AD, cited in John Dominic Crossan, *op. cit.*, p. 229 and pp. 282-283.

BIBLIOGRAPHY

Addams, Jane, *Twenty Years at Hull-House* (New York: Signet Classic, Penguin Books, 1938).

Addams, Jane, *The Second Twenty Years at Hull-House* (New York: Macmillan Co., 1930).

Ansell, Mary, *A Serious Proposal to the Ladies for the Advancement of their True and Greatest Interest* (London: Richard Wilkin at the King's Head in St. Paul's Church-Yard, 1697).

Apsler, Alfred, *Communes Through the Ages: The Search for Utopia* (New York: Julian Messner, 1974).

Athanassakis, Apostolos N., *Hesiod: Theogony, Works and Days, Shield* (Baltimore: The Johns Hopkins University Press, 1983).

Barron, Alfred and Miller, George Noyes, eds., *Home Talks by John Humphrey Noyes*, vol 1 (Oneida, NY: Oneida Community, 1875). Volume 1 was the only volume published although more were intended.

Batey, Richard, *Jesus and the Poor* (New York: Harper & Row, 1972).

Bendiner, Elmer, *The Rise and Fall of Paradise: When Arabs and Jews Built a Kingdom in Spain* (New York: Barnes & Noble, 1983).

Bernstein, Eduard, *Evolutionary Socialism*, Edith C. Harvey, trans. (New York: B. W. Huebsch, 1912).

Bettelheim, Bruno, *The Children of the Dream* (London: Macmillan Co., Collier-Macmillan Ltd., 1969).

Burnet, John, *Early Greek Philosophy*, Fourth Edition (London: Adam & Charles Black, 1930).

Cabet, Étienne, *History and Constitution of the Icarian Community*, Thomas Teakle, trans. (Iowa City: Iowa State Historical Society, 1917).

Cabet, Étienne, *Travels and Adventures of Lord William Carisdall in Icaria*, published in photoduplicate form as *Travels in Icaria*, Robert P. Sutton, trans. (Macomb, IL: The Center for Icarian Studies at Western Illinois University, 1985).

Carden, Maren Lockwood, *Oneida: Utopian Community to Modern Corporation* (Baltimore: The Johns Hopkins Press, 1969).

Cardenal, Ernesto, *The Gospel in Solentiname* (Maryknoll, NY: Orbis Books, 1982).

Castro, Fidel, *Cuba Cannot Export Revolution, Nor Can the United States Prevent It*, Speech, Santiago de Cuba, January 1, 1984 (La Habana: Editora Politica, 1984).

Chirot, Daniel, ed., *The Crisis of Leninism and the Decline of the Left: The Revolutions of 1989* (Seattle: University of Washington Press, 1991).

Clubb, O. Edmund, *Twentieth-Century China*, Second Edition (New York: Columbia University Press, 1972).

Cole, G.D.H., *Socialist Thought: The Forerunners 1789-1850* (London: Macmillan & Co., Ltd., 1962).

Cornford, Francis MacDonald, *The Republic of Plato* (New York: Oxford University Press, 1979).

Crossan, John Dominic, *The Historical Jesus: The Life of a Mediterranean Jewish Peasant* (San Francisco: Harper-Collins, 1992).

Darin-Drabkin, Haim, trans., *The Other Society* (New York: Harcourt, Brace, & World, Inc., 1962), first published in Hebrew by the Hashomer Hatzair, Merhabia, Israel by Sifriat Poalim, Ltd., 1961.

Davidovic, G., *Toward a Co-operative World* (Antigonish, Nova Scotia: Coady International Institute, 1967).

Dawson, Doyne, *Cities of the Gods: Communist Utopias in Greek Thought* (New York: Oxford University Press, 1992).

Delumeau, Jean, *History of Paradise: The Garden of Eden in Myth and Tradition,* Matthew O'Connell, trans. (New York: Continuum Publishing Co., 1995). Originally published as *Une Historie du Paradis: Le Jardin des délices.*

Desroche, Henri, *The American Shakers: From Neo-Christianity to Presocialism,* John K. Savacool trans. (Amherst: University of Massachusetts Press. 1971).

Dmytryshyn, Basil, *A History of Russia* (Englewood Cliffs, NJ: Prentice-Hall, Inc., 1977).

Downs, Michael, *James Harrington* (Boston: Twayne Publishers, 1977).

Eisler, Riane, *The Chalice and the Blade* (San Francisco: Harper & Row, 1988).

Engels, Friedrich, *Herr Eugene Dühring's Revolution in Science (Anti-Dühring)* (New York: International Publishers, 1939).

Engels, Friedrich, *The Housing Question* (New York: International Publishers, n.d.).

Ferkiss, Victor, *The Future of Technological Civilization* (New York: Braziller, 1974).

Florinsky, Michael, ed., *McGraw-Hill Encyclopedia of Russia and the Soviet Union* (New York: McGraw Hill Book Co., 1961).

Fried, Albert and Sanders, Ronald, eds., *Socialist Thought: A Documentary History* (Garden City: Doubleday & Co., Inc., 1964).

Frazer, James George, *Folklore in the Old Testament: Studies in Comparative Religion, Legend and Law*, vol 1 (London: Macmillan, 1919).

Fulghum, Robert, *All I Really Need to Know I Learned in Kindergarten* (New York: Ballantine, 1986).

Gilman, Charlotte Perkins, *Herland* (New York: Pantheon Books, 1979).

Grant, Michael, *Myths of the Greeks and Romans* (New York: World Publishing Co., 1962, Mentor Edition).

Griffin, Donald R., *Animal Thinking*, (Cambridge: Harvard University Press, 1984).

Gutierrez, Gustavo, *A Theology of Liberation: History, Politics, and Salvation*, Sister Caridad Inda and John Eagleson, trans. and eds. (Maryknoll, NY: Orbis Books, 1973).

Harrington, James, *The Political Writings*, Charles Blitzer, ed. (New York: Liberal Arts Press, Inc., 1955).

Hegel, George W. F., *The Phenomenology of the Spirit* in *The Philosophy of Hegel*, Carl Friedrich, trans. and ed. (New York: Random House, 1954).

Himmelfarb, Gertrude, *The Idea of Poverty: England in the Early Industrial Age* (New York: Alfred A. Knopf, 1984).

Horowitz, David, "Socialism By Any Other Name," *National Review*, vol 44:7, April 13, 1992, p. 38.

Hummert, Paul A., *Bernard Shaw's Marxian Romance* (Lincoln, NB: University of Nebraska Press, 1973).

Hyde, Louis, *The Gift: Imagination and the Erotic Life of Property* (New York: Vintage Books, 1983).

Ibarruri, Dolores, *They Shall Not Pass: The Autobiography of La Pasionaria* (New York: International Publishers, 1966).

Jenness, Linda, ed., *Feminism and Socialism* (New York: Pathfinder Press, 1972).

Johnson, Buffie, *Lady of the Beasts: Ancient Images of the Goddess and Her Sacred Animals* (San Francisco: Harper & Row, 1988).

Johnson, Chalmers, "Comparing Communist Nations," in Chalmers Johnson, ed., *Change in Communist Systems* (Stanford, CA: Stanford University Press, 1970).

Johnson, Kay Ann, *Women, the Family, and Peasant Revolution in China* (Chicago: University of Chicago Press, 1982).

Jordan, W. K., *The Development of Religious Toleration in England: Attainment of the Theory and Accommodations, 1640-1660* (Cambridge: Harvard University Press, 1940).

Kanter, Rosabeth Moss, *Commitment and Community: Communes and Utopias in Sociological Perspective* (Cambridge: Harvard University Press, 1972).

Kautsky, Karl, *Communism in Central Europe in the Time of the Reformation* (New York: Russell & Russell, 1959).

Kephart, William M., *Extraordinary Groups: The Sociology of Unconventional Life-Styles*, Second Edition (New York: St. Martin's Press, 1982).

Kephart, William M., *The Family, Society, and the Individual*, Third Edition (Boston: Houghton Mifflin Co., 1972).

Kessler, Carol Farley, ed., *Daring to Dream: Utopian Stories by United States Women, 1836-1919* (Boston: Andora Press, 1984).

Kissinger Report, also known as the *Report of the National Bipartisan Commission on Central America*, GPO, January 11, 1984.

Kropotkin, Piotr, *Mutual Aid, A Factor of Evolution* (London: William Heinemann, Popular Edition, 1915).

Laidler, Harry W., *History of Socialism: A Comparative Survey of Socialism, Communism, Trade Unionism, Cooperation, Utopianism, and Other Systems of Reform and Reconstruction* (New York: Thomas Y. Crowell Co., 1968).

Leakey, Richard and Lewin, Roger, *People of the Lake* (New York: Avon Books, 1978).

Le Guin, Ursula K., *The Dispossessed* (New York: Avon Books, 1974).

Lenin, *Collected Works*, vols 1-45 (Moscow: Foreign Languages Publishing House, 1964).

Lenin, *State and Revolution* (New York: Vanguard Press, 1929).

Lieblich, Amia, *Kibbutz Makom: Report from an Israeli Kibbutz* (London: Andre Deutsch, 1982).

Lichtheim, George, *The Origins of Socialism* (New York: Frederick A. Praeger, Publishers, 1969)

Lowry, Bullit and Gunter, Elizabeth Ellington, *The Red Virgin-- Memoirs of Louise Michel* (University, AL: University of Alabama Press, 1981).

Lowry, Lois, *The Giver* (Boston: Houghton Mifflin Company, 1993).

Macherras, Colin, *Modern China: A Chronology from 1842 to the Present* (San Francisco: W. H. Freeman & Co., 1982).

Mancall, Mark, *China at the Center: Three Hundred Years of Foreign Policy* (New York: The Free Press, 1984).

Mandel, Ernest, *Marxist Economic Theory*, vol 1, Brian Pearce, trans. (New York: Monthly Review Press, 1968). See particularly the opening chapters for a good discussion of the anthropological evidence for primitive communism.

Manuel, Frank E. and Fritzie P., *Utopian Thought in the Western World*, (Cambridge, MA: Harvard University Press, 1979).

Mao Zedong, *Selected Works* (New York: International Publishers, n.d.).

Marx, Karl, "Economic and Philosophic Manuscripts of 1844," in Loyd D. Easton and Kurt H. Guddat, eds., *Writings of the Young Marx on Philosophy and Society* (Garden City: Doubleday, 1967).

Marx, Karl, *Grundrisse*, David McLellan, trans. and ed. (New York: Harper & Row, 1971).

Marx, Karl and Engels, Friedrich, *Marx-Engels Selected Works (MESW)* (in three volumes) (Moscow: Progress Publishers, 1970).

Marx, Karl and Engles, Friedrich, *Marx-Engels Selected Works in Two Volumes* (London: Martin Lawrence, Ltd., 1942).

Marx, Karl and Engels, Friedrich, *Marx-Engels Selected Correspondence (MESC)* (Moscow: Foreign Languages Publishing House, n.d.).

Marx, Karl, *The Poverty of Philosophy* (Moscow: Foreign Languages Publishing House, n.d.).

Mauss, Marcel, *The Gift: Forms and Functions of Exchange in Primitive Societies*, Ian Cunnison, trans. (New York: Norton & Co., 1967).

McCormack, Gavan, "The Cambodian Revolution, 1975-1978: The Problems of Knowing the Truth," *Journal of Contemporary Asia*, vol 10, 1980.

McCormick, Gordon H., "The Shining Path and Peruvian Terrorism," A Rand Paper (Santa Monica: The Rand Corporation, 1987).

McPherson, Natalie, *Machines and Economic Growth: The Implications for Growth Theory of the History of the Industrial Revolution* (Westport, CN: Greenwood Press, 1994).

Melcher, Marguerite Fellows, *The Shaker Adventure* (Princeton: Princeton University Press, 1941), reprinted in 1960 by Western Reserve University.

Melnyk, George, *The Search for Community: From Utopia to a Cooperative Society* (Montreal: Black Rose Books, 1985).

Meyer, Alfred G., *The Feminism and Socialism of Lily Braun* (Bloomington, IN: Indiana University Press, 1985).

Miles, Rosalind, *The Women's History of the World* (New York: Harper & Row, 1988).

Moment, Gairdner B. and Kraushaar, Otto F., *Utopias: the American Experience* (Metuchen, NJ: The Scarecrow Press, 1980).

More, Sir Thomas, *Utopia*, Robert M. Adams trans. and ed. (New York: W. W. Norton & Co., 1975).

Mumford, Lewis, *The Story of Utopias*, (Gloucester, MA: Peter Smith, 1959). Original copyright 1922.

Neubauer, Peter B., *Children in Collectives: Child-Rearing Aims and Practices in the Kibbutz* (Springfield, IL: Charles C. Thomas Publisher, 1965).

Nordhoff, Charles, *The Communist Societies of the United States* (New York: Schocken Books, 1965). First published in 1875.

Noyes, John Humphrey, *The Berean: A Manual for the Help of Those who Seek the Faith of the Primitive Church* (Putney, VT: Office of the *Spiritual Magazine*, 1847).

Ozinga, James R., *Communism: The Story of the Idea and Its Implementation*, Second Edition (Englewood Cliffs, NJ: Prentice Hall, 1991).

Ozinga, James R., *The Relevance of Marx and Lenin to the Soviet Transition to Communism*, PhD dissertation, Michigan State University, 1968, on microfilm from University of Michigan collection at Ann Arbor, Michigan.

Piercy, Marge, *Woman on the Edge of Time* (New York: A Fawcett Crest Ballantine Book, Random House, 1976).

Plato, *The Republic*, Francis M. Cornford, trans. (New York: Oxford University Press, 1979).

Plato, *Timaeus*, R. G. Bury, trans., Loeb Classical Library (Cambridge: Harvard University Press, 1961).

Reeves, B., "Six Milleniums of Buffalo Kills," *Scientific American* 249/4, (October 1983).

Rexroth, Kenneth, *Communalism: from its Origins to the Twentieth Century* (New York: The Seabury Press, 1974).

Riasanovsky, Nicholas V., *A History of Russia*, Fifth Edition (New York: Oxford University Press, 1993).

Robertson, Constance Noyes, *Oneida Community: The Breakup 1876-1881* (Syracuse: Syracuse University Press, 1972).

Roemer, John E., *A Future for Socialism* (Cambridge: Harvard University Press, 1994).

Rohrlich, Ruby, and Baruch, Elaine Hoffman, eds., *Women in Search of Utopia* (New York: Schocken Books, 1984).

Rousseau, Jean Jacques, *The Social Contract or Principles of Political Right*, Charles M. Sherover, trans. and ed. (New York: New American Library, 1974).

Ruether, Rosemary Radford, *The Radical Kingdom: The Western Experience of Messianic Hope* (New York: Harper & Row, 1970).

Ruiz, Ramon Eduardo, *Cuba: The Making of a Revolution* (Amherst, MA: University of Massachusetts Press, 1968).

Russell, Bertrand, *A History of Western Philosophy* (New York: Simon & Schuster Touchstone Book, 1945).

Sandys, George, *Ovid's Metamorphosis: Englished, Mythologized and Represented in Figures*, Karl K. Hulley and Stanley T. Vandersall, eds. (Lincoln, NB: University of Nebraska Press, 1970).

Saxonhouse, Arlene W., *Women in the History of Political Thought* (New York: Praeger Publishers, 1985).

Scott, Sarah, *A Description of Millenium Hall and the Country Adjacent: Together with the Characters of the Inhabitants and such Historical Anecdotes and Reflections, as may excite in the reader Proper Sentiments of Humanity, and lead the Mind to the Love of Virtue*, Third Edition (London: Printed for J. Newberry at the Bible and Sun, St. Paul's Churchyard, 1767).

Shapiro, Herman, ed., *Medieval Philosophy* (New York: Random House, 1964).

Sibley, Mulford, *Political Ideas and Ideologies* (New York: Harper & Row, 1970).

Simkhovitch, Mary Kingsbury, *Neighborhood: My Story of Greenwich House* (New York: W. W. Norton & Co., Inc., 1938).

Sjoo, Monica & Mor, Barbara, *The Great Cosmic Mother: Rediscovering the Religion of the Earth*, (San Francisco: Harper & Row, 1987).

Spense, Thomas, *Description of Spensonia and Constitution of Spensonia* (London: 1795; privately printed at the Courier Press; Leamington Spa, 1917).

Steinberg, Milton, *Basic Judaism* (New York: Harcourt Brace Jovanovich, 1975).

Steinem, Gloria, *Moving Beyond Words* (New York: Simon & Schuster Touchstone Edition, 1994).

Strong, Simon, *Shining Path: Terror and Revolution in Peru* (New York: Random House Times Books, 1992).

Stokes, Gale, *The Walls Came Tumbling Down: The Collapse of Communism in Eastern Europe* (New York: Oxford University Press, 1993).

Timmerman, Jacobo, *Cuba: A Journey*, Tony Talbot trans. (New York: Random House Vintage Books, 1992).

Torres, Father Camilo, *Revolutionary Writings* (New York: Harper Colophon Book, 1972).

Viteles, Harry, *History of the Co-operative Movement in Israel*, vol 1 (London: Vallentine and Mitchell, 1967).

Wald, Lillian D., *Windows on Henry Street* (Boston: Little, Brown, & Co., 1936).

West, Delno C. and Zimdars-Swartz, Sandra, *Joachim of Fiore: A Study in Spiritual Perception and History* (Bloomington, IN: Indiana University Press, 1983).

Wilson, Andrew, ed., *World Scripture: A Comparative Anthology of Sacred Texts* (New York: Paragon House, An International Religious Foundation Project, 1995).

Wilson, Edmund, *To the Finland Station: A Study in the Writing and Acting of History* (Garden City: Doubleday & Co., Inc., 1953).

Winstanley, Gerrard, *The Works of Gerrard Winstanley with an Appendix of Documents relating to the Digger Movement*, Introduction by George H. Sabine, ed. (Ithaca, NY: Cornell University Press, 1941).

Wright, William Aldis, ed., *The Complete Works of William Shakespeare* (Garden City: Doubleday & Co., Inc., 1936).

Index